Praise for *A Reason or a Season*

Dad, thank you so much for writing this book. It gave me a better understanding of your past and everything you have accomplished in your life. It's a combination of feeling happy, sad, thankful and loved. I truly enjoy it.

—Jessica Gourdet-Murray

Many readers will have pleasant memories of sitting around a kitchen table or at their elders' knees, listening to tales of days gone by. This book will evoke those feelings, calling up memories of stories mixed with bits of wisdom that one can use to shape a life. *A Reason or a Season* is a fine autobiography. It describes the story of Jesse's life and it does so by discussing the many people he encountered along the way. This has the remarkable effect of creating a picture not simply of a single life but of a time and world.

—Editor's comment

There are things that you learn from your own experiences, things that you learn in school, and then there's this... the stuff that your parents won't share with you but should.

—A reader's comment

I felt inspired as I read *A Reason or a Season.* I laugh, I cried, I marvel. I thoroughly enjoy the experience.

—Marilyn King-George

I enjoyed reading a *Reason or a Season* which is a heartfelt story of one man's journey through life. The book is interesting, humorous and meaningful.

—Janet Schipper, RN, BS, MSN

I highly recommend *A Reason or a Season.* Readers will learn about life in Haiti, life in the United States, and the similarities and the differences between the two.

—Ernst Albert, Educator

A Reason or a Season

A ma cousine Anicia avec amour.

Jesse

1/31/17

A Reason or a Season

A LIFE STORY

Jesse Gourdet

This book is autobiographical. However, some names and other identifying details have been changed to protect the privacy of the individuals involved.

ISBN-13: 9781533303752
ISBN-10: 1533303754
Library of Congress Control Number: 2016908387
CreateSpace Independent Publishing Platform
North Charleston, South Carolina

For more information, please contact Jesse at jesse@jessegourdet@com.

There are times when all the world's asleep,
The questions run too deep for such a simple man.
Won't you please, please tell me what we've learned?
I know it sounds absurd, but please tell me who I am.

From "The Logical Song" by Roger Hodgson and Richard Davies

I dedicate this book
to
my wife, Yanick Gourdet;
my son, Gregory Jennings Gourdet;
my daughter, Jessica Gourdet Murray;
her husband, Arthur Murray;
and my grandchildren,
Morgan Gourdet Murray
and
Emery Gourdet Murray.
I love you all.

Contents

Foreword

After the publication of *Let It Be Easy,* my father, Jesse Gourdet, didn't think about writing another book until he faced death during an earthquake on August 23, 2011, in Virginia.

On that night, he saw his whole life flash in front of him. Moved by that chilling experience, he decided to write this book as a tribute to the people who had touched his life over the course of seventy years.

He hopes that through the windows of his personal life, a new generation will get a glimpse of life during the latter half of the twentieth century and the first part of the twenty-first century. Perhaps someone may benefit from the lessons he learned along the way.

The book is written in the present moment, about the past, and for the future. It is full of emotionally charged stories that will touch the heart and enliven the spirit. It covers life in Haiti, immigration issues, life in US factories in the seventies, young love, and the quest to experience the American Dream. The book evokes feelings of joy and sadness, love and dreams, fear and hope, passion and power, charity and greed, compassion and destruction, war and technology. I hope it satisfies the curiosity of the reader.

May you enjoy it!

Gregory J. Gourdet

Introduction

By
Wynne S. Wharff

I recall meeting Jesse and his wife, Yanick, for the first time early on New Year's Day after the celebrations of 2014 had subsided. They are friends of my parents—my dad, to be more specific—and they worked together with him at Brookdale Hospital in Brooklyn, New York. They had decided to migrate south after many years of pounding the pavement in the concrete jungle, and my parents had recently followed suit but still had one foot on the cement, as they made it south only during the winter months.

I met many of my parents' friends. I was quite indifferent to some, and I genuinely appreciated others, but when I went along with my parents and brought my own newly born son, Gray, with me to meet Jesse and Yanick for the first time, for a nice New Year's dinner, they truly left an impression.

Jesse struck me as the type of man who was really conscientious about things and who actually took things in; he absorbed the little details and found importance in the things many of us take for granted. I recall him telling me about the book that he had previously written and indicating that he was in the process of writing another. I recall mentioning that I'd like to read that book, but I suppose I'd forgotten about it, as life's many twists and turns happen and one interest takes the place of another.

One day, back in New York, when life was typically busier than usual, my dad plopped a huge manuscript on my counter (with no prior warning) and announced that it was Jesse's book—the one that I had remarked I'd wanted to read. I didn't have time to read any books; I could barely brush my own hair in the morning and make it to work on time! He said Jesse had sent the book for me to have a first read and state my impressions. Along with a nicely written succinct note from Jesse was the contents page, where my name appeared in black and white as the author of the introduction. Had I promised to write that as well? I was honored, to say the least, but also unsure of my suitability for such a role. Had I, too, made an impression of some sort? I wondered if I had and, if so, then when and where.

I had been totally unaware and simply being myself, living life, pondering internally all of my problems and dreams and plans for the immediate future, and imagining what it would be like to perhaps live in such a quiet gated community as the one we were visiting that day. I then discounted the place, along with my parents' own community, for lack of excitement. Sure, it was nice for the retirees, but I was just starting my life at forty! I'd just had a baby.

In retrospect, I realize that what had resonated with me was Jesse's respect for relationships and life. Like the lessons in this book, many of the author's personal influences had murmured words of wisdom—little gems, so to speak—that sounded like simple words but that offered great wisdom once I pondered them in the great scheme of things. When you've really got to appreciate perspective—when the s**t hits the fan—that's when you sit and think about those simple yet powerfully resonating words.

Of course, we all go through our moments when tragedy and sadness propel us toward introspection, and all of a sudden, we ourselves are gurus of wisdom and analysts of life. We become super sensitized to all things around us and find ways to associate whatever is happening with our own personal crises. How self-centered. But isn't that human nature?

As humans, we live via the experiences of others. We make mistakes; we learn lessons from the past and from others. We make more mistakes; we ask for forgiveness. We have faith in a higher power. We teach by doing.

We love; we hate. We forgive; we war. At the end of the day, what's it all about? I suppose we all come to different conclusions about life and the way we've lived ours thus far.

This book seems to tackle life's twists and turns in a very matter-of-fact way that makes us all OK with how things are and leaves us more appreciative of everything around us. It allows us to see life as a plethora of small events that have been orchestrated for us by a higher power—one that gives us the strength and courage to take active steps toward that next level (whether we perceive it to be good or bad)—one that has already set the stage for the way things will go. There is a saying that I hold dear, and I find it to be applicable to this book. I most recently heard a variation of it on television from the famous preacher Joel Osteen. He gave a sermon about how God has a greater plan for us all and has great things in store for you. "This is your due year," he preached. As this book indicates so clearly, one does not know the path one will take, but wow, what lessons that path will teach.

The author, Jesse, commented that he would have liked to meet Woody Allen someday. I had such a unique experience, and that meeting has been a part of some really great opportunities and moments for me—ones that I'd never dreamed would occur. It's human nature to sit and ponder and dream and plan, but as Mr. Allen himself once said, "If you want to make God laugh, tell him your plans."

Part One
The Formative Years

CHAPTER 1

The Day I Left New York, the Earth Trembled

You must begin by knowing that you have already arrived...

Richard Bach, *Jonathan Livingston Seagull*

In the poem "Song of the Open Road," the great poet Walt Whitman writes about traveling on the open road in a spirit of joyfulness, optimism, and openness to new possibilities. It is a long poem; here are a few lines:

Henceforth I ask not good-fortune, I myself am good-fortune...
Strong and content I travel the open road...
All seems beautiful to me...
Allons! whoever you are come travel with me!

These were the thoughts that came to my mind as the alarm on my smartphone broke the silence of the night with the ringtone "New Day." It was August 23, 2011; the time was 4:00 a.m. Indeed, it was a new day; my wife and I were starting our retirement. We were about to leave New York after forty-three years.

We gathered whatever belongings we had in our small apartment on East Ninety-Fourth Street in the Canarsie section of Brooklyn, one of the five boroughs of New York City. Half an hour later, our twelve-year-old red Toyota Camry was fully packed.

Before leaving, we bowed our heads to say a prayer of gratitude, thanking God for the successful life we'd had in New York. Then I took a little key chain with a *hamsa* good-luck symbol that I had bought in Jerusalem years ago, and I recited the traveler's prayer that was inscribed on it. "O Lord, may your love protect us on our journey and guard us from perils on the way. May we reach our destination in joy and peace! Amen."

Then we took off, heading toward the Amtrak Auto Train in Lorton, Virginia, for the 1:00 p.m. car-loading time. Google Maps indicated that the trip would last about five hours. We gave ourselves plenty of time. We wanted a leisurely drive with enough time to rest and have breakfast along the way. No need to hurry anymore; we were about to start a new life as retirees in the Sunshine State—Florida. We had bought our retirement house one year earlier, and a trucking service had shipped our furniture and other personal items to Florida after the sale of our house in Queens. We had rented this little Canarsie apartment near our workplace for the last few months we spent in New York. Ironically, the apartment was on the same street where we had lived when we first moved to Brooklyn years ago, right after we got married. It was like closing a circle.

As we got on Rockaway Parkway, it was quiet. In a couple of hours, it would be busy with public buses, private cars, and people hurrying to catch the Canarsie L train to go to work in Manhattan.

When we merged onto the Belt Parkway, traffic was still light. As we passed Coney Island Hospital, I couldn't help but think that it was one of the many places in New York dear to my heart. I had worked there for twelve years, first as a laboratory technologist and then as a supervisor. I still had friends working there. It was there that I started to mingle with people of different ethnicities and faiths. Besides American-born citizens, I met many who were immigrants like me, such as Chinese, Filipinos, Russians, Koreans, Indians, Pakistanis, and Poles. It was also there that, for the first time, I witnessed the horror of the Holocaust. One of the chemists carried a tattooed number on her arm, a reminder of a Nazi concentration camp.

Nearby was the amusement park with the Cyclone that I used to ride with all the hairs on my body standing on end in fear. As I passed Bay

Ridge, the memory of wonderful Italian restaurants came to mind. One of my favorites was Areo. I ate there many times. The food was so good; I recommended it to my friends.

From the Verrazano Bridge, I could see the skyline of downtown Manhattan with the Statue of Liberty in the distance. The twin towers of the World Trade Center were missing. Terrorists had brought them down ten years earlier, on September 11, 2001, using two passenger planes as missiles, killing about three thousand people. One young woman from my gated community in Queens had lost her life as the World Trade Center collapsed. She had been married earlier that same year. I attended the memorial service in her honor; many people who didn't even know her had tears in their eyes. This event had an impact on the whole world. I was at home in Queens with my daughter as I watched it unfold on television; my wife was at work in Brooklyn. I remember telling my daughter, "This will change the way we live in the future," and it did.

We crossed Staten Island and connected to US highway I-95 heading south. After years of hustle and bustle in the Big Apple, the city that never sleeps, I left New York at early dawn, when most of its eight million citizens were still asleep. I felt like a bird escaping from its cage. Now I was free. To quote Richard Bach again, "There's a reason to life! We can lift ourselves out of ignorance, we can find ourselves as creatures of excellence and intelligence and skill. We can be free! We can learn to fly!"

And the Earth Trembled

On the way to Virginia, we stopped in a little town near the highway to have coffee with cream and sugar, toasted bagels with butter, and blueberry muffins. We arrived at the Lorton Amtrak station around noon. We handed over the car for loading and went inside the station to sit and wait for boarding time. I bought my wife a bottle of water in the little shop at the station. She got busy reading a book she had brought along. More people were entering the station to validate their registrations and get their tickets. Kids were running around playing noisily. Some people were dozing, unaffected by the surrounding noise. I flipped through the pages of a couple of magazines that were lying around. It didn't take me long to get bored, and by half past one o'clock, I decided to go outside. I walked along the sidewalk by the train tracks and then stopped in front of the station. Other passengers were there, watching the cars being loaded onto the train.

Then all of a sudden, I felt a tremor and saw a signpost in front of me shaking wildly. I looked around to see if a train was coming into the station. There was none. And then my cell phone started to light up.

First it was my wife, who frantically asked me, "Where are you? There is an earthquake."

"I am outside," I replied, and I rushed back inside to be with her.

My friends in New York started to call me. They, too, had felt the earthquake, and they knew the epicenter was in Virginia, where they expected me to be at that time, on my way to Florida. The train station's television was set to CNN (Cable News Network). I started to watch the news and learned that the 5.8-magnitude earthquake had been felt along the whole East Coast, all the way up through some Canadian provinces. It was 1:51 p.m. Eastern Daylight Savings time. Fortunately, there were no fatalities.

The train was delayed for a few hours to allow inspection of the tracks for possible earthquake damage. When we finally left, the normal speed of the train was reduced as a precaution.

My wife and I were traveling first class, as we sometimes do. We had a private cabin with sofa beds, a bathroom, and a shower, which made it perfect. We had dinner at five, and then we went back to our room. A movie was being shown after dinner, but we opted not to watch it, preferring to read and to talk. At nine, an employee came to prepare the bed for us and left us a couple of bottles of water. The sofa was transformed into a bunk bed with room for one person on each level. It was nice to have personalized service, which made life more comfortable.

Disaster and Sex

Suddenly, my wife looked very pensive. I asked her, "What's the matter, honey?"

With sadness in her eyes, she said, "What if we had died on our first day of retirement?"

She brought me back to the earthquake in Haiti on January 12, 2010, which killed more than two hundred thousand people in a split second and injured hundreds of thousands more. This catastrophic event awoke the consciences of citizens from every country on earth. People pulled together from around the world to help Haiti cope with that unfortunate situation. We personally knew people who had died in that earthquake.

Then I went back to my wife's question: "What if we had died on our first day of retirement?"

I looked her in the eyes and answered calmly, "It would have been God's will. We had a wonderful life. Forty years together; that's not so bad."

She smiled and melted in my arms. It is a well-known fact that as disaster threatens our survival, we are subconsciously impelled to have sex. I forgot about the upper deck that was set up for me and lay down with her on the narrow sofa bed. After intense lovemaking, enhanced by the rolling of the train, we found sweet sleep in the spoon position, hand in hand. God had other plans for us.

A Feeling of Gratitude

I got up in the middle of the night to go to the bathroom. When I went back to bed, I closed my eyes but couldn't sleep. I started to ponder my wife's question: "What if we had died on our first day of retirement?"

Yes, what if?

Instead of sorrow or regret, a feeling of gratitude overtook my whole body—gratitude for being alive, gratitude for all the people who touched my life and made it worth living.

A couple of questions came to mind: Why are we on this earth? Is it to make life easier for one another? Wasn't it Albert Einstein who said, "The highest destiny of the individual is to serve"?

Here I was, lying on my back with my eyes closed, in a semiconscious state. I started to think of the people who had come into my life to do a little kindness or to help me along the way. One by one, they came to my mind. It started with members of my immediate family, my mother and my father, my aunt who raised me, my grandmother who inspired me, my teachers, my mentors, and many other people I have encountered over seven decades of life. It became like a mind game. Facing death, I had relived my whole life in the space of only a few hours. It began with an incident that marked my life forever, a near-death experience I'd had long ago. It had an impact on me that only love could create.

CHAPTER 2

A Near-Death Experience and the Power of Love

Love never fails.

1 Corinthians 13:8

For three days, the boy lay in the hospital bed in a coma. The doctor had given up any hope of seeing him live. The boy's parents had been called in to be by his deathbed.

Then something extraordinary happened.

While in the coma, the boy saw himself in broad daylight on a wide country road, walking toward a magnificent enclosed garden. He felt so attracted to the garden. As he prepared to enter the garden, a guard at the gate raised her right hand, her palm facing him, signaling him to stop. And then the guard waved her hand back and forth in a motion that he understood to mean, "Go back. Do not enter."

Then nothing!

Bye-Bye, God

Time passed, and he heard women's voices calling his name from the distance. "Jess, Jess."

"Jess, Jess, I am your mother," one of them said.

"Jess, Jess, I am your aunt. Do you recognize me?" said the other one.

They touched his face and caressed his body.

The boy was indifferent to these two women who seemed to care so deeply for him. Still, he felt reassured by their presence and their expressions of love. The women were crying and praying desperately for his recovery.

"Mother Mary, *virgencita*, please give us our son!"

And then they heard him murmur repeatedly, "Bye-bye, God. Bye-bye, God. Bye-bye, God. Bye-bye, God."

Thinking that was the end, they frantically called the doctor. Dr. Phillip, a young physician who had just started working at the newly built hospital, rushed in. Upon hearing these words from the boy, he smiled and told the parents, "He is out of the coma; your son is going to live."

The women's faces radiated with joy. They embraced each other and hugged the doctor, exclaiming, "Thank you, doctor! Thank you!"

The boy slowly opened his eyes and faintly recognized his mother, Mane, and her older sister, Constance. They were leaning over him. Both of them had abundant tears in their eyes, this time tears of joy. Their boy had been saved.

The Power of Love

The story you just read really happened. The boy who had murmured "Bye-bye, God" over and over again while coming out of a coma was me.

While I remember the garden, I do not have a personal recollection of saying the words "Bye-bye, God." My mother and aunt related the story to me later. I was ten years old when it happened. I had come down with typhoid fever, a disease that, according to the Centers for Disease Control, strikes millions of people and kills thousands worldwide every year, due to lack of clean water and good hygiene. The love and tears of the two most important women in my early life lured me to delay my encounter with God.

According to mythology, Ulysses said good-bye to his wife, Penelope, and then went out on a life of epic adventures. He fought in the Trojan War, and he overcame many challenges, including being seduced and held captive by beautiful women. But at the end, he returned to Penelope, his loyal and true love.

On that fateful day at the hospital six decades ago, I said good-bye to God and began a new life of adventures that took me to New York City and many parts of the world. Like Ulysses, I am presently held captive by my own Calypso, my beautiful Yanick. She would like to keep me for herself eternally. But, again like Ulysses, one day I will return home, home to the place of ultimate love. Indeed, God is patiently waiting for my return. Hopefully, the garden I left behind years ago will still be beautiful.

This conception of death has allowed me to live my life without fear. François Cheng, the Chinese-born French Academy member, holds a similar position, exhorting us to look at life from the perspective of death, which is not an absurd ending but the fruit of our being. The great religions of the world teach that life does not end with death. We are sent here for a purpose, and we must fulfill our mission before we die. I do not claim to have the grandeur of the French cardinal Richelieu, who was so sure of his destiny that he boasted, "Heaven can wait," but I had the love of the two caring women who showed up on that fateful day at the hospital. Like two angels, they bargained with God on my behalf to prolong my earthly life. Heaven knows I am not a fast person; that's why I was given a long life and plenty of time to fulfill my destiny. It never ceases to amaze me that over the course of my life, many so-called angels have shown up to get me out of trouble or to make my life easier.

The story that follows is an account of how, at different crossroads in my existence, someone has always shown up—to open a door, to show me the way, or to help me carry my burden. Sometimes they have appeared just for a few seconds, to do a task and then to disappear. In other instances, they have entered my life for a long period of time; whether for a reason or for a season, an angel is always there, each one with a different face. I have come to expect the angels' arrivals. They always come. The first one was no less than the woman who gave me life and taught me the power of love: my mother.

CHAPTER 3

It's Dark Underground; Better Stay in the Light

Now I am become Death, the destroyer of worlds.

JULIUS ROBERT OPPENHEIMER, QUOTING THE BHAGAVAD GITA

MY MOTHER WAS A LOVELY young woman of French and African descent. She had fair skin and shoulder-length hair. She was twenty-five years old when she gave birth to me on Saturday, May 20, 1944, at 11:00 a.m. I was born in Gourdet, a small Haitian village that carries the name of my French ancestor. It is a section of the town of L'Asile, in the arrondissement of Anse-à-Veau, department of Nippes. It is well hidden in the middle of the south of Haiti, between the coastal towns of Anse-à-Veau and Aquin. It was a quiet place that managed to maintain a simple life even while the rest of the world was raging with World War II, the greatest war of all time.

The nations of the world were divided into two camps; the good guys were called the Allies, and the bad guys were called the Axis. It all started in 1939 with one man's ambition to dominate the world, and it ended in 1945, one year after my birth, with over fifty million people dead. The world had never seen such devastation caused by human hands. There are those who believe that aliens from outer space came to earth to instruct the Germans in the development of new warfare technology so that humans could destroy themselves, that it was their way of having fun.

Ultimately, the Americans stole the technology from the Germans and created a new wonder weapon called Little Boy. They dropped Little Boy on an Axis member, killing eighty thousand people in the blink of an eye. And if that wasn't enough, two days later they dropped an even more powerful bomb, Fat Man, on another city, killing about the same number of people in an instant.

When world leaders realized that this new technology had the potential to wipe everybody off the face of the earth, they sat at a table and talked about peaceful solutions to conflicts. The good guys won the war over the bad guys. "Make love, not war" became a slogan for a new generation that was born in big numbers after the war, the so-called baby boomers. I was born just a couple of years before they started to come out of their mothers' wombs.

In that little village of Gourdet, away from the madness, my mother had fallen in love with her second cousin Lecet Lapaix, a handsome young athlete with a dark complexion and straight hair, who was three years older than she was. But unbeknownst to my mother, he had already been chosen to marry a first cousin, based on an arrangement made between his mother and his uncle, the girl's father. My mom's father tried to break the love affair, but by then she was already expecting me. This situation turned into a little family feud involving me, even though I was still in my mother's womb. Anyway, as soon as I was born, my grandfather went to the town's recording office and registered my birth, listing himself as the child's father and his daughter as the child's mother. My grandfather became my father, and I became his son. In other words, I am legally both my mother's brother and her son. Sounds complicated? Fasten your seat belt; you are in for a ride.

A Love Affair That Didn't End

Soon afterward, my biological father went to the same recording office to proudly register my birth under his name, only to be told that my birth certificate had already been issued. He became angry with my grandpa, and he hurried to marry his first cousin as prearranged. An educated family member told me that my father had no choice. In compliance with African cultural beliefs, if your uncle chooses a wife for you, you must oblige. I don't know about that, but it wasn't the end of the story. He continued his love affair with my mother, and later, when she married another man, she was already carrying another son from my father. This was a secret that came to light only after her husband had passed away at an early age.

My mother bore three other children for her husband. Two of them died in infancy during the same week of the same year. In Haiti, there is a mysterious aspect to death. Nobody dies from disease or natural death. The common belief is that someone always causes your death. Most often, neighbors or business associates are the primary suspects. It wasn't any different in the case of the early death of my two siblings. It was believed that a neighbor had cast an omen on these two children. Someone had heard two stones being thrown into my mother's yard the night before the children got sick. My mother's grief was enormous. Happily, she was later blessed with another son.

My Relationship with My Mother

My relationship with my mother was very limited. When I was about three years old, my aunt took me to her house and raised me as her son. In my fifth to sixth year, my father reclaimed me, and I stayed with him. At the age of six, I was sent to boarding school, away from home. When summer vacations came, I went back to live with my aunt. And it stayed like that until I moved to the United States after graduating from university at the age of twenty-four.

Throughout my early life, I saw my mother only occasionally, briefly, when she came to the open market on Thursdays. Her house was miles away. The other times I saw her came when my aunt sent me to spend the occasional Sunday with her family and her during summer vacations.

I have very good recollections of these occasions. Each visit was a very big thing for my mother. She would receive me royally, as a dignitary. Her humble house was spotlessly clean. She set the dining table with an embroidered tablecloth. She properly arranged the bed with a clean linen sheet. She wouldn't allow anyone to sit on it. She reserved it for me, in case I wanted to take a nap. She sacrificed the top rooster to make the best meal in my honor.

Occasionally, she would tell me stories about my life when I was younger. On one such occasion, she pointed to a postcard that she had on the wall. It was the iconic picture of Clark Gable kissing Vivien Leigh in the famous movie *Gone with the Wind*. She told me that my father had given her that picture when they were going together.

Her husband, who was listening, immediately changed the subject by asking me, "Is it true that you're still peeing in bed?"

It was true, and I felt so embarrassed. It wasn't until I was about seven or eight years old that I overcame that condition. Many elders' remedies had been tried unsuccessfully to cure me of this disease.

Three of them come vividly to mind. First, I had to drink a glass of water in which a lizard was allowed to pee. Next, they threatened to tie a snake around my waist at bedtime. Third, they showered me with cold water first thing in the morning.

Obviously none of these barbaric techniques worked. Today, this kind of behavior would be called child abuse. Anyway, I continued to pee in bed, sometimes while dreaming that I was doing it in the field near a tree, like my little dog.

I didn't have to answer my stepfather's question. My mother immediately said, "Leave the child alone."

But, not to be deterred, he had another question for me: "How are you doing in school?"

This time, I beat him to the punch. I answered, "OK."

But my mother came out stronger and proudly said, "My son is first in his class." It was true, and I felt better.

Then my mother said, "Let's go visit a friend." It turned out to be the midwife who had delivered me. She was happy to see me.

"You've become quite a young man," she said. "It's like yesterday when I pulled you out of your mother's womb."

And after conversing with my mother, she turned to me and said, "I did something good for you on your delivery."

"What was it? I asked.

She hesitated, and it was my mother who answered: "She cut your umbilical cord with the precision that allows you to have a big penis."

I was so embarrassed. I turned my head to avoid looking at her. But the two of them were giggling mischievously like two devilish little girls who had happily pulled a successful prank on an innocent little boy.

Another time my mother showed me a small iron pot and told me, "You see this pot? I bought it for you when you were born. This is the pot I used to cook your food." My mother was so proud of me. She loved me so much. I had the feeling that she missed me. But she accepted the fact that I was in good hands with my aunt. Her husband, Etienne Dubos, was a town leader, and they had a successful business.

When the time came for me to leave, she always had a gift for me—a little money or some fruit, whatever she could afford. I felt so close to yet so far from her. I don't remember ever crying upon leaving her, only feeling sad. Her welcoming me into her house with such great honor and love inspired me. I promised myself to take care of her when I grew up, a promise that I later kept after her husband passed away. After I got settled in New York, I applied for and obtained permanent US visas for her and her two sons, my brothers, Gustave and Fritzner. At that time, US visas were easily and swiftly obtained.

Upon arriving in the United States, she spent the first six months with me. I taught her some rudimentary English, which came in handy. After the required stay in this country, she passed the citizenship test and became a US citizen. Being independent-minded, she found her own way in New Jersey, fifty miles away. She lived in this country for twenty-seven years, working and helping my brothers and other relatives raise their young families. Her greatest joy was when I took my kids to visit her in East Orange, New Jersey. She exuded real happiness. Unfortunately, I didn't do that often enough. Crossing Canal Street in Manhattan's Chinatown was such a hassle.

My kids were always amused at the fact that whatever money I gave her on these visits she would in turn share with them. She would tell them, "I pray for your father, and I pray for you every day." She was a very religious person. Morning and night, she would get on her knees to pray. I was glad that someone was communicating with God on my behalf. I could use that.

She was a lively person who made friends very easily. She was blessed with good health all her life. She went to the hospital only once in her entire life. She didn't stay long. She was sharing a room with another patient, and she didn't like the TV program the other patient was watching. She asked for a single room, and her request was granted. The next morning she asked her doctor if she could go home. The doctor complied. She never went back to a hospital. There was no need to.

The Death of My Mother

When my mother reached the age of eighty-six, her health began to decline. One day, she said she wanted to go to Haiti to visit her brother-in-law, my aunt's husband, now a widower. She got her round-trip ticket and traveled to Haiti. She stayed in her former house, which my brother Gustave had rebuilt and modernized. When the time came for her to return to the United States, she said she wanted to stay longer. About six months later, my brother went to Haiti to see her. He found her bedridden. Since my brother was experienced in geriatric care, he used his skills to help her.

One afternoon soon after his arrival, my brother was sitting by her bedside when my mother looked at him and said, "Why do you look so sad? You don't have to worry for me. I am not in pain. I only want to sleep."

My brother took her in his arms. She looked at him one last time and then expired. It was Saturday, August 6, 2005. She had been born on March 18, 1919.

On the day of my mother's death, I was in one of the exclusive villages of Long Island, New York, attending a housewarming barbecue party for a friend of mine. On my way back home, I got a call from my brother in Haiti. He let me know that my mother had passed away. At first, I felt a sense of guilt, thinking that here I had been, having fun while my mother was dying. And then it occurred to me that she was probably smiling at seeing me joyful as she crossed the threshold between life and death. She always wanted me to be happy. She cared more about her children's and grandchildren's well-being than her own. That was my mother.

Then other memories of her came to mind.

It was some years after she had moved to New Jersey. One Sunday a man came to visit me, and he asked to talk to me in private. He was a well-dressed gentleman about my mother's age. His face was serious, and he projected a sense of concern. I was wondering what this man had to tell me.

After we sat down, I asked him, "Would you care for a cup of coffee or a glass of soda?"

"Not now," he replied.

Then, looking in my eyes, he came straight to the point. "The reason I came to see you is because I wanted to ask you permission to date your mother, Mane."

The request caught me off guard. I didn't know my mother had a suitor. I didn't know what to say.

Then he added, "I have a well-paying job. I won't be a burden to your mother."

I looked at him. He was a decent man; I kind of liked him. I thought he would make a good companion for my mother, but I knew nothing about him. Above all, I didn't know what was going on between him and my mother.

I simply told him, "Let me speak to my mother, and I'll get back to you."

When I told her about my conversation with this man, she said, "Tell him that in my family, a woman doesn't take another man when her husband dies."

A Hidden Secret

It was common knowledge in my family that my mother never ceased to love my father, her first love. We teased her sometimes about that, and it made her laugh and be happy.

It was on one such occasion, while I was talking to her about her love for my father, that she revealed to me a secret never before told to anyone. She confided, "When I became pregnant with you, your grandfather was so mad because he didn't want your father for me. I couldn't stand his wrath. I was so desperate that I decided to take my life along with you in my belly. Somehow your paternal grandma, who was your grandpa's cousin, found out, and she talked me out of such a bad idea. As she put it, 'It's dark underground; better stay in the light.'"

I felt a jolt hitting me right in the middle of my heart. I looked at her, but she avoided my gaze by looking down. I could see tears coming out of her eyes.

"I am sorry," she said.

At that moment, I felt closer to her than I'd ever been in my entire life, and it stayed like that.

One day, I showed a picture of my mother that I carried in my wallet to a friend of mine.

She held the picture and said, "Your mother looks sad. Why?"

I had no answer. But from then on I saw the picture from a different perspective. There was indeed an air of sadness about her in the picture. Although my mother exuded a pleasing personality and had many good reasons to be grateful, deep in her heart she was concealing pain, and that was what my friend, who was also a mother, had picked up from the picture. As Longfellow wrote, "Every heart has its secret sorrows, which the world knows not."

My mother survived the ordeal of unwanted pregnancy thanks to my paternal grandmother, Claire, and her advice: "It's dark underground; better stay in the light."

CHAPTER 4

Honor and Respect

Children, obey your parents, for this is the right thing to do.

Ephesians 6:1

Her maiden name was Claircilia Gourdet; she was a tall and big black woman with a round face and short, thin hair. She was very imposing and well respected.

At the gate of her house, people would call, "Honor."

A servant would reply, "Respect."

Then they would be allowed to enter.

As I recall, her favorite words were these: "Who do you think you are, the queen of England?" Perhaps, in some way, she thought she was a queen in her own right.

She was my paternal grandmother and the cousin of my mother's father.

Her husband had gone to work in Cuba, leaving her with the task of raising her children on her own—a task she did admirably. My grandma had no daughters, but she had four sons, of whom she had great expectations. My father studied tailoring at one of the most prestigious shops in the country and became a master tailor before venturing into other businesses. His younger brother Lenord was a saddler who had his own saddle shop, where he also trained other young men in the trade. The third brother, named Robert, enlisted in the police force and became a well-known motorcyclist. For many years, he headed all presidential motorcades. The fourth brother, Joseph, was born after my grandfather came back from Cuba. He is only a few years older than I am. He currently lives in Pompano Beach, Florida. I talk to him periodically.

Who Will Bury Me When I Die?

My grandmother had a great influence over my father. I am sure she urged him to bury the hatchet with my grandpa. The expression "paying alimony" did not exist at that time. My grandma made sure my father took care of me. Her influence over my father didn't stop there. I can see the truth of that in one particular incident.

Starting in the 1950s, many people were immigrating to the United States. My father got caught in the frenzy. He obtained a permanent US visa at a price of $1,000. When he went to tell his mother that he was going to the United States, she instantly passed out and fell down.

When she woke up, she told him, "You're not my son anymore. Who will bury me when I die?"

My father canceled his trip and lost his money. He would never travel in his long life, which covered the span of a century. Looking back, I think it was a blessing for my father. The United States of the fifties with its racial discrimination wasn't the best place for a black Haitian to live. Besides, I doubt that in this country he would have lived to be a centenarian.

Last Words before Dying

My best memory of my grandmother comes from a time just before she died.

She was sick and knew she was going to die. She asked for me to come to see her. I was already eighteen years old. I arrived at her house, and I was ushered to her bedroom. She motioned for me to approach the bed, where she was lying down. As I looked at her, the big and imposing woman I knew looked so frail. She had pain in her eyes, but her voice was strong as she spoke to me.

"You know, you're not going to see me anymore," she said.

I felt sadness in my heart, but I kept quiet.

"I wanted to talk to you," she added. I gave her all my attention, and she said, "I want you to stay in school and do well. When you start working, make sure that you take care of your mother and your aunt. Do you hear me, son?"

"Yes, Grandma!"

Then she added, "I left something for you; your father will give it to you."

She looked at me stoically, apparently somewhat content that she had fulfilled a last duty, and then she dismissed me. "You can go now."

I kissed her on the forehead, and I left the room with a feeling of emptiness. A few days later, on a hot summer day in 1962, she died peacefully in her bed, surrounded by family and friends. It was the first time I had experienced the death of a dear one in such a close and personal manner. I was glad to be in town for such an experience.

When the Boy Scouts Sing

I don't know a lot about comparative religions, but I have attended funeral services given by a few different faiths. And when it comes to pomp and circumstance, nothing that I have seen beats the Catholic Church. And when the funeral service is combined with a ceremony by the Boy Scouts, you have a celebration that stirs every fiber of your being. It was thus at the funeral for my grandma.

It just so happened that my Boy Scouts troop had chosen to hold a summer camp in my hometown that year. Our chieftain was a seasoned *routier*, a leader with years of experience in the Boy Scouts. He guided us through the most elaborate funeral ceremony for my grandma.

We participated in the religious part of the ceremony. I remember being transported to a realm of higher consciousness while inhaling the smoke of the incense being burned in a little device called a *thurible*. It was suspended on chains, and the priest swung it around the casket. It emitted smoke for purification and as a sign of reverence for the dead. I felt a little tingling in my heart when the priest sang the Latin version of Psalm 130, the prayer for the faithful departed.

"From the depths of my despair I call to you, Lord. Hear my cry, O Lord..."

About twenty of us, all in Boy Scout uniforms, performed the scout rituals with songs and movements that touched the hearts of all those in attendance. The grand finale came when we led the mourners in singing the beautiful and sad song "It's Just a Good-bye" in French. The song was almost overshadowed by the intermittent crying and lamenting of the mourning women, and it filled everyone in attendance with grief.

It's just a good-bye, my brothers.
It's just a good-bye.
We will see each other again.
It's just a good-bye.

Then she was laid to rest in a mausoleum built on her property, one worthy of her status. In that part of Haiti, resting places for the dead are often more luxurious than houses for the living. My grandma's grave site has remained a sacred place for me to pause and reflect. I am grateful to her for coming to my mother's aid at a difficult time in her life. She probably saved both of us, my mother and me. I still draw strength from her memory.

Later in the afternoon of the funeral, a woman approached me. She suffered from mental illness and was considered the loony of the town. She touched me gently on the arm and said, "It was really beautiful what you did for your grandma; God will reward you for that."

I said, "Thank you." I couldn't understand how a person with psychological disorders could be so rational. From that day on, she had my utmost respect.

I told my aunt Constance Dubos what the woman had said. She concurred, saying, "It was a dignified ceremony for a dignified lady. Your grandma was buried the way she lived, with *honor* and *respect.*"

CHAPTER 5

Take Care of the Children

There is no greater joy nor greater reward than to make a fundamental difference in someone's life.

MARY ROSE MCGEADY

BY THE TIME I WAS about three years old, one of my aunts, my mother's older sister, Constance Gourdet Dubos, had already been married for a few years. She had lost hope of having children; her husband was purported to be sterile. She decided to take charge of me and took me into her house, which was only a short distance from my grandparents' house where my mother lived. I stayed with her until I was about five years old, when my father took me to live with him in L'Asile, the main town. But my aunt took me again after my father remarried.

I remember being very happy with my aunt in Gourdet, the village that bears our name. It was located on a hill, and behind the hill there were mountains with verdant trees. I remember the shade trees under which I used to sit and dream, the sweet aroma of orange-tree flowers that I enjoyed smelling. The sunsets were splendid. At night, I could see all the stars in the sky. Occasionally, a comet would streak through the night sky. It was not only spectacular but also magical; you could make a wish, and it would come to pass. I liked it even more when it rained because my aunt would allow me to dance naked in the rain. There were many cousins I could play with. Today, most of the original inhabitants have left Gourdet, but it is still a beautiful village with trees and flowers. Its spring, called Source Gourdet, is considered a mystical place that continues to attract visitors. I am emotionally attached to the place; my umbilical cord was planted there under a coconut tree, as per the custom of that time.

A Sense of Hope and Optimism

My aunt showered me with a lot of love. She saw to it that I received a good education. Later, she introduced me to her social and business contacts. She was such a great hostess. She extended herself to the limit to welcome guests. All important visitors to my hometown passed by her house, and they never forgot her.

When I moved to the capital, where I didn't know anybody, she gave me a list of people to visit. Many of them I had met at her home. Some, like Lemieux Gourdet, were family members. He ran a successful food store in the Post Marchand section of Port-au-Prince. His son was a well-known military officer of high rank. Others were business or political leaders who came to my town. On Sundays, I would visit these people, and invariably, they would receive me cordially, sometimes even inviting me to dinner. One such person was a diplomat who lived in the hills in one of the better neighborhoods of the capital. He was so gracious; he told me that the door to his home was open to me anytime. Once he invited me to a party where I met other influential people, including a member of the American consulate who would later prove to be a door opener for me. These encounters gave me a sense of hope and optimism and built up my confidence.

A Visit to a Wise Man

One time my aunt sent me to see a man who lived not far from us in my hometown. He wasn't a voodoo priest, but he had the reputation of being a wise man who knew things. My aunt gave me a small bottle of wine to take with me. When I arrived at his house, he welcomed me kindly. As he opened the package that had the bottle of wine, he looked at me, a little disturbed.

He said, "I think your aunt forgot something. Go back and bring me a sheet of parchment and a brand-new pencil."

It took me another hour to gather the items requested. On my return, he asked me to take a seat at the table. He opened a book of prayers and told me to copy one of the prayers onto the parchment with the newly sharpened pencil. After I finished, he burned the parchment and put the ashes in a glass. He grated a piece of ivory, letting the scraps fall into the glass. Then he poured the wine into the glass and mixed everything together. Then, holding the glass in both hands, he closed his eyes and prayed over it. His face transformed completely. He looked very serene, and he emanated a sense of peace and power. When he opened his eyes, he had a smile on his face.

He handed me the glass and said, "You can drink it now."

I did. That was the first time I drank a glass of wine. A warm sensation went to my head and permeated my whole body.

When I had finished, I returned the glass to him, and he told me, "You can go now, son. *No harm will befall you.*" Here, he was quoting Psalm 91:10 of the Holy Bible.

My aunt wanted to make sure I was well protected. There was a lot of evil out there.

Teaching by Example

I wasn't the only one who benefited from my aunt's good heart. Many of my cousins, especially my late cousin Annette, got a head start in life because of her. I am most grateful to my aunt for the love she showered on me all her life. From her I learned discipline and generosity.

I remember a conversation I had with her once.

Many people of my hometown didn't know how to read and write. Some would come to me to handle their correspondence. I would read and answer letters they had received from relatives living in other towns. It never occurred to me to charge them for this service, and they didn't think it was necessary to pay me anyhow. I considered it an honor to help these people, some of whom were respectable heads of family.

One day my aunt asked me, "How come you're not charging these people for service rendered? Am I sending you to school to be stupid?"

I looked her straight in the eyes and said, "Auntie, I learned it from you. You're the one who is always giving things to people without expecting anything in return."

She turned around and said nothing.

That's who she was.

A Cry in the Night

As much as my aunt was a loving person, she was also a woman of high morals.

There was a young woman who served as the housemaid. She lived with her family some miles away and would go home in the evening. One day, she had to sleep over. I was already a teenager, and she was much older than I was. Instead of making a bed for her on the floor, my aunt told the maid she could sleep with me in my full-size bed. (Big mistake.) In the middle of the night, I happened to touch her. Her skin was so smooth; it gave me a strong erection. She felt my desire and pulled me over her. We quietly made love and slept happily.

The next morning, at the breakfast table, my aunt was somewhat agitated. She said, "I don't know where I got the idea to put the two of you in the same bed." Her husband was hiding a smile.

The maid and I knew what she was talking about; we kept quiet. From that day on, my aunt started to monitor my interactions with girls. She would never let me sleep with other females. And when she saw me get too close to a girl she didn't approve of, she would interject subtle comments for my edification, such as, "If I were you, I wouldn't get into this family."

When I took my wife to meet her for the first time, she approved of her immediately, even without knowing anything about her or her family. My wife was so pretty and exuded such loveliness that everybody liked her. I was so happy.

Later on, when my wife and I visited my aunt, she would tell my wife, "Thank you for taking good care of my son."

On many occasions, I invited my aunt to come to visit my family in the United States. She never did. She wanted to, but her husband didn't like to travel. She couldn't bear the idea of leaving him without her care, even for a few weeks. Ironically, they had not always been close, as I knew from the times as a kid when I heard her fighting with her husband over sex. I slept in the room next door to them, which was how she had heard my cry in the night while making love with the maid and that likewise allowed me to overhear my aunt and uncle.

"Get your hands off me. Go to your whores," she said to her husband one night, after she had found out that he was seeing other women.

With time, my aunt and her husband overcame that hurdle, and they became inseparable.

Talking with the Dead

When my aunt passed away, I was in New York and couldn't attend the funeral. A feeling of sadness overtook my whole being. Soon afterward, I started dreaming about her constantly, at least two or three times a week. It became an obsession.

I couldn't figure out what was going on until I spoke with an old woman who told me, "You need closure. Your aunt wants to see you. Why don't you go to visit her resting place?"

I went to Haiti and held a religious service in her memory, with a Catholic Mass and reception. After the service, I visited her tomb, and I talked to her as if she were right there in front of me.

"Auntie, here I am. I have been sensing the aura of your presence around me. That's why I came to see you. I want you to know how much I love you, how grateful I am for all you've done for me and for the people of this town. Not only did you raise me, but you also took other cousins of mine under your care. Your house was always full of guests. People would come for coffee in the morning, and others would come for dinner and supper. On many summers you allowed me to bring friends from boarding school to be with me. Whatever money you made was spent on charity. You always found a way to uplift a soul or to feed the hungry. Do you know what the priest told me? He said that you should be considered for sainthood because of your charitable work and your great devotion to the church. Cannot beat that, Auntie! Remember, I love you even more than you ever loved me. May you rest in peace!"

She was a fervent Catholic. Her faith was central to her life. At a time when most people in my village were practicing both Catholicism and Voodoo, she totally rejected the latter. Once, there was a voodoo ceremony held in my village. I sneaked in to watch the women dancing. They came in long white robes and red headscarves. Under the mesmerizing effect of the tambour's rhythmic sounds, they fell into trances, one after another, merging into divine essence.

When my aunt found out that I had attended such a forbidden ceremony, she warned me, "You're a church boy. I don't want you to mess with voodoo."

After her death, her husband told me that after she became ill and the doctors sent her home to die, he had offered to have a voodoo priest come to work on her. She had vehemently refused, saying that her faith was in Christ; she wanted to die as a true Christian. Still, her house was open to people of all religious persuasions.

"Passport" Issued by a Secret Society of Sorcerers

I remember an old man in our town who used to come to the house most mornings for coffee and small talk. Once, he told the following story, which covered my skin with goose bumps as I listened to him.

"One night, on the way to the capital on my horse, I came upon a band of voodoo society members who were holding a meeting at a crossroads near a town named Léogane. They stopped me and asked me to show my credentials. It is common knowledge that intruders are not welcomed to these gatherings. The consequences could be severe, from bodily harm all the way to death. I pulled my *laissez-passer* from my pocket and showed it to the leader. He looked at it, and by his smile I knew I was OK.

"He gave the passport back to me and told one of his assistants, 'Give this man a drink. He is one of us.' Someone asked me to turn around and sit on my horse facing backward, and then they handed me a drink."

My aunt was listening, as scared as I was, and she asked, "Did you drink it?"

The man replied, "Yes, I did. I had no choice, and after that, the only thing I remember is that someone vigorously slapped the rear end of my horse with the flat side of a machete. When I returned to myself, I had reached my destination. It was in a fraction of a second. I never knew how I got there."

(Was this a hallucinogenic effect caused by a drug? Or was it time travel through a wormhole that only an initiate can perform? You decide.)

The old man touched his jacket pocket and concluded, "I always carry my *laissez-passer* for my protection. It was issued to me by a secret society of sorcerers. It is valid all over the country."

My aunt went to the kitchen and brought another fresh pot of coffee. In her physiognomy I could read fear. But unlike my aunt, I was mesmerized by the story, and I strongly wanted to see this "passport," but obviously I couldn't ask him to show it to me. Besides, my aunt would have killed me if she had found out that I was interested in esoteric things like that. I forgot about the *laissez-passer*, but as you will see, the *laissez-passer* didn't forget about me. Fate would have it that I would see a copy—but only years later.

After I came to the United States, I took courses at Brooklyn College. One day at the college's library, I stumbled upon a book titled *Voodoo in Haiti* by Alfred Métraux.

I started to flip through the pages, and lo and behold, there was a copy of a "passport" issued by a Haitian secret society of sorcerers. It had to be the same kind of passport the man at my aunt's house had been carrying.

It was written on officially numbered, stamped paper of the Republic of Haiti, indicating a price of ten cents. It included a sketch of a man extending his arms as if to direct traffic.

It was written in imperfect French. Here is my English translation:

Liberty, Equality, Fraternity, Republic of Haiti
In the name of the Father, in the name of the Son
and in the name of the Holy Spirit, Amen.
*Passport issued to the name of*______________________
Recommended in the name of the Master of Crossroads
Recommended in the name of the Master of Highways
[Recommended in the name of other entities]

Holding the book in my hands made me think about my aunt. She welcomed everyone in her house, even if she didn't share the person's religious beliefs. To quote Darwin, "Let each man hope and believe what he can."

A Final Good-Bye

When I returned to New York after the memorial service in my aunt's honor, I had one last dream of her.

I was in my house, and I saw her outside, looking at me through the window. I was both surprised and happy to see her. She waved at me and said, "I am leaving you now. Take care of the children."

Then she faded into the light and disappeared. I have never dreamed of her since.

Here was a woman who never gave birth to a child of her own but devoted her whole life to the care of other people's children. I was happy to learn recently that her house was converted into a soup kitchen where food was provided to the needy. It couldn't have served a better purpose. Even in death, she was still concerned about the well-being of children.

Once, I sent my two children, Greg and Jessica, to visit her. She was ecstatic about it. She took them on a tour of my hometown, introducing them to friends and other relatives as if they were her own grandchildren. She proudly showed them my old Boy Scout uniform. She had kept it all those years as a sign of the joy and pride I had brought her when wearing that uniform. Her love for me extended to my children and maybe to all children.

I pondered over her last words: "Take care of the children."

I couldn't figure out if she was referring to my own children or to children in general.

To solve that problem, I do the best I can for my children and grandchildren, and I also help other children, both here in the United States and in Haiti. As Maya Angelou said, "If you find it in your heart to care for somebody else, you will have succeeded."

My aunt was still providing me with guidance even after her death, as she had in her life. I remember once, I was playing when she noticed that my father was in the neighborhood, overseeing work that was being done on his properties. She called me and said, "Go say good morning to your dad."

That was after she had fixed my hair, tucked my shirt into my pants, and put a book in my hand. She wanted me to make a good impression.

My father looked at the book in my hand and said, "Well, well, we are so studious!"

CHAPTER 6

Zeus's Erotic Escapades

He mated with goddesses and nymphs, princesses and mortal women; he changed into a bull to ravish Europa as she was picking flowers by the seashore; into a shower of gold to penetrate Danaë; into a swan to couple with Leda; into an eagle to catch Asteria who had turned herself into a quail; into Amphitryon to make love to his wife, Alcmena.

ARIANNA HUFFINGTON AND FRANÇOISE GILOT, *THE GODS OF GREECE*

MY FIRST RECOLLECTION OF MY father involves a visit when I was about two or three years old.

I was sitting on my mother's lap on the porch of my grandpa's house when my father showed up on his horse. He looked so gallant, so powerful. But I didn't like it when he said to my mother, "What's this young man doing on your lap?" He was referring to me. I clung a little tighter to my mother.

And she said, "Leave him alone."

Then my father pulled on the reins of his horse to make it dance in a circle. That's when my little dog, Tutu, a gift from my grandpa, started to bark at him. And he left.

A CASE OF DOWN SYNDROME

At some point during my fifth and sixth years, I went to live with my father. He was living alone at that time. His marriage to his first cousin had collapsed. A child of the union had been born with congenital abnormalities. The child had Down syndrome, a disease that is now well understood as a chromosome disorder. The child died in infancy.

There were talks of obtaining an annulment from the church for consanguinity problems due to the couple's close blood relation, but in the end my father sought and got a divorce.

Afflicted by that situation and trying to make sense of his life, my father took me from my aunt. During the time I spent with him, he already had a thriving business as a tailor. In his shop, he had multiple Singer sewing machines and many young men learning the tailoring trade from him. He was also involved in farming, and for a pastime, he organized cockfighting, as they still do in some parts of Haiti.

His live-in assistant, Gerard, took care of me. He made sure that I was clean, well dressed, and properly fed. He accompanied me to school in the morning and picked me up in the afternoon. He was always nice to me.

Feeding on the Plant of Immortality

One morning I noticed that Gerard was feeding my father's roosters with little pieces of aloe vera. I asked him why. He said aloe vera was good for roosters.

"How is that?" I asked.

"These roosters are being prepared for cockfighting. Aloe vera makes them strong and fearless," he answered.

"Give me a piece," I said.

"You shouldn't eat it," he said.

"Why?" I asked.

"It's very bitter."

"Let me try it," I begged.

He gave me a piece of aloe vera. I swallowed it. It was indeed very bitter, but I wanted more of it.

"Give me another piece," I asked.

He gave it to me, and I ate it like candy. He was in awe. He couldn't believe that I tolerated such a bitter taste. From then on, I made sure I was with him in the morning when he fed the roosters. Like them, I wanted to be strong and fearless.

There was a very good reason for that. My father was a very strict disciplinarian, and he used his leather belt to punish me for the least deviation from his rules.

While I was staying with him, he remarried, and his new wife, Gloria, came to live with us. She was strongly opposed to my father's beating me, and on many occasions she hid me under her long dress to help me escape my father's belt.

My father, like many other fathers at that time, followed the example of the God of Moses. He instilled fear and obedience in his children so that they could become good citizens. I developed such a fear of my father that it affected me over a long time. You understand why I took my daily dose of aloe vera, this "plant of immortality," already known by the pharaohs of Egypt. It was to build courage to face the wrath of my father. I was going to learn another secret for developing courage after I met a friend of my father.

The Secret of Robin Hood

My father had a beautiful guitar and an Italian mandolin that he played occasionally. I desperately wanted to play the guitar, but he wouldn't let me. His reason was that musicians don't amount to anything; besides, he said, they get intoxicated and are not taken seriously by society. Little did he know that in just another generation, young musicians like the Beatles, Johnny Hallyday, and members of the mini-jazz movement would empower themselves to such magnitude that, as a group, they would change the very fabric of society worldwide. In Haiti itself, Michel Martelly, a young musical bandleader, would later become president of the country. Although my father didn't allow me to play his guitar and mandolin, he did allow me to sit with him in the evening as he played with a good friend of his named François Vaval.

Vaval was a passionate musician and a fine human being. He was very fond of me, and he would occasionally tease my father by saying, "Lecet"—that's my father's first name—"why don't you sell me your son? He is a good kid."

To that, my father would invariably reply, "I like my son. He is not for sale."

Vaval was playing with my father's ego. It bothered him to see my father punishing me for minor offenses.

One summer evening when my father was away, Vaval came to the house, and he sat on the porch playing his guitar and singing beautiful songs that he had composed. Then he stopped playing, and he said to me, "Can I tell you a story?"

"I love stories," I replied.

Then he told me the story of a knight named Robin Hood.

"Robin Hood," he said, "was a valiant man. He didn't like to see people suffer. He and his men would go around on their horses, taking from the rich and giving to the poor."

Then he looked at me and added, "I must teach you his magic song, the song that gave him power and the courage to fight like one hundred men."

I was very anxious to learn that song. It was called "Mi Mi Do Do," and it goes like this: first, you say, "Do re mi fa sol la ti do."

Then, you sing:

Mi mi do do la la sol
Si si la sol
Do re mi mi mi do do
Si si la sol mi mi do do
Do re mi mi mi do do

I listened to Vaval attentively. It didn't take me long to learn Robin Hood's song. Whatever brought Vaval into my life, he came at a good time. I was at that age when fact and fiction were interwoven in my mind. The song was very useful. It brought me a feeling of strength and inner peace. I would sing it whenever I wanted to muster the courage to face adversity.

François Vaval was a romantic. Some of his songs became national hits under other people's names. One example was the song "Lisa," which was popularized by the famous Haitian singer Gérard Dupervil. Later on, Vaval married my stepmother's younger sister and was blessed with a son and two beautiful daughters. When I started working, I bought him a portable radio/cassette player to record and play his songs. He was so happy. His affection for me never waned. He made my father realize how precious I was, and he instilled in my father a different sense of paternalism, one based on affection and not on harsh discipline.

Later, I would read books and see movies about Robin Hood. What I discovered was a legend that went back to the Middle Ages. Over the centuries Robin Hood came to represent, in an idyllic way, all those who fight in favor of social and economic justice for the oppressed. The problem still exists; that's why the legend never dies, and the song goes on.

A Good Father

I still have some good memories of the time I spent with my father when I was about five or six years old. Whenever he went to the capital on business, he would bring me back a little souvenir. Once, it was a little plastic box with an eyepiece for viewing. When I looked through the eyepiece, I could see two beautiful women in bathing suits by a waterfall. I would spend a long time admiring these two beautiful women. Adults would borrow it from me to enjoy the view, and I was pleased to know that these beautiful girls were mine.

One day, I looked for it and couldn't find it. I realized I had lost it. Later, I found it on the front step of the house. Someone had inadvertently stepped on it and crushed it. I was inconsolable. As you know, the pain of a child is pure and genuine.

Soon afterward, I went to boarding school, and when I came back for summer vacation, I lived with my aunt, who by then had moved to the main town, L'Asile, where my father resided.

Although my aunt provided me with emotional support and showered me with love, it was my father who regularly paid for my room and board, except for the time when he was ill. Throughout my school years, he bought me whatever books I needed for classes. All in all, he was a good father to me. For my part, I made him proud of me by being a good student.

A Subconscious Connection to My Father

Subconsciously, I was attached to my father, and maybe he was attached to me, too. This subconscious connection can be seen in two dreams I had about him during my teenage years. I was in L'Asile, my hometown, when I had the first dream. I was in Anse-à-Veau in boarding school when I had the second dream.

In the first dream, I saw my father in a ditch, like a tomb, and he couldn't get up. I felt so sorry to see him in that condition. The next morning, still with sadness in my heart, I told my aunt about the dream. She listened to me attentively, and then she said, "I hope nothing bad happened to your dad."

He was away on business in Port-au-Prince, the capital. Later that morning we received news that my father had had a terrible accident. He had been in a store when a pile of aluminum roof panels fell on him. He had a broken leg and multiple bruises and required hospitalization for many weeks.

The other memorable dream I had of my father had a happier outcome.

In the dream, I heard the sound of a voice telling me very clearly, "Your father is dead." It was around my fifteenth birthday. I knew then that if you dreamed of someone's death, it meant that the person's age would hit in the lottery. At that time, my father was forty-three. I was so sure of that prediction that I played the number forty-three with all the money that I had. Sure enough, the number forty-three came up as the first prize. I made more money than I knew what to do with. I bought a fancy shirt for myself and a nice gift for my sweetheart, the girl I was in love with. Then I threw a birthday party for myself, inviting my friends. A few bottles of soda and a box of Ritz crackers made everybody happy. Still I had money left over.

In spite of such a happy early experience, I don't gamble. Occasionally I play the lottery but only on hunches. Money has always come to me to meet my needs. All I had to do was work hard, be smart, control my expenses, and invest wisely.

An Expression of Love

After his accident, one of the first things my father did while in the hospital was to request my presence by his side. From my hometown, I traveled to Port-au-Prince to visit him. It was the first time I had gone to the capital. All the lights at night amazed me. Neither my hometown nor Anse-à-Veau, where I went to school, had electricity. To me, it was like having a full moon every night. Although I was there to visit my hospitalized father, my first trip to the capital was an exhilarating experience. The beautiful stores and the incredible items for sale amazed me. On a street corner someone was selling crushed ice in a paper cone and offering multiple flavors of syrup to put on top. The ice was grated from a block with a little apparatus that also served as a measuring device. They called it *fresco.* It melted deliciously in my mouth and made me forget the heat of the sun.

Looking back, I realize that this gesture from my father went a long way toward reaffirming his love for me.

Later on, he made another such gesture. At the age of ninety-eight, he told me over the phone, "I'd like to see you. I have something to tell you. You don't have to hurry; I am not going to die right away." I jumped on a plane and traveled to Haiti from Florida to spend a few days with him. It was one of my most emotionally rewarding visits to Haiti. When I arrived, he was lying in his bed. He asked me to help him sit up on the edge of the bed with his feet on the floor. His face reflected an expression of concern. He told me that he wasn't doing well. I put my hand on his head and ran my fingers through his long, fine white hair. No sign of hair thinning or baldness. Although he had lost his physical vigor, mentally he was very alert. For three days, we talked on a wide range of subjects covering his lifetime. He told me over and over how happy he was to see me, and he also told me about his belief in Christ and nothing else.

At the end, he told me, "I am so very happy that you came to see me. If I die, you don't even have to come to my funeral, unless you really want to. You've done your duty."

I gave him a hug and kissed him good-bye, and I took the plane back to Florida.

How to Quit Smoking

One day when I was a teenager, my father caught me smoking a cigarette. He didn't tell me not to smoke. In fact, he didn't say anything, but I could see on his face that he wasn't happy. Later that day, while I was in his presence with some other people, he told a story.

"When I was a young man," he said, "I went to visit a girl that I was courting. At her house was a friend of mine who was also interested in her. At some point, my friend lit up a cigarette and started to send beautiful puffs in the air in a gallant manner to impress the girl. I asked my friend, 'Can you lend me a cigarette?'

"He said he didn't have any more. But later he pulled another cigarette from his pocket and started to smoke again. All the while, the girl was enjoying this little fight between my friend and me for her hand.

"From that day on," my father said, "I made a determination to quit smoking, and I never smoked again. For this reason, I will never give money to people to buy cigarettes."

Obviously, he was talking to me in the most indirect way. I got the message and never smoked again for the rest of my life. The cold-turkey method of quitting is not for everybody. It is reserved for only a few lost souls who can command the mental toughness needed to succeed. In my father's case, the motivation came from the desire to seduce a girl. In my case, it came from my longing to please my father.

A Man of Extreme Virility

My father was a man of extraordinary virility who engendered children up until his seventies. With his wife, Gloria, my father had one son, who died in infancy, and four daughters. All four daughters, France, Suze, Loline, and Simone, did very well as health care professionals. Additionally, my father had scores of children out of wedlock with different women. Some of them I never met. Obviously, he took literally the message of the Bible in Genesis 1:28, where it says, "Have many children, so that your descendants will live all over the earth."

My father's passion for young women and his cunning ways for getting them into bed were topped only by the erotic escapades of the ruler of the Olympians, the Greek god Zeus.

Like Alcmena—who, according to Greek mythology, slept with her husband and Zeus on the same night to produce Hercules—some women attributed the paternity of their children to my father although they were married to loving husbands. One married woman, he told me, sought him out through an intermediary and asked him to give her a child that her husband could not. There was a condition. He could have only one encounter with that woman. That was all my father needed. They conceived a boy, and my father was allowed to see him only once, in the absence of the husband.

Today, the use of a surrogate mother, the purchase of sperm, and in vitro fertilization are common methods for acquiring a desired child. Traditional couples, same-sex couples, or those who can afford it take advantage of advances in science and technology to obtain a child without copulating. On the other hand, some celebrities surround themselves with young, virile men. My father, who was an athlete, claimed to have benefited from the affection of a famous Cuban singer on her visit to Haiti years ago.

As for my father's escapades, he told me once that promiscuity is a weakness. While it's good pedagogy to teach by example, in this case, he said, "Do as I say, not as I do." I took his advice.

The analogy of my father with Zeus stops right there. While Zeus was a powerful warrior who led the Olympians and won the war against the Titans, my father was a pacifist who didn't believe in taking up arms.

A Man of Peace

I remember one night during the time when Papa Doc Duvalier's dictatorship was terrorizing the country; my father and a friend were conversing while sitting on the wall of a small bridge in my hometown.

The friend asked my father, "Don't you think that something should be done about this regime?"

"Like what?" my father replied.

The man surveyed the surroundings, making sure that there was nobody within hearing distance. Then he said, "If I were to take up arms to change the regime, would you be willing to fight with me?"

I was standing by my father. I could see that the question took him off guard. He looked at me, and placing his hand over my shoulder, he pulled me closer to him. Then, in a straightforward way, he said, "Who would take care of my children if I died?"

The man did not answer.

I didn't like my father's answer. In fact, I was shocked. At that moment I thought he was the greatest coward ever. The story of Robin Hood was still fresh in my mind.

Why can't my father fight against tyranny and oppression, like Robin Hood? I asked myself. Maybe he didn't know the song "Mi Mi Do Do La La Sol," as I sang it in my heart.

But my father knew about arms, I thought. Occasionally he would take me hunting with him. He would go after wood pigeons with his Benjamin air rifle, and I would try to bring down some *tourterelle* birds with my slingshot. These were cherished moments. I never considered my father to be my friend, but he was my dad, and he cared for me. Going hunting with him provided excellent opportunities for conversation between the two of us. He would tell me about the boxing champion Joe Louis—in his opinion, the greatest fighter of all time. He told me that he, too, used to compete in boxing as a young man. Still, he was a man of peace. He wasn't going to use guns to kill people.

As of this writing, my father just celebrated his one-hundredth birthday, and he is living peacefully in his house in Haiti. His health is good except for back pains, which he says are the result of a lifetime of hard work. My cousin Ketty gave me a different reason for my father's back pains.

"He had too much sex while standing up," he confided.

I have no doubt that, had he gone along with his friend to be part of a rebellion, my father would either have perished or been forced into exile, as were countless others who tried and failed to overthrow Papa Doc. The opposition didn't stand a chance. The friend who had urged my father to take up arms wound up in prison and eventually left the country. That was the only way he could stay alive.

Looking back, I think that my father acted out of love. His love for his children and his concern for their well-being were greater than his loathing for the tyranny of a dictator. On the positive side, look at how many flowers wouldn't have been watered and how many children wouldn't have walked on the earth's surface had my father died early in a quest to change his country's history.

Although my father didn't want to take up arms, this doesn't mean that he stayed idle in the face of injustice. He told me a story about an event that happened when he was in his eighties.

"One day," he said, "I saw a man being beaten by an officer carrying a gun. I walked to the officer and told him that was wrong.

"The officer told me, 'Mind your own business, Grandpa.'

"I told the officer, 'I am minding my business; no one has the right to mistreat people like that.'

"The officer continued to beat the man. I jumped on the officer. The officer pulled his gun and brandished it at me, yelling, 'I am going to kill you. I am going to kill you.' Other people came just in time and pulled me away from the officer.

"After that incident, my blood sugar levels became erratic. I just couldn't tolerate such an injustice, even if it had cost me my life."

That was my man!

A Belief in Astrology

My father was a versatile businessman who knew how to change with the times.

In the early sixties, a new phenomenon happened in Haiti. Shopkeepers started to import used clothes from the United States and sell them in Haiti. They were conveniently called "Kennedys." The resulting effect was devastating for professionals like my father who made their living mostly from tailoring. He and his wife then opened a successful grocery store.

One day he was reading a French magazine when he came across an advertisement for an astrologer named Sirius. The ad indicated that by mailing Sirius your demographic data along with some cash, you could get a psychic reading from the world's greatest astrologer. My father put the required cash payment in an envelope and mailed it to the given address. I thought he was wasting his money. A couple of months later, my father received a letter in the mail that contained his astrological reading. It was a lengthy report. He asked me to read it for him. (I had regained my duties as official correspondence consultant; should I have charged him?)

It contained advice on topics such as love, health, investments, and finances, even a list of numbers to play in the lottery. My father disregarded all of the advice, except for one bit. Sirius advised that, in accordance with the location, date, and hour of my father's birth, the stars indicated that his best investment vehicle would be real estate. That was the only thing my father retained from the whole report, and it made him financially secure over his long life. He bought whatever real estate was available for sale in his hometown. Later he would resell these properties at a hefty profit and reinvest the proceeds in rental houses in the capital.

It took the words of a renowned psychic (or charlatan) to convince my father of something that most businessmen take for granted. Sometimes, in order to be heeded, a truth must come from an authority figure, like Sirius, who took his name from the brightest star in the sky.

But I found out that my father wasn't the first or last to use guidance from the stars. History books abound with successful people who have relied on astrologists and psychics. Financial mogul J. P. Morgan consulted his psychic adviser before making important financial decisions.

Anyway, whether the advice came from a psychic or from the Wharton School of Business, home ownership was a financially rewarding practice until the collapse of the US real-estate market in 2007 and its ripple effect in other countries.

My father invested in real estate at the right time. He didn't have to worry about a fluctuating market. His investments grew steadily and provided him with the means to support himself and his family. Once he told me that he heard people say that he had found a hidden treasure of gold on his land. He confided in me that the only gold he'd found was the fruit of his hard labor and his good luck, which he attributed to God by the intercession of his mother from heaven.

Protection from Above

My father had a profound veneration for his mother. In remembrance of her and as a symbol of protection, he wore a medal of Saint Clare on his necklace.

This happened to be his second necklace with a Saint Clare medal. He lost the first one at the hand of an intruder. One day, a couple of young thugs entered his house and demanded money. His wife, who was at the store counter, gave them the few dollars that were in the drawer. As they were insisting on getting more money, one of them noticed my father's gold necklace with the gold medal. He tried to yank it from his neck.

My father looked him in the eyes and said, "Son, if you want the chain, let me give it to you. If you break it, you'll have to repair it."

Then he calmly unlocked the chain and gave the necklace to the young thief. The two robbers left in a hurry. My father smiled. He had $3,000 cash in his pocket.

In his usual way, he said, "That's the way it was meant to be."

When I heard that story, I immediately sent him another Saint Clare medal. You don't want to break such a pattern of high protection for too long a period of time.

When I visited him on his ninety-eighth birthday, in accordance with old customs, the arrangements for his funeral had already been made. His wife had acquired a burial plot, coffin, and suit. The only item left was the reception. It had to be commensurate with the man and the occasion.

I don't know if my father ever made peace with my maternal grandfather. The few times he mentioned his name, he did so with profound reverence.

CHAPTER 7

What's in a Name?

A rose by any other name would smell as sweet.

SHAKESPEARE, *ROMEO AND JULIET*

WHEN I SAY "GRANDPA," I always mean my maternal grandfather, whose name was Dor Gourdet, my legal father. I had very little interaction with my paternal grandfather.

I mentioned earlier how I came to bear my grandpa's last name, Gourdet, in spite of my father's attempt to give me his last name, Lapaix. Now, about my first name, I will say that if Grandpa triumphed in giving me his last name, he was overruled when it came to my first name. Considering that my grandpa didn't want to have anything to do with my biological father, he decided to legitimate me—in other words, to make me his natural son under the law. What better way to express this situation than to name the child "Legitime?" Nothing wrong with that!

My people didn't know about feng shui, but they were practical in the choice of a name that would bring good luck to a child. My father was born on the seventh of May. He was called Lecet (phonic French for "the seventh"). He did very well in life. His younger brother was named Lenord ("the north" in French). It had something to do with the north direction of the compass; one of my grandma's cousins, Benjamin Gourdet, was a land surveyor. Lenord became a successful saddler.

But this time, following the tradition of practicality in the choice of a name didn't resonate too well with other members of my family. Everybody disagreed with Grandpa.

He didn't say a word until one of my grandaunts told him, "Brother, I have a beautiful name for the child."

"Whatever you say, Sister," Grandpa replied.

And my grandaunt said, "Gesner is the name."

"Gesner, that's fine," said Grandpa.

And that's how I got my *first*, first name—Gesner. It came with two nicknames, Jess and Nènè. My mother called me Jess. My little cousins called me Nènè.

When my grandpa went to register my birth certificate, the officer wrote "Jusnet" as my first name. Nobody noticed the change. However, I carried the name "Gesner" in primary and secondary school. No one ever looked at my birth certificate until I applied to law school at the age of twenty. I then discovered that my name was Jusnet. I contacted a friend of mine named Enaph Hyacinthe. As a lawyer, he petitioned the court for a name change on my behalf. A judgment was rendered, and my name officially became Gesner.

When I arrived in the United States, I found out that people could not say Gesner with the French pronunciation. I didn't like the way they pronounced it, with the hard *G* instead of the soft *J* sound. I told them to call me Jess. But it was easier to say Jesse. Not to make an issue of a name, I changed it officially to Jesse when I became a US citizen. Still, most of my family members continued to call me Gesner, including my wife, who claimed that she married Gesner and not Jesse. I like the name Jesse. It is a biblical name. King David's father was named Jesse. It is a common name in this country. I thought the issue was settled. But I soon found out that nobody knew how to spell Jesse; it was Jessie, Jessey, or Jessy. I gave up! Maybe one day I'll go back to the name *Legitime*, just like Grandpa wanted; after all, it was Shakespeare who said, "A rose by any other name would smell as sweet."

Just kidding!

CHAPTER 8

Trial by Fire

I asked for courage. God gave me dangers to overcome.

Author Unknown

One day, my grandpa was sitting on the front porch of our house. He pulled out his wooden pipe and filled it with tobacco. And then, with a whimsical look on his face, he told me, "Go in the kitchen, and fetch me fire to light my pipe."

This request shocked my mother. She looked at my grandpa and said, "What?"

I must have been about three or four years old. The kitchen was a one-room structure separated from the main house. A fire pit was in the center with three stones to hold the cooking pots when food was being prepared. Small children like me were not allowed in the kitchen by themselves. One of my cousins had suffered severe burns after falling into the fire pit while playing.

My grandpa Dor looked as if he hadn't heard my mother's question. He just motioned to me to carry on. I went in the kitchen and took a red-hot burning log and brought it to my grandpa. All the while my mother was watching me with constant awe, ready to make a move if it became necessary.

My grandpa took the log from me. In a very slow and casual way, he lit his pipe, throwing a few puffs of smoke in the air in a satisfying manner.

"Go put it back," he said, returning the log to me.

My mother's heart was clearly pounding.

I went to the kitchen, placed the log in the fire pit, and went back to my grandpa, who received me with his arms wide open to hug me. He threw a furtive look at my mother, who by then was showing signs of relief. Addressing me, he said, "You're a big man now."

That gave me self-confidence and a sense of worth at a very early age.

Village's Community Work

When I was about four years old, I saw my grandpa Dor, along with the men of my village, build a house for a young family. It was the first time I had seen so many people working together. There was a lot of activity. Men were cutting large pieces of wood with long saws that required two operators, one on each side. They would move it back and forth until the wood was cut. Other people were using big hammers to put the pieces together. There were no metal nails, only notches and long wooden pegs that were inserted into holes made with a long drill. I had never seen anything like that before. I was enthralled by this technology that was so new to me.

The young family made no payment to the workers. Everybody worked for free. It was cooperative work, as you would call it today. At the end of the day, a meal was served to everyone. That, by itself, was another novelty to me. I had never seen so much food being prepared by so many women. The kitchen pots were huge. The meal was typical. Millet was cooked like rice but so hard that the pot was turned over and the millet came out like a cake, and everybody received a slice of cooked whole millet covered with black beans in sauce and fried pork cubes. After dinner, the people sang and danced until late evening, and then everybody went home to sleep.

Another time, workers brought the cows to the front yard of my grandpa's house, where a big fire pit was being constructed. A branding iron with the letters DG (for "Dor Gourdet") in big uppercase characters was being heated in the fire.

One by one the cows were tied up, placed down, and branded on their backsides with the initials. I watched with consternation at this horrific but customary act that was being inflicted upon these animals. I can still smell the odor of burning cowhide and hair. I made a decision never to do this to my cows and horses when I grew up. Fortunately, I have lived in cities all my adult life; I never had any animal to be branded.

Grandpa's Funeral

I don't have any other memory of interacting with my grandfather. I went to live with my aunt and then with my father, and later I was sent to boarding school. He died while I was in boarding school. Out of respect for my grandpa, my father sent for me so I could attend the last services in his memory. After all, Grandpa was my legal father, and he loved me very much.

From boarding school in Anse-à-Veau, I went back home. It was on the ninth day after my grandpa's death. According to ancient African beliefs, a person has two souls, a little soul representing your ego, your identity, and a big soul responsible for the bodily functions. Upon death the little soul rises before God. The big soul sits by the grave for nine days before it departs. During that time, it can be stolen and put into a bottle to be used for magical purposes.

For that reason, my family held prayer sessions each night for nine consecutive days following the death of my grandpa, to liberate his soul. The ninth day was a day of great celebration. Friends and relatives came from all over to honor his memory and pay respect to the family. A cow was slaughtered to feed the many people who had come for that occasion.

As I was coming to my hometown, Gourdet, on horseback, I met many people on their way to the service, or the "ninth," as it was commonly called. They would move aside to make room on the narrow pathway for my horse to pass, along with the worker who accompanied me. Those who knew me personally told me how sorry they were about the passing of my grandpa. One woman said to me, "You know Dor loved you a lot. He always talked about you."

It was late in the evening when we arrived. Grandpa's house was set on a hilltop. The sun was setting on the western horizon, intermittently hidden by breathtaking clouds of yellow, orange, and red. As I approached the house, high on my horse, people saw me, and someone said, "Dor's son has arrived."

"Jess, Jess, you see what happened? Your grandpa is gone."

Many women came to help the family with chores. They started to express their grief by wailing and crying. Before I knew it, it was a big commotion. More people were approaching me and calling my name.

"Oh, Jess, your grandfather is gone!"

"Dor is gone forever!"

"You know he loved you."

"Yes, he loved you."

I felt I was hearing a lot of *blah blah blah*. I couldn't handle such an outpouring of sympathy. I felt a tightening in my throat, and tears started to pour out of my eyes.

I got off the horse and embraced my mother, my aunt, and a few other relatives. I was so happy to reunite with my dog Tutu, who by now was showing his old age. As I was playing with my dog, my aunt grabbed me by the arm and pulled me into the living room, where a table was set. She placed a huge plate of food in front of me, saying, "Eat, son. You must be very hungry."

It wasn't the first or the last time that I would hear such words. My aunt always made sure that I was well fed.

The distance from my boarding school to my hometown was about fifteen miles, but because the road conditions were bad, and the person who came to pick me up was walking, it had been an exhausting five-hour ride. I was indeed tired and hungry. I ate the whole plate of food. Then I went straight to bed and fell asleep immediately.

I woke up in the middle of the night to the sound of dominoes falling on wooden tables and the tirades of drunken card players. The rum was flowing freely under the tent that had been erected to accommodate the many people. Not all who came wanted to mourn the departed; some were there just to enjoy a good time at someone else's expense. As I said above, it was a tradition to say Catholic prayers for the soul of the departed for nine days after death, followed by a huge celebratory dinner on the ninth day; the higher the dead person's status in the community, the more people showed up, and the bigger the celebration. This custom is now in decline; most people cannot afford such high expenses for funerals.

A Small Inheritance

Since my grandpa had adopted me as his son under the law, it was natural that I became one of his heirs. After the funeral services, my aunt told me that my grandfather had left me a small inheritance. The money was used to buy my First Communion suit and a pair of very nice white shoes that earned the admiration of my fellow classmates. One kid told me later that he had asked his mother why she hadn't bought him a pair of shoes like mine.

However, the best compliment came when a young lady told me on that day, "You look very handsome, like a gentleman."

I was so happy. I felt as if Grandpa were right there with me, saying, "You're a big man now."

I don't remember much about my maternal grandmother. I have only a blurred vision of her holding me in her arms. She died while I was still small.

Both my maternal grandparents are buried on their land in the village of Gourdet, where they were born. One can still see their tombstones side by sidc. I know they had high hopes for me. They wanted me to get a good education.

CHAPTER 9

"And Then They Sent Me Away"

Education is the key to unlock the golden door of freedom.

George Washington Carver

On a hot summer day in July 1950, when I was six years old, I was playing with a friend of mine, a boy named Voltaire Israel, when Brother Francis, the headmaster of the Catholic school for boys in the coastal city of Anse-à-Veau, happened to be visiting my hometown. My friend Voltaire was a year older than I was, and he was already attending the school, so Brother Francis knew him. The Catholic brother inquired about me and asked to meet my father. He told my father that he would like me to attend his school. Since my uncle Joe, my father's youngest brother, was also in that school, my father agreed.

When October came, I was placed on a mule with some provisions and sent to boarding school. I became separated from my family, but it was an unstructured family. My mother and father were not together, and at that time, I didn't have any siblings, only some cousins whom I played with occasionally. However, I missed my little dog, Tutu, whom I loved very much. I wanted to take Tutu with me, but I was told that was not allowed. This made leaving home to go to an unknown destination so much more painful. But I discovered something in the new town that made it all worthwhile.

My birth town, L'Asile, was located midway between the two coastal cities of Aquin and Anse-à-Veau. The town was built at the convergence of three large rivers—the Maho, the Serpent, and the Despins. Like most kids, I loved water, and by the time I was six years old, I was already an accomplished swimmer. When I arrived in Anse-à-Veau, I discovered the sea, to my great satisfaction. It was the largest body of water I had ever seen. I was bowled over. To make it even more awesome, on the water there were small canoes and what appeared to me like odd-looking houses. Later, I was told they were called boats or ships, used as a means of transportation of goods and people from one coastal city to another, especially from Anse-à-Veau to the capital city of Port-au-Prince.

I was too young to know about Christopher Columbus. Now, I can imagine the amazement of the Indians when they saw his ships—the *Niña*, the *Pinta*, and the *Santa Maria*. The water was so blue, and the sand leading to it was so white. Calm waves moved gently over the surface of the sea, illuminated by the sun's brilliant light. I entertained the idea of swimming all the way to the horizon in the far distance. But my dream was soon dampened by the admonishments of older people who decided that I couldn't go swimming whenever it pleased me; the sea was dangerous. In other words, there were rules. I was getting acquainted with a new form of constant adult supervision and discipline. Besides, I found out that the water was salty. I didn't know that the sea contained its own salt. *That's a lot of salt,* I thought. But it was long before I went swimming in Israel's Dead Sea, years later, where the salt content is almost ten times that of the ocean, and I was floating on the water.

Boarding School

The city of Anse-à-Veau was divided into two sections: the lower town and the upper town. The Catholic church, the two Catholic schools, and most city offices were in the upper town; still, the distribution of residences for the elites of the town was about the same for both upper and lower towns.

It was an old city that dated back to the Spanish and French colonists. It was the hometown of many historical figures.

A general named Guérin fought in the war for Haiti's independence against the French. Historians report that for him, "even in the eyes of the law the son of a peasant could not be considered as equal to his" (Manigat 2001, 327).

That was before Abraham Lincoln's Gettysburg Address, in which he restated the basic tenet of the US Declaration of Independence, "that all men are created equal." Dr. Martin Luther King Jr. reiterated this theme in his speech "I Have a Dream," on August 28, 1963, at the Lincoln Memorial in Washington, DC. However, these words are still relevant today.

A second important personality who called Anse-à-Veau home was Fabre Nicolas Geffrard. As president of the country, he negotiated the concordat with the Vatican in 1860, restoring Catholicism as the official religion in Haiti.

A third important historical personality of the town was Sud Dartiguenave, the first president under the US occupation of Haiti in the early part of the twentieth century.

I spent twelve years studying in Anse-à-Veau. It was a fundamental part of my early life. The houses were beautiful. Many of them were two-story colonial-style houses with balconies and attics. Anse-à-Veau was the seat of government for the arrondissement. There was a prefecture, a general inspector of schools, a small unit of the national army with a captain at its head, a court with judges, and at least half a dozen well-educated and bar-certified attorneys. The church was built in the old Gothic style and could seat well over two hundred parishioners. The city was placed under the protection of Saint Anne, the mother of Mary and the grandmother of the baby Jesus. There were two French-born priests administering to the faithful. Later on, there would be a Haitian priest. Most people were Catholic, but there was an emerging Protestant following, supported by US Baptist churches. Voodoo was always in the background. It was overtly practiced but mostly in the villages. Many fervent Catholics had a devotion to the gods and goddesses of their African ancestors.

The city boasted three primary schools. The all-boys school was run by the Catholic Brothers of Christian Instruction, with the assistance of a few lay teachers. The all-girls school was run by the Catholic sisters. The mixed-gender public school was run by lay teachers. A greater percentage of students at Catholic schools passed the seventh-grade national exams the first time. This was important because most students' formal education stopped right there in the seventh grade. There was no secondary school in the city or in the immediate surrounding towns at that time. It would be another six years before members of the clergy and town intellectuals decided to join forces to establish a free secondary school for the town's underprivileged youth, those whose parents could not afford to send them to the capital for further education. I benefited from that secondary school after I graduated from seventh grade. I was able to continue my education in Anse-à-Veau, with expenses that my father could afford.

My room was in the lower town, and my school and the church were in the upper town. I went to the school to complete my registration on my first day in Anse-à-Veau. There, I met Brother Francis, who welcomed me warmly and assured me that I would like the school and have a good time. But it took me some time to adjust to this new environment. Luckily, my uncle Joe was attending the same school. He had another two years to go. He and I were in the same rooming house, which accommodated up to twelve kids. I was the youngest one.

A couple named Cedric and Anna Morgan, or Mr. and Mrs. Morgan, ran the rooming house. They had no children of their own. They surrounded themselves with other people's children. The Morgans were good people. A couple of the children boarding there were from Mrs. Morgan's relatives who couldn't afford to raise them. She took them in and provided for them as if they were her own children.

Mr. Morgan had three brothers. One of them was living in the capital, Port-au-Prince. He had one son, Willy, and one daughter, Ada. They would occasionally come to spend a couple of weeks during summertime. Willy later became a doctor. The other two brothers, Leon and Leonce, were twins. They had immigrated to the United States. Leon came once to visit his brother Cedric in Anse-à-Veau. I remember two things about his visit. One, he came with a beautiful suitcase that had a satin-finished interior; he left it for his brother. I would use it on a couple of occasions. The second thing I remember is that, one morning during his stay, Leon looked at my school shoes, which were full of dirt.

He asked me to clean them, saying, "A young man should always wear shining shoes."

I thought that was the rule in the United States where he came from. The lesson stayed with me forever—or at least until the advent of fancy sneakers.

Mr. Cedric Morgan held the office of city registrar. He kept big ledgers provided by the government, where he recorded all new births for the city and surrounding villages. He issued official birth certificates on governmental forms that came with the printed stamps of the republic: "*Liberté, Egalité, Fraternité, République d'Haiti.*" Later, after I learned calligraphy in school, I would help him to transcribe those birth certificates into a second book. One would stay in the town's archives, and the other one was sent to the capital to be stored at the national archives.

Mr. Morgan was very formal. He never received anyone without his jacket on. If he was relaxing in his rocking chair and someone showed up at the door, he would invariably put on his jacket before receiving that person. Kids in the neighborhood knew that they couldn't whistle or create a ruckus when passing in front of his house. They had to show respect.

The large house was built in the railroad style. From the street, you stepped onto a front porch that had two doors. They opened into a large living room that had Mr. Morgan's office desk and chairs, along with his rocking chair. Mrs. Morgan had a grocery business, and many of the items for sale would be on shelves in a section of that same room. There were basic necessities such as sugar, olive oil, spaghetti, cigarettes, razor blades, soap, spools of thread, paper and envelopes, and alcohol.

The second room contained the stairs up to the second floor. Mrs. Morgan forbade all boys to look up when a girl was going up the stairs, to prevent them from peeking at the girl's panties.

The third room followed in straight line. It served as the dining room. It had a large round table, able to seat up to twelve of us. In one corner of that room was a big pottery jar of cool drinking water. Against the wall, there was a garde-manger where certain food items were kept. The Morgans didn't have a refrigerator. My father had one, but that was in my hometown, miles away.

Both the second and third rooms had doors to the right that opened onto a corridor coming from the street to allow maids and other people to enter the premises without passing through the house.

The layout of the second floor was the same as that of the first floor. There were two bedrooms and a formal living room with a balcony facing the street. It was nicely arranged with imported chairs and another rocking chair. The walls were decorated with wallpaper that had a very nice floral design. From the middle room on the second floor, you could go up to an attic where the Morgans kept items not in use.

In the back of the house, there was a small garden with flowers and a cherry tree. The cherry tree provided enough cherries to make delicious jam every year. Another structure came after the garden. It had two rooms. One room was used as the kitchen. The other room was a storeroom where Mr. Morgan kept his tools and apparatus for beekeeping. It was there also that our cat gave birth under the eyes of an understanding big dog named Zazou.

There's an interesting story regarding our cat. Mrs. Morgan warned us never to accept anything from or give anything to a certain woman who lived nearby. It was believed that she was a sorceress. One day Mr. and Mrs. Morgan were not at home, and this lady showed up at the door of the house. In her humblest way, she requested a small favor. She wanted a little cat litter to make a remedy. We knew right away that she was up to something. We remembered Mrs. Morgan's warning, and someone told her that the cat didn't make any poop that day. She left empty-handed, with her head down.

About twenty feet away from the structure that held the kitchen and the tool shed was a separate small outhouse that served as a toilet.

We kids used the space between those two structures to play marbles and other games. It was there that, one day, a kid named Syla was trying to cut a tree branch with a machete. Instead, he chopped off one of his fingers. I took the piece of finger and preserved it in a small jar filled with alcohol. I then totally forgot about the incident until I started to work for New York City's Office of Chief Medical Examiner (OCME), dealing with biological specimens.

The sleeping accommodation at the Morgans' was a little strange, but we got accustomed to it. The girls would sleep on beds. Some of the boys would sleep together on straw mats that they set on the floor just before the evening prayers. My father bought me an army cot that could be folded. I used it for most of my time in boarding school. Sometimes in the morning, I would put it outside in the sun to dry because, as I mentioned earlier, I used to pee in bed. I was better off at my aunt's house, where I had my own bed. Here, there were too many kids to have individual beds. The house had no indoor bathroom. We had chamber pots to relieve ourselves during the night.

The town had running water, but it was limited to one faucet per house. We collected water in vases and shared it among us for washing and bathing. There was no electricity. We used kerosene lamps to illuminate the house at night and to provide light in the evening for us to study by.

There were lots of frogs, and sometimes in the evening, they would jump on us as we studied. That would create a little diversion for the boys and great panic for the girls. One night, one of the boys fell asleep while studying. An open book was lying on his lap. His head was bent backward. His mouth was wide open. All of a sudden one of the frogs jumped and landed on his forehead, missing his open mouth by a few inches. We woke him up. He never realized that he had almost swallowed a frog.

On weekends, we didn't have to study in the evening; instead, we studied during the day. The Morgans didn't have a radio. It would be years before I saw a television. The evening was left to tell stories and riddles. We would sit on the front porch, and one person would say, "Tim Tim."

Someone would reply, "Dry wood."

Question: "What is round without a bottom?"

Answer: "A ring."

Whoever got the right answer would ask the next question.

Question: "What has four legs in the morning, two legs during the day, and three legs in the evening?"

Answer: "A person."

Sometimes Mr. or Mrs. Morgan would tell us the story of Bookie and Malice, two characters in Haitian lore. One of them was very smart and shrewd; the other one was very dumb. Malice, the smart one, always took advantage of Bookie, the dumb one.

At night, Mrs. Morgan would lead us in loud prayers for protection and good luck. Besides the regular Catholic prayers, which included a full rosary, there were prayers to Saint Charlemagne and to Saint Michael the Archangel to weed out evil. There was also a prayer to the four Evangelists, Saint Matthew, Saint Mark, Saint Luke, and Saint John, to watch over us as we slept. We had to recite certain psalms, like Psalm 23, which I later found out was recited at both Jewish and Christian funerals. I always felt that the prayers were too long. I just wanted to go to sleep. But Mrs. Morgan was very strict about evening prayers. Night after night, we would recite these prayers until they were ingrained in our psyche, until they were part of us. Once, I had a nightmare, and I woke up in the middle of the night with Psalm 23, a psalm of David, in my mouth. I was reciting it in my sleep.

> *The lord is my shepherd; I shall not want. He makes me lie down in green pastures. He leads me beside still waters. He restores my soul. He leads me in the paths of righteousness for his name's sake. Even though I walk through the valley of the shadow of death, I will fear no evil, for you are with me; your rod and your staff, they comfort me. You prepare a table before me in the presence of my enemies; you anoint my head with oil: my cup overflows. Surely goodness and mercy shall follow me all the days of my life, and I shall dwell in the house of the Lord forever.*

It had a calming effect on me that made feel better. Obviously the prayer was hidden in some part of my memory, ready to reappear in time of need.

As I grew older, I did away with reciting long prayers, preferring meditation. I came across a short prayer said to have been written by James Dillet Freeman. It summarizes my relationship with God, and I embedded it in my subconscious mind:

The light of God surrounds me;
The love of God enfolds;
The power of God protects me;
The presence of God watches over me;
Wherever I am, God is.
All is well!

The Morgans served three meals every day. We never went a day without food Breakfast consisted of light coffee or chocolate with a single bread roll or half a cassava spread with peanut butter or fruit jam. Sometimes we had *acassan*, a delicious beverage made with corn flour, milk, sugar, star anise, cinnamon, and vanilla. There were no such things as Special K, Honey Nut Cheerios, or Honey Bunches of Oats. On special occasions (and invariably on New Year's Day, which is Independence Day), we would have *soupe giraumon*, a delicious soup made with pumpkin. This was a tradition that came from the founding of our country. Apparently, *soupe giraumon* was a delicacy reserved only for the white French colonists. Slaves were forbidden to have it. On the day of the celebration of our independence, Jean-Jacques Dessalines, Haiti's first president, ordered it to be served in every household and to be shared with neighbors.

Mrs. Morgan made her own butter and cottage cheese in small quantities.

Dinner, the biggest meal, was served at midday. Every day before noon, we would set the large round table, whether we were going to have a meager meal or a festive dinner. Mrs. Morgan would join us after serving the meal, which was prepared by a daytime maid. The meals were salty on two occasions: when the sea salt was almost gone and when a new batch of sea salt had been bought.

Mrs. Morgan taught us the rules of etiquette, including how to sit and behave at the table, how to hold our arms at all times, and how to eat with a fork and a knife. I still remember her whenever my wife reminds me that my elbow is not supposed to be on the table or that I am using the wrong fork for salad. The menu at the Morgans' varied depending on the day, but the short list of dishes rotated indefinitely. It consisted of corn, millet, rice with beans, plantains, sweet potatoes, yams, and meat or fish. Meat consisted of beef, pork, and goat; chicken was always reserved for Sundays. Occasionally there were treats like black rice with shrimp or fried plantains with roasted pork cubes.

When I was ten years old, I liked to accompany the maid to the seaport on Saturdays to buy fish. It was a good opportunity to play and swim in the sea while waiting for the fishermen to return with their catch in their boats. Sometimes on Saturdays we would have bouillon, which was always delicious. We always drank water, reserving soda for special occasions. We never had wine or other alcoholic beverages. Even at Holy Communion, only the priest drank the wine that represented the blood of Christ in the Eucharist. At that time, wine was not served to the communicants. Only the host, or the bread that represented the body of Christ, was given to the faithful. I had wine only once on a very special occasion, as described earlier in the chapter "Take Care of the Children."

Supper was a light meal served in the evening. It consisted of leftovers from the midday meal or a repeat of the morning meal without coffee. Sometimes we had *la bouillie*, a hot cereal. I remember one evening after my arrival in Anse-à-Veau, I started to cry. Mrs. Morgan asked me why I was crying. I couldn't tell. I didn't know myself. She decided to give me my portion of the next morning's meal. I ate it voraciously, and I went to bed happy. The same thing had to be done for the other kids, who were also very happy. The next morning there was much talk about what we were going to eat. But something was found for breakfast. Mrs. Morgan taught us one thing that remains with me until now. Whatever there was to eat should be shared among all of us, whether it was a small or large quantity. However, I must admit I didn't see it that way at the time. My father was paying for my care and sending enough food so that I didn't go hungry. But there were many mouths to feed in that house, and I wasn't such a happy camper in that flock. Neither was I happy in school. But slowly I adjusted to this new environment, and I finally discovered what happiness could be.

CHAPTER 10

How to Spell Happiness

Happiness is the only good.
The time to be happy is now.
The place to be happy is here.
The way to be happy is to make other people happy.

Robert G. Ingersoll

While I was in first grade, one day during break time, my teacher, Mr. Ray, noticed that I was standing alone in a corner and not playing with the other kids. He came to me with a candy in his hand. He took off the wrapping and asked me if I could read the word embedded on the candy.

When he noticed that I showed no particular interest, he raised my attention by saying, "I will give you the candy if you read the word."

I looked at it; it was one of those big words that we had just started to learn in class. At first, I thought I couldn't read it.

Then he said, "The word has two parts. Let me separate them for you." He covered one part with his finger, and I could see "bon."

I said, "Bon."

"Very good," he said. Then he covered "bon" and left the second part uncovered: "heur." By that time a small group of my classmates had formed half a circle around us.

Addressing me, Mr. Ray then said, "We learned a similar word in class today. It had to do with time."

Then I said, "*Urr.*" (That's more or less how you pronounce *heure*, the French word for "hour.")

"Perfect," he said. "Now put the two parts together."

Before I opened my mouth, another student shouted, "Bonheur."

"That's it," said the teacher. "Bonheur." (*Bonheur* is the French word for "happiness" or "good times.") "The two of you will share the prize," he added. He then brought the candy to his teeth and broke it into two pieces. He gave me one piece, and he gave the other piece to my classmate Yves Boucher.

Then Mr. Ray said, "Happiness is sharing."

I enjoyed my piece of candy. I also learned a lesson that stayed with me all my life: "Happiness is sharing."

Later on, I found out that the pursuit of happiness was an even greater concept than I could ever imagine. It was so important that the founding fathers included it, along with life and liberty, in the US Declaration of Independence as an inalienable right.

Like a cut diamond, happiness is multifaceted. It can shine in personal achievement or in service to others. Lofty ideals such as beauty, love, and kindness are also part of it. Happiness is what everybody wishes for but never fully obtains. That's why, year after year, we wish people a Happy New Year, a Happy Anniversary, or a Happy Birthday.

The incident with the candy had a major impact on my life in the school. First, it established a personal bond between my teacher and me. The fear instilled in me by my father had extended to all authority figures, including Mr. Ray. My out-of-class interaction with him dissipated that fear. I came to see my teacher not as a distant authority figure but as a kind individual willing to share a piece of candy with a student.

Yves Boucher and I became best friends. We played together, and we talked to each other all the time. On more than one occasion, we defended each other against older students who tried to bully us. Little by little, I was gaining the self-assurance needed to survive in this intimidating environment.

Sometime in secondary school, my friend Boucher left and moved to the capital, and I lost contact with him. Later I heard he had established a big private school in Port-au-Prince.

On a recent visit to Haiti, I asked my cousin Ketty, "Do you know someone by the name of Yves Boucher?"

"Yes," he replied. "I know where his school is. I can take you there."

We drove to the school. When we arrived, we entered a reception room. There were two gentlemen talking, and one was wearing a dark suit with a red tie. We paid no attention to them, and we went to the receptionist, who was sitting at a desk. I told her I was there to see Mr. Boucher.

She pointed to a door in front of us and said, "You can knock at the door."

I did, but nobody answered. Then my cousin Ketty started to hit the door really hard.

At that point the gentleman with the dark suit walked to us and said, "I am Yves Boucher. How can I help you?"

I looked at him. "I am Gesner Gourdet. It's been more than fifty years—"

I didn't finish my sentence. He gave me a big hug. He called the other gentleman he was talking to and told him, "You remember I always tell you about my childhood friend Gesner Gourdet? That's him, a man you could always count on."

We used to help each other as kids; that's how he remembered me.

We talked for about an hour and promised to stay in touch. The story of the candy with the word "happiness" written on it did not surface in our conversation, but it was the incident that initiated our friendship in the first grade.

Chasing Butterflies

The year went by pretty fast. Classes were held Monday through Friday. They started at 8:00 a.m. and ended at 4:00 p.m. with a two-hour break from 11:30 a.m. to 1:30 p.m. so we could go home for lunch. The distance between the school and my room and board was about two miles. I did it walking with other students four times a day, sometimes kicking a can down the road until we reached home, making sure that the couple I lived with wouldn't notice that activity. Kicking a can could wear out our shoes much faster than our parents could afford to buy us new ones. So it was a reprehensible activity.

There were two shorter break times, one in the morning and one in the afternoon. We would play soccer, flag, or other games. One of my favorite pastimes was chasing yellow butterflies, especially around the feast of Saint John the Baptist on June 24, when the butterflies were in their greatest numbers. It was also the day when you could predict the future by looking into a well or a glass of water at exactly noon, when the sun was right above your head, leaving no shadow. I did it one year. The only thing I saw was a very tall house; no one could tell me what it meant.

Infant Jesus of Prague

I did very well in the first grade. At the end of the year, I came out near the top of my class. Brother Francis, the headmaster, congratulated me for my school achievements and rewarded me with a small image of the Infant Jesus of Prague, which I cherished very much. Brother Francis had a vested interest in my success; he was the one who had brought me to the school. This little gesture of encouragement went a long way in boosting my self-confidence, and I continued to do well in school. But it was summer vacation. I went back home to enjoy the summer at my aunt's house and to be with my family.

CHAPTER 11

A Touch of Genius

$E=mc^2$

EINSTEIN

WHEN SUMMER ENDED, I WENT back to school. I made sure I carried my Infant Jesus of Prague image along with me. In the next few years it would be my good-luck charm. The year was uneventful. I followed the same routine, and I progressed well. The school year started at the beginning of October and ended at the end of June. July, August, and September were summer vacation months. All students went back home. We spent the time playing soccer, swimming, playing cards and board games such as checkers, or doing nothing. On Sundays we would have a picnic, dance, or some kind of party. One such party was the celebration of the baptism of a girl's new doll. It was an occasion to pair girls with boys as godfathers and godmothers of the doll, and this usually established opportunity for closer relations between them as boyfriends and girlfriends.

I spent Christmas, Easter, and summer vacations at my aunt's house. My father lived a few yards away with his wife and their daughters. I also spent a lot of time at his house during the day, in the company of my little half sisters. Some days, I would have two midday meals, one at my father's and the other at my aunt's house. My stepmother, Gloria, didn't have any problem with that, and as far as my aunt was concerned, I could eat as much as I wanted.

One day in the summer after my second year in school, I was at my father's house when I saw him tinkering with a lock that he couldn't open. He had forgotten the combination code. There were three digits placed horizontally. I told him I could open it. He said I could not.

I said, "Give it to me."

As he gave it to me, he said, "If you open it, you can name your prize."

My father was one of the few people in my hometown who had a refrigerator. They were called Frigidaire. It was the name of the brand.

I said, "What about anything I want in the Frigidaire?"

"That's fine," he said. He didn't set a time limit.

I imagined that the code had to be a number between 000 and 999. All I had to do was to move the numbers sequentially until I reached the code number that would open the lock. No need to be a genius to figure that out.

I took the lock and started to change the digits really fast, making sure I didn't miss any number. It didn't take me long to reach number 777. I heard a click. I pulled the handle, and lo and behold, the lock opened. My father couldn't believe it when I brought the open lock to him.

As I was opening the refrigerator door to collect my prize, he said, "Wait, there is one more test."

I felt I was being cheated. After all, I had won my prize.

Then he said, "How many times is this refrigerator door opened in a day?"

"As often as needed" was my instantaneous answer.

"You can have your prize," he said with a smile. The guy thought I was a genius. I had my soda.

CHAPTER 12

There Is No God

I know that God will not give me anything I can't handle.
I just wish He didn't trust me so much.

Quote attributed to Mother Teresa

When October came, I went back to Anse-à-Veau, on that same mule, with the usual provision of a couple of chickens, plantains, bananas, yams, ground corn, cassava, and my special treat, a jar of grapefruit-pulp jelly prepared for me by my mother, a delicacy I still enjoy today.

We were in Anse-à-Veau for less than a month when disaster struck. On October 27, 1952, I woke up in the middle of the night with the house shaking violently and people crying. I found myself against the wall on the other side of the room from where I had been sleeping. The tilting of the house had thrown me off my cot and from one side of the room to the other. In Mr. and Mrs. Morgan's bedroom, the armoire landed on their bed; it narrowly missed crushing them. Luckily they were not seriously hurt.

The bedrooms were on the second floor of the two-story house. We hurried down to the first floor and moved quickly to an empty lot across the street. The house next door had completely collapsed. The people there had managed to escape but had severe injuries. Many houses fell down, and people had to be rescued from under the rubble.

That was the first time I heard the word "earthquake." It was the first time I experienced it. It was very scary, especially with the aftershocks that would throw me off balance. As I stood on that empty lot, I wondered whether the earth was going to open up and swallow me. There were many fatalities. People were crying. One woman was walking up and down the street yelling repeatedly, "There is no God. There is no God."

I was shocked when I heard those words. I thought it was blasphemy. But when she added, "My son is dead. My son is dead," I empathized with her pain and her suffering.

Many people had their rosaries in hand, praying to a God who for some reason was turning a deaf ear. The town was devastated. My school was completely destroyed. For the next few days, everybody slept in open fields. It would be months before we could return to normal life. The school was later rebuilt, but the beautiful two-story colonial houses that were destroyed by the earthquake never regained their original splendor. They were replaced with one-level houses, everything on one floor. The town would never be the same.

Sick with No Hospital

A few days after the earthquake, my father sent a couple of his assistants to pick up my uncle Joe and me. The earthquake had severely damaged the roads. The usual four-hour horseback ride turned into literally a whole day of travel.

When I got home, I fell ill. There were no doctors or nurses in my hometown. My family brought in the woman who managed the town's closest thing to an infirmary. She recommended that I receive immediate professional care and warned that I could be in for a serious problem. The nearest hospital was miles away. With despair in my heart I asked, "Why did this happen to me?" The answer to that question would come only years later when I read the book *When Bad Things Happen to Good People*, by Rabbi Harold S. Kushner.

"No one ever promised us a life free from pain and disappointment," he wrote. "The most anyone promised us was that we would not be alone in our pain, and that we would be able to draw upon a source outside ourselves for the strength and courage we would need to survive life's tragedies and life's unfairness...The question we should be asking is not 'Why did this happen to me? What did I do to deserve this?' That is really an unanswerable, pointless question. A better question would be: 'Now that this has happened to me, what am I going to do about it?'"

While in New York, years later, I asked the question, "How come there is no hospital in my hometown?" And I wasn't the only one to ask that question. A few of us from my hometown formed an IRS 501(c)(3) organization to help our town, and one of the goals was to build a hospital. Many of us felt there was a need for it. However, it would take another twenty years for that dream to be realized, this time with the dedication of other young people committed to the development of our hometown. A regional hospital was built and staffed with Cuban doctors and nurses, and it presently serves many patients a day.

During my illness, I would learn another important lesson that would shape my vision of what the future could bring me.

CHAPTER 13

The Shaping of a Vision

Dream lofty dreams, and as you dream, so shall you become.
Your vision is the promise of what you shall one day be;
your ideal is the prophecy of what you shall at last unveil.

James Allen

Michel Chaptini was a Lebanese man who immigrated to Haiti. Unable to penetrate the commerce business in the capital, which was already monopolized by other foreigners, he married my father's sister-in-law Therese and established himself in my hometown. He must have been in his early forties when I knew him. He always wore a suit. He opened a series of businesses in the town. He had a soda-bottling company, a bakery, and a lucrative coffee-export business. My hometown was a heavy producer of coffee, dating back to the French colonization. He would buy coffee from the growers and export it by cargo boats from the coastal city of Petit-Goâve, where he had business associates and a depot.

As a member of my extended family, he became aware of my predicament when I was sick. He immediately offered to use his truck to take me to Petit-Goâve for medical attention. The roads being what they were, it took the greater part of a day to make the trip. We arrived in Petit-Goâve late in the afternoon. Michel and his driver took me straight to the hospital.

The doctor examined me, gave me some medications, and sent me home for rest. It didn't take me long to get better.

After about a week, Michel returned to my hometown, but as a precaution, he left me in his house in Petit-Goâve so I would be close to a hospital. His assistant, a gentleman named Tony, took care of me. Tony was also the manager of Michel's gaming business. There were two pool tables in the house, and at night, people would come to play pool and card games.

Petit-Goâve was a major city located a short distance (about forty miles) to the south of the capital. The streets were wide, and the houses were similar in size to the bigger houses in Anse-à-Veau. The city boasted a magnificent church, and to my delight there were many young people of my age, some of whom I played soccer with.

Michel's depot was right on the seashore. From the house, I could admire the big cargo ships, and I was amazed to see men carrying on their shoulders huge coffee bags to be loaded onto the boats. At night, it was such a delight to see these illuminated "palaces" on the sea. Their lights reflected on the water. I was impressed by this magnificent view, and I could have stayed there forever. Luckily, upon his return, Michel told me that my father had agreed to let me stay longer. When he realized how much I liked the place, he allowed me to stay there for nearly two months with Tony while Michel traveled back and forth between my hometown and Petit-Goâve and sometimes to the capital. There was no reason to hurry back; the earthquake had destroyed my school in Anse-à-Veau.

Learning How to Eat Crabs

A maid came in daily to prepare the meals, do laundry, and take care of other insignificant house chores. Tony was experienced in Middle Eastern cuisine, and he coached the maid in the preparation of special dishes. My favorites were kibbe, stuffed grape leaves, and hummus.

Since we were right on the shore, I spent a lot of time swimming and fishing in the sea. Tony taught me how to build a crab trap using wooden sticks and cord. He placed a couple of stones and small pieces of fish in the box and dropped it to the bottom of the sea, which wasn't too deep by the house. Before long, crabs would go into the box, and we would pick them up.

He also showed me how to eat them with my hands after steaming them. First, you remove the legs and claws, and then you separate the top and bottom part of the shell to expose the delicious white meat. After that, you spend more time breaking the legs and claws to enjoy the hidden meat. It always amazed me to see how the crabs would turn an appetizing red color as soon as they came in contact with hot water. Sometimes the maid would make crab soup. Very delicious!

A Glimpse of the Future

One day Michel took me to dinner at the house of a friend and business associate. My experience there would have a profound impact on my life. It gave me a glimpse of what the future could be. The man's company controlled the coffee export business in the region. His house was unlike anything I had ever seen before. Not only was it beautiful and well furnished, but to my surprise, it had an indoor kitchen and indoor bathroom. I was only eight years old, but I spent the whole night trying to figure out how, by the grace of God, they managed to put a kitchen and toilet inside a house.

The meal was finalized right there in front of us, on what I later learned to be a gas stove. A warm crème brûlée was served as dessert. I was not only impressed but inspired. I wasn't going to let this day pass without taking full advantage of it. It was a lucky day to mark with a white stone, following Roman traditions. I closed my eyes and sent a message to the universe: *When I grow up, I will have a beautiful house with an indoor kitchen and bathroom!*

It was Ralph Waldo Emerson who said, "What lies behind us and what lies before us are tiny matters compared to what lies within us." God was listening to a child's prayer; the universe knows how to make things happen, even if it takes many years.

Soon after I arrived in the United States at the age of twenty-four, I started saving money to buy a house. Within seven years of my arrival, I bought my first house in a nice section of Queens, New York. Since then, I have owned and lived in four expensive houses. I am happy to report that all my houses had electricity, indoor kitchens, and bathrooms, which, of course, is the norm in the United States. But I didn't know that when I was eight years old, growing up in Haiti.

In a twist of fate, when Michel became seriously ill years later, I was there by his side on the daylong journey from my hometown to the hospital Canapé-Vert in the capital, where he later expired. I felt that I had repaid him for what he had done for me. He was one of the pioneers of my hometown, connecting the business leaders of the country with the people of my town. He created economic opportunities for the town by providing an outlet for the coffee export business. He showed people that they could build better and stronger houses using blocks instead of wood and mortar. Unfortunately, he didn't have any children. Upon his death, it was revealed that he was associated with the Jehovah's Witnesses even though he had never set foot in any house of worship. His wife, Therese, who had an ax to grind with the Catholic priest then serving in town, established a Kingdom Hall of Jehovah's Witnesses in my hometown. A few members of my family became members, and that's how he is remembered.

For my part, I felt fortunate I was afforded the opportunity to give back a little bit to a man who had cared for me at a time when I needed it most. He contributed to the shaping of my vision of the future when I was young.

CHAPTER 14

Dr. Jekyll and Mr. Hyde

The fault, dear Brutus, is not in our stars, but in ourselves, that we are underlings.

SHAKESPEARE, *JULIUS CAESAR*

AFTER THOSE ENJOYABLE TWO MONTHS in Petit-Goâve, I went back home. Soon afterward, it was time to go back to Anse-à-Veau to resume my third-grade studies, which had been interrupted by the violent earthquake. Major changes took place when I went back to school. Makeshift classrooms were erected to accommodate the students. At break time, we received a glass of milk made with powdered milk, courtesy of the United States. There was a new headmaster. My protector, Brother Francis, a tall and jovial man, was replaced by Brother Gerard, a short, stocky, middle-aged Frenchman who inspired fear in everyone. The black robe he wore over his street clothes and the large crucifix that hung on his chest didn't cause any problems; all Catholic brothers wore the same accoutrements. I was already accustomed to that. What frightened me were his somber demeanor and the no-nonsense look in his eyes. He had managed Catholic schools in other cities. For any offenses, students would be sent to his office for discipline. The student's head would be placed between Brother Gerard's knees to expose his behind for a good spanking with a wooden ruler.

After my eye-opening stay in Petit-Goâve, I was running wild. I can't remember what I did wrong. I can only speculate that the offense was so severe that a good spanking wasn't enough. I got a note for my father, who lived miles away, requesting his presence at the school. My father's low tolerance for misbehavior was going to be reaffirmed, this time in a stronger but more diplomatic manner.

Upon receipt of this note from the school, indicating my disregard for established rules, my father sent five leather whips to the school with a signed note giving full power to the headmaster to straighten me out. The note also expressed his regret that, because of his busy schedule, he couldn't make the trip to see the headmaster. (My father told me later that he hadn't wanted to humiliate me by coming to the school and making a scene.) Fortunately for me, this action from my father had the reverse effect on Brother Gerard, the religious man. Upon receipt of that "correctional gift" from my father, he called me into his office and talked to me. From then on, Brother Gerard took me under his personal care and, by acts of kindness toward me, changed me totally for the better. He gave me a little book, called *Ali Baba and the Forty Thieves*, which opened my eyes to a brand-new world.

Occasionally people have asked me, "What book had the greatest influence on your life?" For me, it was definitely *Ali Baba and the Forty Thieves.* It was the first book I read in its entirety. I was so enthused to learn the magic words, "Open, Sesame!" and "Close, Sesame!"

I took delight in the maid's clever plans to outwit and kill the thieves by pouring boiling oil over their heads. At the end, Ali Baba got all the gold and married his nephew to the resourceful maid.

That book opened me to the pleasure of reading as a key can open the door to a treasure. Brother Gerard gave me more books from the Arabian Nights, and from there on, I was reading nonstop. I became an avid reader. *Aladdin's Lamp*, *Sinbad's Voyages*, *The Magic Carpet*, *Gulliver's Travels*, and *The Last of the Mohicans* are some of the stories that ignited my imagination.

My passion for reading and Brother Gerard's new attitude toward me resulted in a significant improvement in my grades. It didn't take me long to position myself at the top of my class. My relationship with my father took a turn for the better. He didn't have to straighten me out anymore. He had abdicated his rights over my behind by assigning them to someone else. Furthermore, he was pleased that I was getting good grades. He stopped playing the role of a strict disciplinarian; he became my father. On many instances, he told me he was proud of me. That made me happy, and I continued to do well.

As I showed improvement in my studies, the headmaster became even more lenient with me. Occasionally when I was reciting a text and got stuck, he didn't hesitate to tell me the next few words to get me back on track. That didn't go over too well with other students, who felt he was playing favorites.

I remember once a student got stuck while reciting a text. He asked Brother Gerard to tell him the next words. The brother did not. The student lamented, "Dear Brother Gerard, if it was Gourdet, you would have helped him out."

Somehow I felt privileged.

On another occasion I got in trouble for unruliness with a teacher, another Catholic brother named Brother Genole. He sent me to the headmaster to be spanked. To my great surprise, Brother Gerard asked me to sit down and asked about the problem. I told him that I hadn't done anything wrong and that Brother Genole was the one creating all the problems.

He listened to me attentively, and then he said, "Go back to class, but make a sad face as if I had spanked you."

I went back to class. When Brother Genole asked me what happened, I did not answer. He knew that I was a favorite of the headmaster. He never bothered me after that, but I also tried not to push my luck.

"The Fault, Dear Brutus..."

On Sunday mornings, we attended the eight o'clock Mass with the school as a group. Instead of the khaki uniforms we wore during the week, we had white long-sleeved shirts and white short pants, with light-blue ties bearing the white embroidered inscription "FIC," the French acronym for Brothers of Christian Instruction (*Frères de l'Instruction Chrétienne*). The boys would sit on the right side facing the altar. The girls would sit on the left side, dressed in their white Sunday uniforms, hair properly combed, faces powdered with an all too visible coat of talcum powder; lipstick was forbidden. It was the best opportunity for boys and girls to evaluate one another, in the hope of making a match. Some students would come to me to help them write love letters. In the process, I became good at the art of love-letter writing. For that, I would pay dearly later on.

A few students lived in villages about ten miles away from the school. They studied with their books open while running on their way home in the evening. They needed to know their lessons before dark. Their parents couldn't afford the kerosene to keep the lamps on for a long time at night. Occasionally, some of these students would miss a Sunday Mass. It angered me to see them being spanked on Monday for such an offense by the same headmaster who was so kind to me, the same one who taught us many songs, two of which I still remember. One was "The Legend of Saint Nicholas." The good old saint was able to revive three boys seven years after they were killed by a butcher and made into bacon (in French, *petit salé*).

The other song was very funny; Petula Clark would sing the English version. All of us students liked it. It was "The Little Shoemaker," and it was about a shoemaker who wanted a bride. He made a pair of magic shoes and offered them to a young lady. The little shoemaker was very stupid, but he danced the night away and married the girl.

I began to develop ambivalent feelings about Brother Gerard. Was he good, or was he bad—Dr. Jekyll or Mr. Hyde? I never came up with a satisfactory answer. I guess he was a human being, caught in the prejudices of his time and exhibiting both strengths and weaknesses. His new assistant, Brother Godfroy, was a totally different person.

CHAPTER 15

An Irish Toast to Long Life

Blind belief in authority is the greatest enemy of truth.

ALBERT EINSTEIN

BROTHER GODFROY WAS A YOUNG Canadian Catholic brother who came to replace Brother Genole, the one with whom I had had a little skirmish. Brother Godfroy was a very humble brother. He told us that he was the twenty-first and last child of his mother and father. As an infant, he suffered poor health, and his mother made a vow to Saint Joseph that if her son was saved, she would make sure that he devoted his life to missionary work. Sure enough, when the time came, the young man joined the Catholic brothers' organization and became Brother Godfroy.

It didn't take long for me to learn a lesson in humility from Brother Godfroy.

There were workers on school grounds finishing some of the work on the temporary classrooms. One day, a classmate and I were playing before class when one of the workers told us to behave. We paid him no attention.

Then he said, "I bet that as soon as Brother Godfroy shows up, you won't be able to say 'oink' like a little pig."

Now, you don't tell kids things like that without eliciting an appropriate response. So, not only did we call him "oink," imitating the sound of a pig, but we also went around and around him, singing, "Oink, oink, like a little pig."

He got mad, and as soon as Brother Godfroy showed up, he told him that we had called him a pig. We tried to explain that the worker had been the one to come up with the word in the first place, but to our frustration, Brother Godfroy wasn't moved. He gave us a long lecture on humility and respect for humble workers. Then he told us to kneel, apologize to the worker, and beg for his forgiveness.

There was no way I was going to do that. That was too much to ask, too high a price to pay for an offense I didn't commit. He was the culprit, not us. He had come up with the word "oink," not us. Both of us refused. Then Brother Godfroy told us we would stay outside on our knees and not attend classes. My friend and I were adamant in our position. We were not going to beg for forgiveness for something we hadn't done.

We spent the whole class session outside on our knees. After the morning break, there was going to be an exam that would count toward trimester grades. My friend gave up and said he was sorry. I held firm and got zero for the exam.

Lunch break came. Brother Godfroy told me I couldn't attend afternoon classes until I apologized to the worker. When I came back from lunch break ready to spend the afternoon on my knees, the worker went to Brother Godfroy and told him that I had apologized to him and that he was satisfied. I never told him I was sorry. In fact, I never said a word to him. His own feelings of guilt motivated him to pardon me. I went back to class, but I lost my usual first position by missing the exam.

This incident taught me two lessons. First, I discovered that I had the inner fortitude to stand my ground and not give up when I thought I was right, even if I had to pay a price. Second, I learned about virtues. By forgiving me, the worker had shown more humility and forgiveness than I was able to muster. High on the pedestal of my pride, I wasn't going to change my conviction. I insisted that he was wrong and I was right. Therefore, I refused to lower myself in front of him and beg his pardon.

Faced with this situation, Brother Godfroy, a true humble servant of God, used the opportunity to lecture us on the virtues of forgiveness, humility, and charity. He would use all kinds of examples to instill these virtues in us. I felt as if he were addressing me personally when he lectured, and I made sure I read the nuggets of wisdom that he posted on the walls. Here are some of them:

- Weak people don't forgive; only strong people do.
- If you look down on people, you cannot see God above.
- We can sit on a throne, but we're still sitting on our behinds.
- Women wear proudly on their head what a rooster carries humbly on its tail.
- Stealing from the state is stealing; therefore, it is a sin.

I made a decision to practice humility, forgiveness, and charity. Still, I didn't believe everything Brother Godfroy said.

Don't Believe Everything You're Told

On the playground one day, Brother Godfroy was reading students' palms to predict their future. I went to him and tendered my hand. He looked at my palm and indicated the major and minor lines, the ones that supposedly correlated to my heart, head, life, and fate. He told me about events that would take place in my life regarding relationships, marriage, offspring, health, travels, and so on. I paid little attention until he said I would die at the age of fifty-two. Now, my great-grandma, my father's grandmother, had just died at the age of 103. Why shouldn't I live that long?

I couldn't get that prediction off my mind. It stayed with me over the years. And I made a request to God to allow me to care for my children and to play with my grandchildren. Still, when I turned fifty-two years old, I was scared to death. I thought I was going to die. Then, I found out that the best way to counteract an idea that had been planted in my mind was to replace it with another idea.

Around that time I came across a saying said to be an Irish toast. I proposed it to myself and posted it on my refrigerator door so that it could be embedded in my subconscious mind. It read:

Jesse,
May you live to be a hundred years, with an extra year to repent!
Signed,
Jesse

I must say that either the Irish toast is working or that God has his own plan regarding my life. Otherwise, you wouldn't be reading this little story. Like Juan Ponce de León before me, I have found the Fountain of Youth in the Sunshine State of Florida. A little golf, a little writing, an alligator in the sun, a dolphin jumping out of the intracoastal waterway, and a breathtaking sunrise or sunset will keep me occupied for hours. Time goes pretty fast when you're enjoying nature, and I am not in a hurry to die.

A Taste of Heaven

Once, Brother Godfroy told us that when we died and went to heaven, we would be contemplating God for eternity. I thought that was so boring.

I asked him, "What is eternity?"

"I am glad you asked that question," he said. "Let me explain it to you by telling you a story."

And here is the story he told:

"Once upon a time," he said, "there was a monk in a monastery who asked the same question. 'What is eternity?' He thought it was an awful long time to do only one thing, such as contemplating God. One morning the monk went for a walk in the forest near the monastery. He heard a bird singing. He stopped to listen, and although he had enjoyed birdsong before, this time it was different. It was as if this little bird was glorifying God in its own way, and he became captivated by the bird's song. Time passed, and the monk didn't realize it, until one day he opened his eyes, as if coming out of a long sleep. He noticed that his beard was touching the ground. His clothes were all torn. He walked out of the forest to the monastery. There were only ruins. He asked a passerby what had happened to the monastery. He was told that it had been destroyed during the war. What war? The passerby hurried to get out of the sight of this lunatic, who looked, indeed, very strange. The monk then realized that, with only a small bird's song, he had experienced a glimpse of eternity."

Here in Palm Coast, I take time to listen to a bird's song.

Am I contemplating God?

Is it a glimpse of eternity?

Brother Godfroy was a good teacher and the humblest person I have ever met. The virtues of humility, forgiveness, and charity that he instilled in me constitute the building blocks of my character. For that I am grateful. However, I don't think that palm reading was his forte. His prediction, I suppose, was based on statistical analysis that indicates the life expectancy for an average person in Haiti at that time. I left Haiti at the age of twenty-four.

I studied with Brother Godfroy until the seventh grade. Then I left primary school and moved on to secondary school with different teachers. But before I get to that, let me tell you about my love life around that time and my own discovery of how the universe works.

CHAPTER 16

When God Closes a Door, He Opens Many Windows

Out of my great despair came my greatest joy.

RHONDA BYRNES, *THE SECRET*

WHEN I WAS TWELVE YEARS old, I fell in love with an adorable girl who was attending the nuns' school. Her name was Annie; she was about my age. Not sure how to approach her, I decided to send her a love letter through one of her friends. I placed all my knowledge of love writing into the letter, making sure it expressed in a poetic way my admiration for her angelic beauty, the deep feelings she inspired in me, and my desire for her to be my sweetheart. I waited anxiously for her reply. One grueling week passed.

On Sunday morning, as I went to church and entered the sacristy to put on my altar-boy dress, I noticed the other boys were laughing. I asked what was so funny. Someone said, "Nothing." I didn't pay much attention. I put on the red robe that reached the ground, topped by the surplice, a white tunic that reached below the knees. The boys were still laughing, and I saw that one of them was holding what looked like my letter in his hand.

"What's this?" I asked.

They started laughing more loudly, and the one holding the letter said, "Hey, lover boy." Having read the letter, he knew its contents, and he had shared it with the others.

I yelled, "Give me my letter."

But he wouldn't give it to me. Instead he was scoffing at me, saying, "Lover boy is rejected."

Finally, another boy took the letter from him and gave it to me. I then found out that Annie had left it for me on the way to Catholic Mass.

It was indeed my letter, and it had been meant for Annie's eyes only; now the whole world knew about it. My heart was torn into pieces. All kinds of thoughts started to race in my mind. I shouldn't have sent her the letter. I lost face in front of all my friends.

I was so humiliated. Later, during Mass, I rang the little altar bell. The joyful sound that brought the attention of the faithful to the miracle of the Eucharist was transformed into a sound of sadness for me. This was the worst day of my life. I didn't know how I would survive.

I did survive, and years later, I would learn an invaluable lesson about how the universe works. "Adversity carries with it the seeds of greater benefits" (Hill 1963).

Within days of my "tragedy," I received a written note from another girl, this one named Angie, asking me to be her boyfriend. I immediately answered, "Yes!"

During that same week, a second girl, by the name of Marie, sent me a verbal message: she would be more than happy to be my sweetheart if Annie didn't care for me.

I said, "Yes, yes!"

Now, instead of one, I had two girlfriends. But neither of them was Annie, the ultimate object of my admiration. Secretly, I was still yearning for her love. A few months later, during summer vacation, I finally got an opportunity to talk to her. She apologized for hurting me, explaining that she liked me very much but was afraid that her father would have killed her had he found out that she had a boyfriend at the age of thirteen. She then said she was willing to defy her father and be my sweetheart if I still wanted her.

I said, "Yes, yes, yes."

Obviously, when it rains, it pours.

I was able to manage my three newly found girlfriends, Angie, Marie, and Annie, without much difficulty. We did not have much interaction anyhow. It was more holding hands if we happened to meet on the way to school, the touching of a sprouting breast, and an occasional kiss when nobody was around, especially with Marie. She surprised me with a deep-tongue kiss. I later found out that she was so self-conscious about making a good impression that she asked an older female friend to teach her how to kiss. She became an expert, and I benefited from it. (By the way, according to AOL.com, in 2014, "How to kiss" was the fourth most frequent "how-to" search inquiry people made.)

As for Angie, she enjoyed writing as much as I did; our relationship boiled down to the exchange of love letters almost daily.

Things became a little more complicated with Annie. When her parents found out that she was in love with me, she suffered dearly. While her mother was sympathetic, her father absolutely forbade the relationship and scolded her whenever he suspected that she was with me. It didn't take him long to find her a suitable husband, with whom she had many children and a happy life. Over the years, I lost contact with Angie and Marie, and I never saw them again.

This story may give the impression that I was an outgoing and extroverted young boy. Far from it. I was rather timid and awkward with girls. But for unknown reasons, some of them were attracted to me. One day, when I was in my Boy Scout uniform, I stopped at a friend's house. She was a lovely young girl of about thirteen, a couple of years younger than I was. Her mother was out. I could tell by the way she looked at me that she had a crush on me. After talking with her for a little while, I told her I was leaving.

She said, "What happened to my kiss?"

I didn't know I had promised her a kiss, but we joined lips, and by that simple gesture, we became officially boyfriend and girlfriend. And that was the end of that. Years later, I met her again, and she told me how much she had been in love with me when we were young.

And so it is. "When God closes a door, he opens many windows." This is a lesson I learned on my own, through my own experiences. None of my teachers taught me that one, not even Father Jestin.

CHAPTER 17

Take Nothing for Granted

Anything that can go wrong will go wrong.

MURPHY'S LAW

FATHER AIMÉ JESTIN WAS A French priest in his late thirties. Born in Paris, he fought against the German occupation of his native land during World War II. After the war, he came to serve in Haiti as a priest in accordance with the Haitian concordat, which the Vatican signed in 1860 during the presidency of Fabre Nicolas Geffrard, who (as mentioned earlier) was born in Anse-à-Veau, where Father Jestin was assigned. The concordat provided trained priests and religious educators for Haiti.

From the independence in 1804 until that treaty, Haiti was without Catholic priests. The French priests had left Haiti after the war for independence. There was never any attempt to train Haitians for the priesthood. It was not unlike the United States, where the first black priest couldn't even attend seminary in that country because of racial discrimination. Augustus Tolton had to study and be ordained as a priest in Rome in 1886.

In the absence of Catholic priests, the African voodoo religion mixed with elements of Catholicism was practiced in Haiti to fill the void of human beings' deep-seated need for the spiritual.

With the 1860 concordat, the Vatican had finally recognized the State of Haiti. It should be noted that while France had accepted the loss of its former colony and recognized Haitian independence in 1825, it took the

Vatican another thirty-five years to finally accept the independence of this first black nation, a country that won its war against Napoleon's army and declared its sovereignty in 1804. Still, the Vatican didn't do it for free. The Haitian government had to cover certain costs.

For my part, I was gratified to learn in 2014 that Pope Francis had elevated a Haitian, Bishop Chibly Langlois, to the College of Cardinals. After nearly 150 years of Catholicism, a Haitian religious leader now has a voice at the table.

The Body of Christ

I am grateful that there were good teachers like Father Jestin to give me an adequate education. It allowed me to break the cycle of poverty that is still the lot of my people. I was familiar with Father Jestin, since he was the parish priest from whom I received the sacraments of First Communion and confirmation. By the time I was ten years old, I had become an altar boy, serving Mass with him almost daily.

Once, I managed to both amuse and annoy him on the same day, at the same Mass. It was before Vatican II, the big change in the Catholic Church that was carried out by Pope Paul VI but initiated by Pope John XXIII—"to open the windows of the church to let in some fresh air," as he is purported to have said.

At that time, people receiving Communion would kneel along the altar rail, and the priest would put the host on their tongues while saying a prayer. The altar boy would hold a small tray under their chins to collect whatever bits of bread might fall so that they wouldn't reach the ground. I slightly touched the chin of my sweetheart with the tray as she received the Holy Communion, scaring the hell out of her. This little mischievous act didn't go unnoticed by Father Jestin, who looked at me with his lips outlining the beginning of a smile, as a partner in crime.

After Communion, I gave him the tray. He inspected it for little pieces of the holy host, the bread that represents the body of Christ, and he dropped them in the golden chalice that had the wine that represents the blood of Christ. Then he returned the tray to me. I noticed that there were still a couple of tiny pieces of bread on the tray. I brought the tray back to him. He cleaned it and returned it to me. But I saw that there was still one more speck of bread on the tray. I brought it back to him a third time because, as far as I knew, each one of those tiny specks of bread represented the body of Christ and couldn't be discarded; it had to be treated with the utmost respect only a priest could provide.

Father Jestin looked at me, very annoyed, cleaned the tray for the third time, and told me through clenched teeth, "Don't come back."

Then he drank the wine that contained all those tiny pieces of bread, each one representing the body of Christ. The Eucharist is at the center of the Catholic Mass. It's not something to understand. As Christians, we are asked to believe it through the mystery of faith.

All of this was happening under the watchful eyes of the bewildered congregation. Luckily at that time the priest stood with his back to the congregation; most people couldn't figure out exactly what was happening at the altar.

Later on, the church did away with that little tray and the altar rail. Now communicants receive the holy host in their hands, not only from the priest but also from trained laics, who hold the host up and say, "The body of Christ."

The person receiving the Communion says, "Amen."

Once I attended a church service while on vacation, and during Communion, I presented my hand to receive the holy host, but to my astonishment, it was withheld from me. The situation became a little awkward for a moment. I didn't understand why. It turned out that I hadn't said amen. Now I make sure I say amen.

The scene at the altar with Father Jestin wasn't the last time he and I would have a little skirmish.

The Sword of Damocles

Father Jestin was my secondary-school teacher for five years. In my second year, he taught writing. One day, he gave us an assignment to write a paper on "the physical and moral description of a person, dead or alive."

I did my work about another teacher with whom I had an ax to grind. He had failed to give me an A when I thought I deserved it. I portrayed him as uglier than he in fact was, and I also wrote a moral description indicating that he didn't care much about the well-being of the students.

The next day, I was playing in the schoolyard at break time when, from the window, Father Jestin called me to his office.

"Sit down," he said, with a very concerned look on his face. "What's gotten into you?" Then he said, "Who wrote your assignment?"

I said, "I did." I didn't know where he was heading.

Now, Father Jestin wasn't just anybody. He had been a French officer in World War II, trained in the art of interrogation and the value of a compromising secret document.

He said to me, "Do you realize what you've done?"

I thought it was just a class assignment.

"This is defamation of character; if this paper ever comes to light, you could be in for a libel lawsuit."

I still didn't know what he was talking about.

As if to protect me from some unseen danger, he tore the page of my assignment from my notebook with a single quick gesture. He then folded it and put it in the pocket of his white cassock.

I left his office thinking, *What have I gotten myself into? Libel lawsuit? What's that?*

Whatever it was, it was bad.

I went back to the yard. I had lost all desire to play. But it wasn't the end of the story.

A few days later, some of us members of the choir were by the organ in the church, rehearsing songs for the expected visit of the bishop to the parish. The songs were boring, and to enliven the atmosphere, one student flicked the earlobe of another student, landing a strong blow. It didn't take long for a little brawl to develop.

The organist got angry and took us to Father Jestin, who started ranting and raving. He expressed his disappointment in us. He complained that for all he'd done for us, we failed to do our part in the preparation of something as important as the bishop's visit. Then he put his hand in his cassock's pocket and pulled out a piece of paper.

Looking at me, he said, "Gourde*ttt*." (The *t* in my name, usually silent, became very, very pronounced.) "The sword of Damocles is here; here it is." He brandished the folded paper in the air.

No one except he and I knew what the paper was or why the priest had addressed me personally, but after that my nickname became "the sword of Damocles."

Years later, I met an old classmate; he greeted me warmly by saying, "Hi, the sword of Damocles. How nice to see you!"

He didn't remember my real name.

Anyway, we went back to rehearsing without any further disturbance. The day came for the bishop's visit, and everything went very well. Bishop Collignon was a tall, big man with a sense of humor. In his homily, he congratulated Father Jestin for the masterly performance of our wonderful choir, made up of well-behaved young men.

Father Jestin smiled, but in his heart he was saying, "O Bishop, you don't know what I am going through with these little devilish boys!"

At the reception that followed, the bishop and other dignitaries sat at the dinner table, enjoying a good meal. While I was serving as waiter, I couldn't help but picture in my mind another dinner that took place a long time ago in ancient Greece. Our world history professor had told us the story of Damocles and King Dionysius.

"In Greek legend," he had said, "there is a story about a man named Damocles, who was jealous of the king. He believed that the king was happy because he had so much abundance; everything was going well for him. It was as if the universe was created for him. The king prepared a surprise for Damocles to give him a taste of what it was like to be a king. He invited Damocles to a banquet, urged him to sit in the king's chair, and entertained him royally. Damocles enjoyed himself until he saw above his head a sharp sword held by a single horsehair. A shiver ran through his spine. He then realized how fragile the king's happiness was. He panicked and fled the palace to live a simple life in the country."

My teacher concluded that the king had wanted to teach a lesson to Damocles: "Don't take anything for granted; danger always hangs over our heads."

The Helmet of Darkness

You would think that I had learned the lesson that one should take nothing for granted in life.

No!

I was going to be in trouble again with Father Jestin, this time on a matter of faith. I refer to it as the Helmet of Darkness. According to legend, the Greek hero Perseus wanted to save his mother from a bad king. He embarked on the challenge of defeating Medusa, a Gorgon from whom a single look could mean death. Luckily for Perseus, he had a little help from the gods. They gave him a helmet that made him invisible; it was called the Helmet of Darkness. With that helmet, Perseus was able to do what no other human being had done before him: he defeated Medusa.

As young people, we were always fascinated by the supernatural, and when we discovered a technique that allowed us to perform impossible tasks, we jumped on it. It was such a case when my friend Jake stumbled upon a book of magic.

Jake was poking around in the attic of his house one day when he was attacked by a flock of bats that had been hanging from the ceiling. They started to fly all over him. Overcome by panic, he tried to retrace his steps back to the stairs, but instead, he fell on a box that contained old books. The bats left the attic through a broken window. He was alone.

He searched the box and came upon a book called *The Little Albert Handbook of Magic*. He took the book and hid it under his shirt. Then he left the house and came to show the book to me. With high emotions, we frantically read these magic formulas. We were delighted to possess such wonderful secrets. This book would give us the power to do anything we wanted. It had secret procedures for all kinds of useful things:

- how to make a girl love you;
- how to catch birds;
- how to find treasures;
- how to win in a game of hazards;
- how to be invisible; and
- how to transcend space and time and be in two places at the same time.

(It sounds farfetched, but according to quantum physics, this might one day be possible.)

We started to experiment with the procedures contained in the book. Because we had to buy certain ingredients that raised the suspicion of the shopkeepers, before long it reached Father Jestin's ears that some kids were practicing magic. Confronted by Father Jestin, we repented and gave him the book. In his sermon the following Sunday, he made a major speech attacking all nonbelievers, including the Freemasons and practitioners of voodoo. He threatened with excommunication anybody who got involved with magic or other satanic practices. My friend and I were scared of being excommunicated by the church, because if we died, we would go straight to hell, where we would burn eternally. We went to confession and did penance to expunge all our sins.

These incidents didn't in anyway alter my good relationship with Father Jestin. He still looked at me as his protégé.

You Cannot Be a Bishop

Occasionally we would put on a play under the direction of Father Jestin, and all the parents would be invited. Once I had this long monologue to act. It was about a taxi driver who didn't know his way around town. He kept on getting lost, to the exasperation of his passenger, who was running late for an important meeting. Many incidents happened along the way, including the hitting of a couple of chickens that were crossing the street. I had my French beret tilted on one side of my head; I looked like a real taxi driver. The audience loved it and gave me a lot of applause. Afterward, Mr. Morgan congratulated me and told me he was proud of me for memorizing such a long monologue. Father Jestin was very pleased.

One day I was in his office when he was grading homework assignments. He looked at me and said, "I go over yours really fast to avoid seeing mistakes because I don't want to deduct points from you."

At the end of the school year, he would reward the top three students with monetary prizes. I never failed to get one. Once, I got five dollars from him. That was a lot of money then. Most workers didn't make that kind of money in a month. But the parish did well.

I remember going with Father Jestin to a church dedicated to Saint Yves. It had a beautiful waterfall, and it had become a major pilgrimage site and sanctuary. It had the power to bring miracles into people's lives. Many healings and instances of good fortune in business were attributed to this site. Pilgrims in large number visited the place on the celebration of the feast of Saint Yves. On that occasion, Father Jestin would say the Mass for the intention of many deceased loved ones, to get them out of purgatory and into paradise. Upon request from the faithful, he blessed all kinds of items, from rosaries to statuettes to images of saints to candles. All of this came with contributions to the church. Bad-mouthing people would say that at some point, Father Jestin would have to stop the blessings; his horse's *sacoche* couldn't hold any more money.

Anyway, I felt grateful that he was generous to us. For my part, I used the money from the prize at the end of the school year to buy the most expensive pen at that time, an Esterbrook fountain pen.

I guess Father Jestin had big plans for me in the future. One day I was sitting on the balcony of the presbytery with him, looking over the city below us and the blue sea in the distance. The church and the presbytery were built on top of a small hill overlooking the city with a view of the sprawling sea that extended all the way to the horizon.

As I was enjoying the view, I saw him reflecting for a moment; then he looked at me and said, "You know, if you should become a priest, you wouldn't be able to make it to bishop."

"Why is that?"

"Because your mother and father were not married," he answered.

Now, I had never told Father Jestin that I wanted to be a priest. Even though I was an altar boy for many years, the idea had never crossed my mind. I wanted to keep my girlfriends. Besides, I already knew the joy of sex. Still, I surprised him with my quick answer.

"What about Jesus?" I said. "His real father and mother were not married."

"It's not the same thing," he said, brushing me off. Then he talked about other things.

Well, since I didn't go into the priesthood, I didn't have to worry about not being a bishop.

The irony of life would have it that many years later I visited the parish, and in that same place where I had spoken with Father Jestin, who by then was long dead, I met a new priest. As I introduced myself to him, he said, "You look like a bishop."

I instantly remembered my conversation with Father Jestin. I couldn't believe it. Was it a voice from the other side?

An Immersion in Greco-Roman and French Literature

As I mentioned earlier, Father Jestin was my teacher for five years. By the time I reached the fifth year of secondary school, I was well versed in ancient and modern classical literature. Names such as Cicero, Virgil, Pluto, Ovid, Horace, Homer, and others were familiar to me. We studied *The Iliad*, *The Aeneid*, and Marcus Aurelius's *Meditations*.

As a punishment, one student was expelled from the classroom until he could recite in Latin the first one hundred lines of a text called *De Viris Illustribus* (a biography of illustrious men of Greek and Roman antiquity written by a fourteenth-century Italian writer named Petrarch). It took that student almost a week to memorize the text, but after that he would talk Latin on the street to the amazement and consternation of everyone. People who didn't know why he was speaking Latin on the streets thought he was going nuts. He later became a devoted teacher.

Still, he wasn't the only one who was versed in Latin. Sometimes in the schoolyard you could hear a student shout at a friend in Latin, "How long, O Catilina, will you abuse our patience?" He would be using a Latin phrase from the Roman writer Cicero to settle an argument. We got a lot of fun out of these incidents.

With Father Jestin I studied French classics from the sixteenth, seventeenth, and eighteenth centuries, putting me one year ahead of schedule. The seventeenth century was my favorite. I enjoyed reading Racine, Corneille, Boileau, and Pascal. We memorized the *Fables* of La Fontaine; we put on plays by Molière. We learned about serendipity, when something good happens by chance. For instance, Ronsard's most quoted verse was changed by accident. In a poem written in memory of his friend's daughter, Rosette, who died at an early age, Ronsard wrote, "And Rosette had lived what roses live, the space of a morning."

However, the publisher thought he wrote, "And rose she lived what roses live, the space of a morning."

This little change has made all the difference. The poem became a great success because of its universality.

My favorite writer was Descartes. With him, I learned that *cogito, ergo sum* ("I think, therefore I am"). One must erase old concepts and start from scratch to come up with fresh ideas that are not tainted with preconceived notions. In other words, it's good to have your own mind.

Good Administrators Leave Marks

Father Jestin was a great administrator. He managed the church with professionalism. When I went through my papers while writing this book, I came across a card that he had given me in 1958. It is a summary of my religious demographics. Here is the information on the card:

> #145
> Parish: Anse-à-Veau—Town
> Name: Gesner Gourdet
> Place: In town
> Date of birth: 5-24-44
> Date of Baptism: June 1944
> Date of Communion: 6-8-52
> Date of Confirmation: 1-15-56
> Date of Renovation: 5-30-57
> Marriage:
> Wife's name:
> Children:
> Year 1958: Catechism Good. Signed, Father Aimé Jestin, Curé.

I didn't even remember I had Renovation. I don't think the Catholic Church does it anymore.

A Priest Disguised as a Woman

After I left the school to attend classes in the capital, Father Jestin discovered that the teacher I had used as the subject of my classroom assignment wasn't really a saint. He denounced Father Jestin to the authorities, accusing him of subversion and plotting against the government. Father Jestin, the former World War II officer who fought against Hitler's army in his native France, narrowly escaped arrest by disguising himself as a woman to leave the town and flee the country.

I tried to contact him some years later. I got his address in France from another priest, named Father Henry Guimard. I wrote a letter to him. I never got a reply. I wanted to express my gratitude to him and let him know that I was doing well and that I had finally realized how frail life is, that one cannot take things for granted; danger is always hovering over our heads.

Father Jestin wasn't the only one who experienced the nefarious effect of the sword of Damocles. Two of my other teachers became victims of the evil that was sweeping the country at that time. Perhaps their fate had something to do with a haunted house. Let's find out.

CHAPTER 18

The Curse of the Haunted House

It's better to light a candle than to curse the darkness.

Old proverb

On top of a hill overlooking the sea, waves crashing against the rocks below, stood a majestic two-story mansion. Once the private residence of a former political leader, the house had survived the earthquake of 1952, but it was too big to maintain. It was left unoccupied for some time. When the town intellectuals decided to give a secondary school to the city, this house became a good choice for a school building because of its many rooms. However, not everybody agreed on the suitability of this house for young people. Rumor had it that strange things happened in the house at night. People often heard footsteps when they could not see anyone. Tables and chairs moved on their own for no apparent reason. The house guardian had seen a woman peeking into the garde-manger, but she would vanish as soon as someone approached. In one room on the lower level, the emaciated corpse of a long-dead baby was found in a closet. It was thrown in the nearby sea as a form of burial.

Briefly, everybody knew that the house was haunted. But it became the secondary school anyway, and the students loved it. I especially liked the winding staircase rail. I could slide down it unobstructed for two levels. Each classroom bore the name of a historical personage, like Solon Menos, a Haitian writer who was born in Anse-à-Veau and obtained a doctorate in law from the University of Paris in the early twentieth century, or Anténor Firmin, who wrote a book, *On the Equality of Human Races*. A picture of each person hung in the relevant classroom.

The school's headmaster and prefect of discipline were practicing lawyers. One was my Greek teacher; the other one was my world history teacher. They both paid the ultimate sacrifice.

The early 1960s was a time of national chaos and student uprisings against the government. Somehow the school building caught fire. Even though neither teacher had anything to do with the fire, they were picked up by security and brought to prison in the capital. From then on they were never heard from again. Some say they were summarily executed. We never stopped mourning these two young lawyers who provided education to the town's underprivileged children without any compensation.

I still remember the day when I was having difficulties with the translation of a Greek sentence, and I started to cry.

My teacher told me, "Don't worry; with time you will be good at it."

And then, raising his eyes in the air, he pronounced these words by Anatole France, which I never forget and can still recite in French:

> *Si les grains jetés dans la terre noire peuvent produire de si belles fleurs, que ne doit-il pas être permis au cœur de l'homme à devenir au cours de son long voyage vers les étoiles?*
>
> ("If seeds thrown into black soil can produce such beautiful flowers, what shouldn't be allowed for the heart of man to become in its long journey to the stars?")

Inspiring words by a caring man—unfortunately he was assassinated in the prime of his ascension. He never had the pleasure to witness the flowering of his seeds. I remain confident that the spirits of that haunted house who permeate both the dead and the living worlds will communicate the good news to him: "Dear master, the seeds you planted in the black soil have produced beautiful flowers."

As for my world history teacher, his memory came back to mind many years later when I visited Tallinn, the capital of Estonia, a former Soviet state by the Baltic Sea. While dancing with a beautiful Estonian girl, I whispered in her ear, "I love you," in her native Russian language. She was elated and would have followed me to the end of the world. However, my wife was with me. I had to behave.

It was my world history teacher who told us, "As citizens of the world, you should learn how to say 'I love you' to a woman in any language." This advice has served me well. That's how I remembered my teacher.

For that I am grateful.

Another teacher who made a great impact on me was a young Haitian priest named Father Willy Romulus. From him I would learn another important lesson.

CHAPTER 19

The Power of Focus

It is with the heart that one sees well. What is essential is invisible to the eye.

ANTOINE DE SAINT-EXUPÉRY

WHEN FATHER ROMULUS CAME TO Anse-à-Veau, he struck me right away as a young Haitian priest with a mission and a vision to match. He was tall and skinny, and his strong power of focus and the intensity of his determination distinguished him from other people. It was as if he had a blueprint for life, and he wasn't going to let people or circumstances get in the way. He was full of passion for his pastoral work. Father Jestin was the curé, the priest in charge of the parish. Father Romulus, the young priest, was the vicar, the assistant to Father Jestin. He implemented many new programs Father Jestin either didn't have the time for or simply wasn't interested in. I never saw him socializing with other priests or with the other religious educators such as the Catholic brothers or the Catholic sisters who were white French and Canadians. He was all business. While Father Jestin would enjoy a cocktail on a hot summer afternoon, Father Romulus never drank; instead he concentrated on his work.

When he wasn't attending to priestly affairs, I would see him in his office translating the little catechism book from French to Creole, the language spoken by all Haitians. He had realized that most people could not understand the instructions for Catholic life written in Latin and French, and he set out to give it to them in their own language. This was years before the Catholic Church came to the same conclusion and allowed for Mass to be celebrated in vernacular languages in the mid-1960s. He was ahead of his time. For my part, I still enjoy a Mass in Latin with Gregorian chant.

Father Romulus created a group called Catholic Youth Students, of which I became the president. This was an opportunity for us students to meet outside the classroom and learn public speaking. He trained us in religious instruction. And on Sundays after Mass, some of us would go to the surrounding villages to instruct the people on the life of Christ and to teach them religious prayers.

A Woman Named Jeanne

It was on one such mission that I met a young woman named Jeanne. She introduced me to the pleasures of life in the suburbs. I had gone to her village to teach religion on a Sunday. She attended the religious class, and on my way back home, she accompanied me. When it was only the two of us on the road, she held my hand and started to get really close to me, caressing my hair and kissing me on the face. It didn't take me long to realize that things could go further soon. She asked me to stop at her house, which was on the way. Nobody was home. We hit the bed right away. That was such an unexpected and pleasing experience! But my joy would soon turn to trepidation.

It was mandatory for us to go to confession during certain times of the year. You couldn't escape it. I dreaded the day. I didn't want to tell Father Romulus what really happened during my tour of religious education. And I was afraid to go to confession with Father Jestin because I thought my sin was too big. Contrary to religious beliefs in some non-Christian cultures, the Catholic Church teaches that sex outside marriage is sinful. Even in marriage, sex should be used only for procreation, not for pleasure. I was battling with a feeling of guilt, and finally, after an agonizing self-deliberation, I went to confession with Father Romulus.

In the semidarkness of the confessional, I told him that I had had sex. I feared that he was going to give me a long lecture.

But luckily for me he was compassionate. He didn't get upset, and he didn't lecture me. He simply asked, "Was it with an adult or with a young girl?"

"With an adult," I quickly responded although I had some doubt. But I convinced myself that I hadn't lied because the girl was older than I was.

"Any other sins?" he asked.

"No," I answered.

He then told me to ask God for forgiveness, and he absolved me with the Latin phrase "*Ego te absolvo a peccatis tuis...*"

And I made the sign of the cross. Then he asked me to say one Our Father and three Hail Marys.

I left the confessional to kneel down at a bench, and I recited the requested prayers. While I was praying, it suddenly dawned on me that the good father had omitted to tell me not to do that again. I was relieved; I could see Jeanne again.

God Will Speak Tonight

Father Romulus not only taught us religion, but he was also our math teacher. With him, I learned algebra, one of the courses in which I excelled. It served me well later when I took calculus in college. Under him, I became the librarian for the little library of the school. I read almost all the books, from Alexandre Dumas to Émile Zola. *The Count of Monte Cristo, The Three Musketeers, Les Misérables,* and a host of other books kept me awake most nights. In *Candide,* Voltaire challenged the idea that "all is for the best in the best of all possible worlds" while the world was crumbling around us and human beings were subjected to abject sufferings. In *The Stranger,* Albert Camus expressed the idea of the indifference of the universe toward us.

These two books left me with a lot of unanswered questions about our existence: Does God really care about us? What is my place in society? Do people have a right to judge others?

One book Father Romulus personally gave to me was *Dieu Parlera ce Soir,* (God Will Speak Tonight), by Jean Marie de Buck, a Jesuit priest. That book, along with another, *Le Petit Prince* by Antoine de Saint-Exupéry, had a great influence on me. They inspired me to look inside myself for communication with God. That's where I found answers to universal questions.

On a visit to Haiti, long after I was living in the United States, my father asked me, "Have you seen Father Willy Romulus?"

I answered, "No, I haven't seen him, but I know he comes to New York occasionally."

Then my father addressed me personally as he told me a story.

"It was during the time when you were still in Anse-à-Veau," he said. "One day, I got a phone call from Father Romulus. He said, 'I have something very important to discuss with you regarding your son Gesner, but I can't do it over the phone. It has to be done in person.'

"'Can you come this Thursday?' I asked him.

"'Yes, I'll travel this Thursday,' Father Romulus answered." The distance between the two towns was a three- to four-hour horse ride.

"Father Romulus came on that day," my father said. Then, he said that Father Romulus told him, "Your son Gesner has learned all that can be offered in his present school. It is time to put him in a more advanced school in the capital."

And my father concluded, "That's why I decided to send you to school in the capital."

At that moment, the memory of Brother Francis, who had brought me to Anse-à-Veau, came to my mind. And I told my father, "What a coincidence. One religious man brought me to Anse-à-Veau; another religious man took me away from it."

"That's the way it was meant to be," my father concluded.

I didn't know that Father Romulus, now Bishop Romulus, had been watching over my good upbringing. I felt grateful. And I took advantage of one of his visits to New York to thank him in person. I met with him in Queens and reminded him of the book, *God Will Speak Tonight*, that he had given me as a teenager. I told him how the book's message had guided me over the years. Then, our conversation turned to human-rights violations in Haiti.

Bishop Romulus was an outspoken critic of the regime. He even served time under house arrest. He worked hard to promote social justice and economic improvements for the Haitians. However, his elevation to bishop and the work he did within the Catholic Church are better testimony to the power of focus that he exemplified and that I learned from him. Thanks to him I was able to move to the capital and attend a more challenging school, ensuring that I got the best possible education. For that I am grateful to him.

Part Two
A Little Fish in a Big Pond

CHAPTER 20

O God, Come to My Aid; O Lord, Hasten to Help Me

The most certain way to succeed is always to try just one more time.

Thomas A. Edison

When I arrived in Port-au-Prince, the capital of Haiti, in October 1962, I felt like a little fish in a big pond. That feeling stayed with me for a good couple of years. Finally, I realized that I was just as good as—or in some regards, even better than—the people who were born in the capital and who looked down on people from the provinces.

My first problem came on the first day of classes, when I found out that I wasn't registered in the public secondary school I was supposed to attend. All my papers had been submitted on time, and I had a verbal acceptance from a school official. It was a time of great turmoil, and members of the government were bringing additional students to the school and demanding their admission. School officials could not reject them. Classes had more students than the school could accommodate.

My class was supposed to have sixty seats. It had already reached over one hundred students. Many students had to stand up to attend lectures. Some of them would take notes by putting their notebooks on the shoulders of the students in front of them. In other words, the class was overfilled.

One sympathetic school secretary told me to continue to go to my classes while she tried to pull some strings to get me officially enrolled. I wasn't the only one in that situation. The students in my class, which was Rheto B, met in one fixed room. Teachers for the different subjects came to that room to deliver their one- or two-hour lectures according to their schedules. They paid little attention to attendance. The school's administration made periodic roll calls. Any student not on the official list for that class had to vacate the classroom. Those of us who had to leave would come back in the afternoon or the next day to attend classes until the next roll call.

In the meantime, I contacted the few people I knew to see if they could help me to be admitted to the school. My father and my aunt knew some people, but they couldn't help.

Finally, I tried to appeal directly to the minister of education. I went to his office, but I wasn't allowed to see him. Someone told me he had a mistress whom he visited every day and gave me the address. I went to the house one afternoon around three and asked to see him. A servant told me that the minister was resting and couldn't be disturbed. I told her that I would wait outside on the street in front of the house. His car was there.

I waited and waited until about five, when I saw the minister getting in his chauffeured car with his gorgeous mistress. I approached him and stretched out a hand while attempting to talk to him. It was in vain. He told me that he was on his way to the theater and didn't have time for me. My heart was broken. That was my last resort. I had already exhausted all my resources. I went home like a wounded bird that couldn't fly. I had to limp around.

Beaten but not broken, I kept telling myself that things would be all right. Still, what do you do when you come to the end of the tunnel and there is no light? You get down on your knees and pray, hoping that someone will hear you. That night, I remembered a prayer Father Jestin used to say: "O God, come to my aid. O Lord, hasten to help me."

I closed my eyes and said it loudly with all my heart. A few days passed, and nothing happened.

I attended classes for a couple more days, and then there was another roll call. I had to leave the classroom. I went home again. I was reaching the paroxysm of desperation. It had been almost a month already since school had opened, and I hadn't been admitted. Why hadn't God answered my prayer? I didn't realize then that within that experience there were lessons to be learned. First, it's always darker before sunrise. Second, the universe has its own agenda; it takes its sweet time to make things happen. You just have to be patient.

And the Angel Came

When I arrived home, a gentleman named Yvon just happened to stop by to say hello to the people at the house. He knew of me, but it was the first time we had met. He asked me, "Why are you home so early? Shouldn't you be in school?"

"They kicked me out," I replied. And then I explained to him what had happened.

He listened attentively, and when I was finished talking, he said, "I am the assistant to the assistant director of the Department of Education. Why don't you come tomorrow morning at eight thirty? I'll see what I can do for you."

I said, "Thank you." Finally, a glimmer of light was showing at the end of my dark tunnel.

That night I slept very well. I woke up early, and by 8:00 a.m. I was at the Department of Education. I met Yvon, and he took me to see his boss, the assistant director. Yvon told him that I was his nephew. In a few short words, I explained my situation to the assistant director, and I showed him my report card from my previous school.

He looked at it and commented, "Hmm, you're an A student."

I didn't think it was a question, so I said nothing.

He then looked at me and asked, "What class do you want to be in?"

I told him the class, and on my report card, he wrote, "Accept student Gesner Gourdet in Rheto, B Section."

He signed it, put the seal of the department on it, and gave it back to me, saying, “Good luck in your studies, Mr. Gourdet.”

I immediately took my new document to the director of the school.

He looked at it, and in a resounding voice, he said, “Now, it’s the assistant director who sent him! The assistant director!”

I went to class. The school did a roll call that afternoon. My name was finally on the official list of students. Hurray! I was very happy.

I never saw the assistant director again. I heard that he had left the country to work in Africa. Someone with the same last name was a suspect in an attempted political kidnapping. Carrying the same last name as the president’s enemy makes you automatically guilty by association.

As for Yvon, my benefactor, I met him years later at a funeral service in New York; his son accompanied him. I was happy to see him again after so many years. I told the son what his father had done for me.

He said, “That’s how my father is; he always likes to help other people.”

I thought it was the best compliment I could ever pay him. Yvon looked at me with a smile on his face. I could see he was proud of the good deed he had performed years ago. Through him, God had come to my aid. The Lord did not hasten to help me. He came in his own time, but he came. I was grateful to all involved for helping me to continue my studies. I was especially grateful to Yvon. Like an angel, he came to my rescue and opened the way for me to shine.

CHAPTER 21

You Can Do It

Whether you believe you can do a thing or not, you are right.

HENRY FORD

NOW THAT I WAS OFFICIALLY accepted in the school, my next challenge was to establish myself at the head of the class. This was a position that I had occupied in my previous years in school, and I had become accustomed to it. The only problem was that I had never had more than thirty students in any previous class, and that was way back in elementary school. In my secondary school, the maximum number of students I competed with had never reached twenty. In fact, my last class had counted only eight students. This new class had well over one hundred students. Some of them had been in the school for up to five years. I had just arrived. And to make it even more daunting, there were a number of girls in the class. I wasn't used to that. I was scared.

Our French teacher was a recent graduate of the Sorbonne in France. He gave us a homework assignment, an essay on the writers of the seventeenth century. This was a subject I was well versed in, having studied it at my previous school with the well-educated French teacher, Father Aimé Jestin. I prepared my assignment, doing the best I could.

One week later, the teacher came back in class and said, "Student Gourdet, please come to the front of the class."

I was way in the back of the jam-packed classroom. Some students had to get up to allow me to jump over the benches so I could reach the front. Less than three feet separated the first bench from the front wall. All along I was asking myself, *What did I do wrong this time?* The sword of Damocles came back to mind.

The teacher handed me my paper and said, "Read it to the class."

This time I panicked. Something was really bad with my essay. Was I being humiliated? A thousand thoughts were running through my mind. My hand started to shake. I looked at the paper, but I couldn't see a thing.

"Go ahead," the teacher reiterated. "Read your paper."

Meanwhile, over a hundred pairs of eyes were fixed on me. One student said, "He cannot read?"

Hearing those words made me feel even worse. I was standing right in front of a couple of girls who were seated on the first bench. One of them was an eighteen-year-old of stunning beauty; her name was Vivian. I had noticed her before, but I had been told to keep my hands off because she was engaged to a teacher.

Anyway, Vivian took my hand and squeezed it a little bit. In a soft voice, she said, "You can do it."

I looked at her with a blank face. So much for the secret of Robin Hood that was supposed to give me courage; I totally forgot about it.

Vivian smiled at me and repeated, "Go ahead. You can do it."

I managed to return a little smile. And then I read the paper.

When I had finished, the teacher took the paper back from me and told the class, "This is exactly what I expected of you, class. This is how an essay should be done."

I hurried back to my little place to hide myself mentally. And I heard a voice saying, "But he can't read."

That was the voice of the same student who had made the previous comment. His name was Dave; he was a fixture at the school. He was the star athlete, and he controlled the class.

Member of an Elite Group

Later that day, one student came to me and said, "I have a large chalkboard at home. A small group of students comes to my house to study. Why don't you join us? Here is the address."

That afternoon I went to the student's house. The star athlete was there, too. We became friends. It wasn't a secret society, not even a fraternity. There was no hazing. I wasn't subjected to any rituals of initiation. I simply became a member of a group of elite classmates. We did homework together, especially math, covering geometry, algebra, and trigonometry, and also physics, in which we were studying electricity and optics. We had the master's edition of some of our textbooks, which made a big difference. We tried to be ahead of the teachers.

Not long afterward, our physics teacher called me to the chalkboard with these words: "Let's try the newcomers. Student Gourdet, go to the blackboard."

Why me all the time? Does he intend to humiliate me? I asked myself.

However, by then I had regained my confidence by doing daily practice with my friends. I wasn't afraid anymore to be in front of the class. In fact, I was starting to enjoy it. I was poised.

The teacher asked me to solve an optics problem, something to do with a light beam's transmission.

It turned out I had just practiced that problem with my newfound friends. I had no difficulties at all. And when I had finished, I wrote in Latin on the chalkboard in big white letters, "*Quod erat demonstrandum, QED*!" (That which was to be proven.)

The teacher got upset, and in a strong and angry voice, he told me, "Go back to your seat, Mr. Gourdet." He never called on me again.

I felt vindicated. He was one of the people I had unsuccessfully appealed to in my quest for admission to the school.

The Power of a Pretty Woman

Things were going pretty smoothly for me until I got in trouble in Latin class. The class was taught by a dignified man whose first name was

Rockefeller. He was also a radio announcer, and he did a commercial for a product called Maggi Cubes, a food flavor enhancer made by Nestlé. In the commercial, he had a way of saying "Maggi" that was designed to catch attention.

As the teacher was lecturing, a voice said, "Maggi," imitating the voice on the radio. The teacher stopped and asked who had spoken. Nobody answered.

Then he said, "Class will stop until the perpetrator shows his coward face."

No one volunteered. Then he looked at my bench, on which sat four students, and he said, "All of you on that bench, come with me."

He took us to the school director, who asked us to tell him who had said the *word*, which by now could not be uttered. None of us said anything. He then sent us home and asked us to come back with our parents. I knew who had said "Maggi" because he had been sitting right by me. He was a member of my study group (you can probably guess who he was), and I wasn't going to denounce him.

I went home and asked a female friend of mine to come to the school with me the next day. She was a young administrative assistant in a big office. She was pretty, and she dressed impeccably.

When we arrived at the school, the director, who was a bachelor in his late thirties, took a look at my "parent's" lovely face, attractive demeanor, beautiful dress, and cadenced walk in her high-heeled shoes. He was instantly smitten. He offered a chair to my friend.

"Mademoiselle, or is it madame? Please sit down; please sit down."

"It's mademoiselle," my friend said.

And, in well-choreographed slow motion, my friend let her naturally padded posterior reach the chair, to the bewilderment of the director.

In a soft voice, she said, "I have come to represent Gourdet's parents. They couldn't make it due to prior engagements; I hope this is acceptable to you, Mr. Director."

Under the charm of this wonderful maiden, the director became apologetic. "I am so sorry you had to be disturbed, Mademoiselle. Student Gourdet is not at fault; he would never do such a thing. He can go back to class."

The director wanted to continue with some small talk, but my friend got up and said, "Thank you, Mr. Director!"

As we left his office, the director was still in a daze.

On that day I learned to appreciate the power of a pretty woman. I never knew what happened with the other three students, but they all came back to class.

The So-Called Virtues of Communism

The rest of the year went pretty much uneventfully in class, except for occasional literature affirming the so-called virtues of communism. Pamphlets were left in the classroom for students to find in the morning. A friend of mine tipped me that government officials were placing them in the classrooms as bait for communist sympathizers. I knew the danger that such articles posed, and to protect myself, I developed a habit of getting to school a little late. That way I wouldn't be the first one to find them.

However, there was a student I took home with me at lunchtime to share my meal on a couple of occasions because he had nothing to eat. One day he came with an article that had been put out by the Haitian Communist Party. He asked me to review the article with him. I read the article, and we talked about how courageous Fidel Castro was and how we all admired him. And he asked me if I wanted to join the Communist Party. I told him emphatically no, and I warned him of what could happen to him if the officials found out. I think I must have scared the hell out of him. He never talked to me about communism again. It turned out that the government had secretly created its own Communist Party to entice predisposed young people to become communists. Officials then arrested them and put them in jail to gain favors with the Americans, by showing that the Haitian government was cracking down on communism.

I lost contact with this classmate, and one day, years later, while I was attending a concert with my daughter at York College in New York, I came upon him. We were happy to see each other, and he told my daughter that I used to feed him when he was hungry, which I immediately declared was an exaggeration.

The Therapeutic Property of Sex

Not to be deterred by communist sympathizers, I continued to study with my group, and I continued to do well in class. On weekends I would go to the movies and occasionally to a nightclub where the famous Jazz des Jeunes was playing. I didn't have a girlfriend at that time, but my older half sister, Mama, would find me a friend to dance with. The music was so lascivious, it was sexually arousing. However, I was concentrating on my studies and didn't have time for girls.

Still, I was getting exhausted. One day I didn't feel well, and I developed a fever. A friend of mine who was in his first year of medical school stopped by to see me and realized I had a temperature.

He asked me, "When was the last time you had a girl?"

"I cannot remember," I told him.

"That's the problem," said the young future doctor, feeling proud of his diagnosis. And he also had a prescription. "I am coming to pick you up tonight. I know someone who can help you."

Later that night, he took me through a dark alley to a hooker residing in a shanty. She was a decent-looking young woman, dressed in a provocative skirt that revealed her well-rounded shape. I fell for her right away. We didn't have much of a conversation. She just asked me to relax and be comfortable. In no time, she made me sweat my fever away.

On my way out, she said, "Don't hesitate to come to see me whenever you don't feel well."

I thought she was a real doctor in her own right. She helped me release the overflow of sexual energy that was causing my discomfort.

Encounter with a Fortune Teller

My schooling followed the standard education system administrated by the state. It comprised seven years of primary education and seven years of secondary education.

The last two years of secondary education prepared students to take the examinations given by the Ministry of Education. They were called

Baccalaureate Part I and Baccalaureate Part II, taken in two consecutive years. Successful completion of these two exams opened the doors to the university for higher education and a profession such as medicine, law, or engineering. Only a small percentage of the Haitian population reached that level of education in my time.

As I was readying myself to take the first national test, one day a woman stopped by my house and claimed she was a psychic who could predict the future. She offered to do a reading for me; I told her that I wasn't interested. She replied that she wasn't going to charge me; it was free. I agreed to do it.

She had me sit in front of her. Then she took my hands, closed her eyes, and said, "Your father has a lot of money hidden somewhere."

I knew that she was aware that my father was well off. But I wasn't sure about hidden money. Next she told me, "I see that you're going to take a very important test, but there is a problem."

"What kind of problem?" I asked.

She didn't answer.

"You're talking about my final exams, aren't you?"

She acquiesced with a nod of the head.

"Am I going to pass those exams?" I asked.

"It would be better if I speak to your father," she replied.

That's when I realized that she was after money. I got angry and pulled my hands from hers. Like Alexander the Great with the Oracle at Delphi, I wanted to drag her by the hair until she told me the answer I wanted to hear. But I wasn't setting out to conquer the world, and she wasn't Pythia, the Oracle at Delphi. I just wanted to pass my exams. I dismissed her.

Just to be on the safe side, I redoubled my studying effort. But somehow, by nine that night, I was falling asleep. I couldn't keep my eyes open in spite of multiple cups of coffee. Instead of fighting it, I decided to go along with it. I went to bed at nine in the evening and got up at one in the morning. I studied until four. Then I went back to bed again to wake up at 6:30 a.m. I never told my father about the encounter with this woman. It was a wise decision; things could have gotten complicated.

I took the state exams. They were given in the capital to students from across the nation. The students came from all major cities with secondary schools. Since the exams were given in July when school had already closed, the students from outside the capital were lodged in schools that were not used for the exams. They came with their own food and other supplies. Many of them were accompanied by family members who came to cook for them during the weeklong exams. They couldn't afford to eat in restaurants, and the government didn't provide alimentation.

Passing these exams meant a great deal for students. It allowed them to enter university, to learn a profession that would later lead to a well-paying job. It was the door to a better life for the whole family. In large families, very often only one made it to that level of education. The responsibility then fell on that person to help provide for the other siblings. There was great pressure on these students to pass the tests.

One student, a pretty, young girl, was sitting near me during the exams. She had come from a small town in the northern part of the country. It was the first time she had been to the capital. She was nervous. She sent me a distress signal. She needed help in the math exam. I watched for the proctor, whose job it was to make sure that nobody was cheating, and when he was looking the other way, I slipped the answers to a couple of problems to this student. She looked so confused. I don't know if my help was even useful to her.

The exams were both written and verbal. The written exams covered French literature, plant physiology, Haitian history, English, Latin, Haitian literature, physics, chemistry, and mathematics. The verbal part covered English, world history, world geography, and Haitian geography.

Immediately after the exams, I went back home for summer vacation. It would be a couple of weeks before I received my test results. The night before the announcement, I dreamed that I was happily swimming in a crystal-clear body of water, like a lake or the sea. I felt so good in the dream. When I woke up, I knew something good was going to happen on that day; I just didn't know what. I had received no previous notice of the date for the announcement of the exam results.

I was playing soccer with my friends when my father came to tell me that I had passed the state's exams. He had heard my name on the radio. That was the way the results were given at that time. Names of students who had successfully passed the exams were read on national radio, to be heard by the students and their families wherever they might be in the country. Since the radio announcement was repeated all day long, I was able to hear the calling of my name, with a little twist of happiness in my heart. My aunt and my mother were elated. My father was so proud of me that he gave me his Benrus gold watch. I still have it. I have kept it all these years as a symbol of his love for me.

Nationally only a small percentage of the students passed the exams on the first round. Many in my class didn't make it. All the members of my study group made it successfully. My classmate Vivian's words—"You can do it"—came to my mind. I felt grateful to have the support of a great woman. But watch out for fortune-tellers; they can be so ambiguous.

Summer vacations ended, and the fall season started. It was time to go back to the capital to resume my studies. I was anxious to meet my friends and exchange congratulations with the members of my study group, but it wasn't going to happen as fast as I had thought.

CHAPTER 22

A Helicopter Ride

Life isn't about waiting for the storm to pass;
it's about learning to dance in the rain.

TONY ROBBINS

AS I MENTIONED EARLIER, THE last two years of secondary school prepared the students for the exams given by the state after each year's classes. I had successfully passed the first one. Flush with my success, I was poised to return to the capital to complete the last year of secondary school and take the second examination given by the state. It was the beginning of October, and as was typical for that time of year, there was plenty of rain; however, nobody foresaw the destructive hurricane that was to reach our town.

I said good-bye to my family and took the overloaded bus to the capital. My father had reserved a front seat for me, near the driver. It was a special seat with a cushion and more legroom, away from the brouhaha of the forty or so passengers in the main part of the bus. This had cost him a little more, but he felt I deserved it. I was moving up in the world.

Soon after we crossed the River Maho by my hometown, the town's authorities ordered us to return. They had received official word that our region was going to be hit by a major hurricane. It was October 2, 1963.

I went back home hoping that I could travel the next day, on Thursday, October 3.

School was scheduled to open the following Monday, October 7.

Starting in the afternoon and throughout the evening, strong gusts of wind hit the town. Our house was made of blocks and therefore could resist the winds; many people abandoned their frame houses to seek refuge at my aunt's house. We couldn't even make coffee; the wind was so strong it blew out the flames, and it became too dangerous to keep the fire pit on. My aunt's yellow cat, Mimi, went to hide under a bed. She couldn't handle all the commotion. Children were crying; women were praying; the men were talking loud; some were even telling jokes. Nobody really slept the whole night; the noise caused by the wind was too frightening.

The bells of the village's church, propelled by the wind, continued to ring furiously in a sinister carillon that threw people into greater panic. A strong burst of wind finally brought down the structure that held them and silenced their gloomy sound. After that, we could hear the lamenting of residents whose houses had been blown away. Slowly, the night passed as nature pounded this little town with the fury of an angry god.

When morning came, the sun exposed the ugliness caused by the hurricane. The damage was colossal. Many houses were destroyed, including a brand-new elementary school that had been the pride of the community. It was supposed to be a model for other elementary schools to be built in the country.

The immense flooding of the nearby rivers carried the trunks of large trees and all kinds of debris. Rushing water cut through the cemetery and unearthed the coffins. The bodies were carried away, to be left on the streets in front of people's houses. The rushing waters also carried many people away. Aluminum roof tiles were scattered all over. One of them had cut the waist of a young man who later passed out for lack of medical care. There were multiple casualties.

It was the most damaging hurricane that had ever hit our region. My family suffered property losses. My father injured the same leg bone that had been broken some years earlier. Still, every cloud has a silver lining.

A few days after the hurricane, we heard a strong noise coming from the sky. Something was approaching the city. People went outside to look at the sky. We were happily surprised. It was a US helicopter that landed on our soil. It was the first time the people in my hometown had ever seen a helicopter. To my supreme enchantment, out of the helicopter came a young officer in military uniform; I recognized him right away. It was my uncle Joe, my father's younger brother.

Following the tradition of other family members, he had enlisted in the police force. He was entrusted with the duty of accompanying the US Marines to our town, in order to assess the damage caused by Hurricane Flora and to provide humanitarian assistance. While we felt indebted to these young Americans who came to our rescue, it was gratifying to see one of our own taking part in this important mission. The marines evaluated the damage and reassured the town's officials that more aid would be coming. The helicopter took along two severely injured people for urgent medical care in the capital. My uncle made sure I got a ride. Here again, he appeared like another angel who came to my rescue in time of need.

As the helicopter lifted up and hovered overhead, I could see my aunt making the sign of the cross with an expression of fear and gratitude: fear of seeing me lifted into the sky in this machine she knew nothing about, and gratitude in knowing that I was on my way to continue my studies. For my part, I was thrilled to be up in the air looking at the earth from above. For a moment, I forgot about the suffering that was around me, and I enjoyed my bird's-eye view of the landscape.

As we flew over the land, I was able to see the devastation that extended all along the way. The plantations were totally destroyed, and so were the huts that served as homes to people in the surrounding villages. One of the marines was taking pictures; however, he couldn't capture the human affliction that was hidden in the people's hearts. It was a time of great sorrow.

After a few minutes, the helicopter left the inner land and began to travel along the coastline. I became spellbound by the magnificent view of the coastal landscape. The sea was such a deep blue, and the sand was so white. Occasionally I would see a fishing boat with men throwing their nets in the water. Despite all this tragedy, I had never seen something so beautiful. Everything was so calm, as if nothing had happened. It was such a moving experience. My uncle, who was with us, offered me a sandwich and a bottle of soda. I consumed them voraciously. The helicopter continued on its path along the seashore, giving me a view of the many small communities and occasional towns. Finally, in less time than I would have liked, we landed in the capital. I took a taxi home. I would be staying with one of my father's friends, who had a young family. That's where I would learn of a great tragedy that changed the course of history.

CHAPTER 23

The Death of US President John F. Kennedy

We do not comprehend that in punishing us, in overturning our plans and in causing us suffering, He (God) is doing all this to deliver us, to open the Infinite to us.

VICTOR HUGO

MY NEW CLASS WAS CALLED Philo for Philosophy. The name left me a little puzzled because, besides philosophy, we were taught ten other subjects. They were animal physiology, chemistry, cosmography, English, Haitian geography, Haitian history, mathematics, physics, world geography, and world history.

Due to the hurricane, I had missed a few school days, but it wasn't too bad.

As it had been in my previous class, the room was too small to accommodate all the students. There were no alleys between the benches. The first bench was near the entrance door, and students and teachers had to climb over it to enter the classroom. One teacher was short and chubby. His legs were too short to climb over the bench; he always drew our giggles as he struggled to enter the classroom.

One day our philosophy professor came to class and in a stoic mood told us, "All the great philosophers are dead. Socrates is dead. Plato is dead. Aristotle is no longer with us, and your servant is not feeling too well."

We all cracked up laughing. The consensus was that our professor was losing it. On many evenings, one student had seen him walking by the seashore in a slow and calm pace, head down, talking to himself. A sign of genius, or was it something else?

The Irony of Socrates

The professor told us about Socrates and what he called the irony of Socrates.

"Socrates," he said, "was a philosopher who lived about four hundred years before Christ. He personified the expression, 'There is a method in his madness.' In order to extract the truth from people, he would pretend ignorance and ask them logical questions that would elicit the answer he really wanted. He perfected this method so well and used it so indiscriminately that he ended up annoying the political leaders of his time. Ironically, they used his own method to get even with him. They asked him a series of simple questions that led him to the logical choice of either looking stupid or drinking hemlock poison. He chose the latter, thereby confusing his foes, who had wanted to humiliate him.

"At the end, Socrates told them, 'The hour of departure has arrived, and we go our separate ways. I to die and you to live. Which is better, only God knows.' He became famous after his death and earned himself a place in the book of immortality for his contribution to the art of questioning."

My professor concluded, "Today, most lawyers use the Socratic method to win their cases by confusing the ignorant, as if the ignorant needed a lot to be confused."

His course covered psychology, ethics, and logic.

I really liked psychology, and it was while I was preparing for an exam on that subject, on the afternoon of Friday, November 22, 1963, that I heard the news of the assassination of President John F. Kennedy. As was my custom, I was listening to music on the radio while studying. Then, all of a sudden, the music was cut in the middle of a song.

The announcer said, "Flash, latest news, received by telecast from the French Press Agency. The president of the United States, John F. Kennedy, was shot in Dallas, Texas. Repeat, the president of the United States, John F. Kennedy, was shot in Dallas, Texas. Please stand by for further announcements."

At that time, I knew very little about President Kennedy, but a shiver ran along my spine, and I stopped studying to listen to the news updates. Later on, it was announced that the president had died as a consequence of an assassin's bullet.

The Nature of Evil

I don't know if it was because I was studying psychology or because it was a universal concern, but the following questions came to my mind upon the death of President Kennedy: What is the nature of evil? What motivates God and people to do evil things?

In less than two months, I had witnessed evil in two different forms.

In October, I saw the destruction of my hometown by natural disaster, followed by unimaginable human suffering. This was caused by the hand of God.

In November, I learned of the senseless murder of the greatest leader of the time, changing the course of history. This was caused by the hand of man.

There was so much evil going on in the world. Where would it stop? Were natural disasters a way for God to compel us to evolve? Were acts of violence, committed by a few, nature's way of forcing us to discover our inherent goodness? Did that mean that we live in a perfect universe where everything is an expression of God's divine order? Perhaps evil is necessary for some unknown greater purpose. Many technological advances are created because of wars that destroy cities and kill millions of people. Throughout human history, civilizations have taken giant leaps after the destruction of previous ones. Doesn't the phoenix rise from the ashes of its former self? Suffering must be our way to evolve. No pain, no gain.

After much internal deliberation, I came to the notion that God's role in our lives is not to prevent suffering but to empower us to adapt to challenges.

I couldn't discuss these lofty ideas with my philosophy professor; he had his own agenda. Anyway, my mind became preoccupied by a more mundane matter after I met Margarita.

CHAPTER 24

Lesson from a Practitioner of the Oldest Profession

Prostitution is the world's oldest oppression, which stems from the world's oldest inequality, that of women.

NORMA RAMOS, LETTER TO THE *NEW YORK TIMES*

IT WAS 1963, THE YEAR of President Kennedy's assassination, and I was in my last year of secondary school. That's when I made contact with her.

A GIRL NAMED MARGARITA

On my way to and from school, I had to pass a brothel. I never paid it much attention. But one day during lunch break, as I passed the building, I saw two beautiful young women sitting in front of it. When they saw me, one of them murmured something to the other. They couldn't contain their loud laughs.

I threw a furtive look at them. I could tell they were young Hispanic girls from a neighboring country who had been either smuggled or brought to Haiti under false pretenses, to work as prostitutes. At that time, many US Marines were stationed in Haiti. The girls provided entertainment and sex for them. Periodic medical checkups ensured that they were not carriers of sexually transmitted diseases (STDs).

The girl who had spoken to the other one called me and said, "Come. I'd like to talk with you."

I stopped and looked at her. Beautiful face, nice body shape, light chocolate skin, and dark shoulder-length hair—she was probably in her late teens or early twenties.

As I approached her, she asked me in a soothing voice, "Do you want to give me the best?"

I was taken off guard. "What's that?" I said in all my innocence.

With a twitch in her eyes, she replied, "You know what I am talking about." As I stood there, not knowing how to answer, she added, "I like you. You don't have to pay me."

"I am going for lunch at home and back to school," I told her.

She dismissed my argument by asking, "Don't you like me?"

She was a gorgeous young woman, and I was starting to feel the attraction. But I wasn't going to compromise my classes. I was caught in a dilemma: school or pleasure?

Timidly I said, "You're very beautiful."

"Then?" she said with inviting lips and piercing eyes that went deep into my soul. I was enraptured.

Still I held on and told her, "I really have to go."

"I am not holding you," she claimed. But she wasn't going to be deterred. "Why don't you come after class?" she proposed.

"I will come," I said.

Somewhat disappointed but still cordial, she extended her hand to me for a handshake and said, "My name is Margarita. What's yours?"

"Gesner," I said.

"See you later, Gesner."

"Bye." And I left.

My head was spinning, and I felt hot. It wasn't the heat of the Caribbean sun that was causing my discomfort. It was Margarita. I went home, and I couldn't take my mind off her. I didn't even feel hungry. Throughout my afternoon classes, I was still thinking about her. Never had a woman come on to me so strongly. Her passion was contagious. I couldn't wait for the evening.

When the night came down, I took a shower, put a splash of French perfume on my face, grabbed a change of clothing, and went back to the brothel. *Ranchera* music was blasting inside. With some trepidation, I walked up the stairs that led to the bar.

What a disappointment!

There she was, sitting at a table, joyfully having a drink with a young US Marine in uniform. I was in shock. I turned around to leave, but she saw me. She got up and came to me.

"I am very sorry," she said. "Can you come back another time when I am free?"

I was devastated. Why had I gone there in the first place? I hated her. I hated myself. Never would I let another woman play with my feelings. I went back home. I couldn't study. I went to bed, but I couldn't sleep.

The next day, on my way home from school for lunch, I passed by the place again, but this time I walked on the other side of the street, with my head straight, in the hope of not seeing her. But she was waiting for me. She called my name, but I ignored her. She crossed the street, almost getting hit by a speeding car that she avoided just in time, and she caught up with me.

"I am very sorry about last night. I really like you," she said. "Come tonight, and I'll wait for you."

"You won't see me," I answered with a firm voice.

She looked at me with pleading eyes, yet her intonation was unyielding when she took my hand and said, "Then come now. I really like you."

I couldn't escape her gaze. There was something in her eyes that made me believe that she was sincere when she said she liked me. And without being fully conscious of what I was doing, I let her lead me to her place.

It was a small room. A full-size bed was spread with a deep-red sheet. There was a chair in the left front corner and a bench in front of a small dresser with a mirror. She pointed to the bed and said, "Please sit down."

I ignored her gesture and sat on the chair.

Then she said, "Wait for me a moment." And she exited before I could say a word.

Here she goes again, I thought.

I waited for her. Her clothes were neatly arranged in an open closet. It was a simple wardrobe, with some short pants and a few dresses on hangers. One glitzy evening gown was the only item of value. In the far right corner, there was a fan that I had failed to notice until now; it was off. On the dresser lay a few beauty supplies, such as lipsticks, deodorant, and perfume bottles. A large comb was stuck in a hairbrush. Another item definitely caught my attention. It was a framed picture of Margarita with a nice-looking young man. Was he her brother or a former boyfriend? I was feeling jealous.

Then, she came back carrying a tray of food and a soda. She placed the tray on my lap and genteelly said, "You must be hungry. I brought you something to eat." They say the way to a man's heart is through his stomach. She knew that.

I said thank you and started to eat. She sat on the bed and looked at me intensely with an expression of tenderness. *Girls have a way of getting into you,* I thought. I continued to eat. She continued to look at me tenderly. It never occurred to me to ask her if she wanted to share the meal with me. It was probably her own ration that she had given me.

As I finished eating, she removed my shirt and started to play with me, kissing me. Before I knew it, we were both naked on the bed, making love. It was pure ecstasy!

I went back to her on other occasions. She never asked me for the two dollars that was the going rate for such a service, and I never volunteered to pay her. Once I brought her a small bottle of perfume. She accepted it happily, but she told me I didn't have to buy her any gifts.

"You are my gift," she said.

Her body had a price, but her soul did not.

I stopped seeing Margarita for a while, and then one day I went back to the brothel and looked for her. With disappointment, I learned that she wasn't there.

Her friend told me, "You didn't know? Margarita went back home."

Back to the guy in the picture, I told myself with a feeling of loss.

Being a student of history, I couldn't help but think of yet another practitioner of the oldest profession who liberated herself from the oppression of prostitution and left to follow a young teacher some two thousand years ago.

I never set foot in the brothel again. It was the end of an adventure.

With the establishment of marriage, the young girls who provide this kind of service are shunned by society, and all kinds of moral stigma are attached to them. The debate over prostitution is very much alive. The March 23, 2015, issue of the *New York Times*, on page A20, featured a couple of letters to the editor under the heading "Has Sweden's Prostitution Law Lived Up to Its Promises?" One letter writer, Norma Ramos, stated, "Prostitution is the world's oldest oppression, which stems from the world's oldest inequality, that of women."

In a profession that started with religion and dates back to the cradle of civilization in ancient Mesopotamia, whether it was in dedication to the goddess of love and fertility, or to boost a soldier's morale, or even to guide a young man in his rite of passage, the sacrifices of these young women cannot be ignored.

Now that Margarita was gone after fulfilling her mission, it was time for me to redirect my focus to the many courses in my Philo class and prepare for university.

Some people come into your life for a reason; others for a season. Margarita came into my life for both, and I was grateful to her.

There were other hurdles to overcome, one of which was dealing with politicians.

CHAPTER 25

Dealing with Politicians

Honesty is the first chapter in the book of wisdom.

THOMAS JEFFERSON

MY LAST YEAR OF SECONDARY school went pretty smoothly. Still, I studied hard, following the same routine I had developed earlier by going to sleep early and waking up at about one in the morning, to study until four and then go to sleep again until about six thirty. I didn't tell my friends about this schedule; they thought I was so smart that I didn't have to study. There was no point in making them believe otherwise. It was Ernest Hemingway who said, "Let them think you were born that way."

I took the exams given by the Ministry of National Education. While I was on vacation, my name was called another time on national radio, informing me of my success. I was the second person in my family who had ever made it that far in school. The first one was an older cousin. It was also an honor for the town. At that time, my hometown counted only a handful of people who had reached that level of education.

It was time to think about university and a profession.

Like those of many other secondary-school graduates, my two choices were medicine and law, in that order. There was only one medical school in the country, and in order to be admitted, you had to take an entrance exam, which I was sure to pass, but more importantly, you had to have a recommendation from one of the leaders of the regime or from the president himself. My father wasn't a Duvalier supporter; I had to connect with high-powered politicians who could give me those much-needed recommendations. I contacted three people.

The first one was a person of influence whom I knew personally. I went to see her, and she quickly asked me for an unspecified amount of money. I brushed her off.

The second one was a national political leader who had passed through my aunt's house. When I went to see him, he received me politely and presented me to his staff, telling them how gracious my aunt had been when he visited my town. He told me that my aunt had already spoken to him about me.

Then he said to me, "As you know, I travel throughout the country on behalf of the president, and many people ask me for recommendations. Here is what I am going to do. I'll put your name on my list of recommendations; it's about ten names. However, I cannot guarantee that they will take all ten of you."

I told him, "Good enough!"

As I left his house, a feeling of sadness overtook me. I realized that I couldn't rely on this man. It was a waste of time. However, I appreciated his forthrightness, and to this day, I remember him with great respect because it's rare to find a politician who exhibits such a high degree of frankness.

The third person I relied on to get me into medical school was a friend of my father. He was a top henchman of the president. He even saved the president's life on one occasion. When in town, he would occasionally come to my aunt's house for supper.

I had every reason to believe that with this man's recommendation I would be admitted to medical school. Once, he had been sick, and I had visited him in the military hospital where he was a patient.

When I went to see him about the recommendation, he told me, "It's too bad you didn't arrive sooner. The president was here. He came to visit me. He left about an hour ago. I would have presented you to him."

Then he said, "I will introduce you to Dr. Roger Lafontant. He is the one who decides who is admitted to medical school. He owes me a favor."

A few days later, he gave me an appointment at the southern gate of the National Palace. There, we met Dr. Lafontant, and he presented me in these terms: "This is Gesner Gourdet. His father is a chief bookman (a leader) in L'Asile. Can you recommend him for medical school?"

Dr. Lafontant shook my hand and said, "Of course."

As we were about to leave, I said to Dr. Lafontant, "Doctor, you didn't write my name. Will you remember it?"

He replied, "Gourdet, right? Don't worry."

Now, you don't have to be an expert in human nature to understand that when someone tells you not to worry, that's when you should definitely worry.

When the list of admitted students was posted at the medical school, I checked it a hundred times to make sure, but my name wasn't on it.

My father's friend was out of town. Nothing could be done. Later he apologized to me and told me that if I still wanted to apply next year, he would go directly to the president. However, during the course of the year, someone put a bullet in his stomach and killed him as he was coming out of a restaurant. The president gave him a state funeral with full honors.

As for Dr. Roger Lafontant, he later staged a failed coup d'état and was sent to jail, where he was subsequently eliminated.

I thought that the little saga about my failed admission to medical school had ended there, but I was wrong. As I was writing this book, I consulted with many people who knew me at different stages of my life to compare what I remembered with other versions of events in my life. An older cousin of mine was one such person I spoke with.

He asked me, "Do you know why you were not admitted to medical school?"

I answered, "Yes," and I told him the story I related above.

He listened to me, and then he said, "That's not the way it happened."

Then he told me the following story.

Sometime after the medical school results were given, and I wasn't admitted, the regional political leader happened to visit our town. During this visit, he told my aunt that during his conversation with Dr. Lafontant, he had found out that there was a candidate to medical school from my town. That candidate didn't make it because the person who was supposed to recommend him told Dr. Lafontant not to accept him on the basis that his father didn't support the regime. The student had successfully passed the exam, but they removed his name. My aunt was in shock.

She told the political leader, "The student you're talking about is Gesner, my son." At that point, the regional political leader became afraid and went to see my father in the middle of the night. He begged my father not to reveal his name if this story ever came to light. The regional leader feared that if my father's friend, the Duvalier henchman, found out that he had accused him of lying to my father, he (the regional leader) would be a dead man.

My cousin concluded, "That's the reason your father sent you to the United States. He didn't know whom to trust."

I listened to my cousin with awe. I didn't know what to think. Medical school was long gone from my mind. I had a successful career in the medical field. I retired at the top of my profession as a hospital laboratory administrator. In the course of my professional life, I held lectures attended by young doctors. I even had the privilege of providing moral support for a couple of young students who made it into medical school. Dr. Wladimir Gédeon graduated from the Columbia University College of Physicians and Surgeons, and Dr. Sabrina Carrié graduated from Harvard Medical School. I just couldn't believe that there was so much intrigue regarding my life.

I guess this kind of behavior should be expected when dealing with politicians. My case is not unique. In his book *An Hour before Daylight: Memories of a Rural Boyhood*, former president Jimmy Carter related a similar incident that happened to him. For two years, his local congressman had given him the runaround in his quest to enter the US Naval Academy.

I asked my father about the story concerning my admission to medical school, and he replied with his usual stoic phrase: "That's the way it was meant to be."

Anyway, after learning of my defeat in attending medical school, I moved to my second choice, which was law school.

CHAPTER 26

Law School Years

We cannot direct the wind, but you can adjust the sails.

Bertha Callaway

As I mentioned above, a couple of my secondary-school teachers were lawyers. They provided me with the inspiration that drew me to that field. One of them told us that according to the Greek philosopher Plato, the field of law was the ultimate profession. I read *The Republic*, and I was fascinated with the concept of truth. From my original notion of the truth as a certainty that could be proven in a court of law with the rigidity of mathematical certainty, I came to the understanding that litigating was an art that could define the truth. I realized that the establishment of the truth is a power game that has occupied humanity over the centuries. Whether it's about religion, politics, law, or daily living, we are concerned with the truth, and I wanted to play my part in this crucial game. I also realized that the perception of truth could elicit very emotional responses.

Once I told my girlfriend at the time, "The truth of today may not be the truth of tomorrow." She became despondent and started to cry, thinking I was leaving her. It wasn't my intention.

I was always captivated by the trials taking place in the town of Anse-à-Veau. I used to hang out by the windows of the courtroom, mesmerized by lawyers litigating important cases. Once, there was the trial of a man who had murdered a rival. He bought a machete and sharpened it really well on a sharpening stone. To verify the machete's sharpness, he cut off one of his own fingers. Then he went to his rival's house and chopped off his head with a single swift blow of the machete. It was a very important case that raised high emotion in the community. I wasn't going to miss such a case.

I was watching through the window of the courtroom when the prosecutor opened the case with these words. They were so impressive, I never forgot them: "On June second of this year, the most odious crime was perpetrated by the most audacious criminal this town has ever seen. I will prove to the court that it was premeditated murder."

I admired the prosecutor, and I thought he was super. I could see myself litigating similar cases. However, I never did. My dream of being a prosecutor was shattered, and it never became a reality. Life would take me on another course.

Still, I attended law school, and in July 1967, after three years of study, ninety-four of us graduated in my class. The names of the new graduates were announced on national radio and published in newspapers such as *Le Matin*, which had a motto that read, "If *Le Matin* says it, it's true," as compared to the motto of the *New York Times*: "All the news that's fit to print."

These mottoes make me laugh, as they bring to memory other mottoes I learned in law school. Some of them came to us from the Romans and were supposed to be eternal truth, such as "The mother is always certain. The father is always uncertain."

With advances in medicine such as in vitro fertilization and DNA testing, these mottoes hold no water.

A More Competitive Environment

During my years in law school, I worked as a teacher at one of the upscale private secondary schools. I taught French literature in the humanities classes. The owner of the school would often skip my payments, complaining that the students were not paying their tuition. The truth was that he had a house full of his own children, and indeed, money was scarce.

He wished to marry me to one of his many daughters, but I was not interested, as I was seeing a beautiful young divorcée from a well-established family. She took care of my sexual needs. One day a friend of mine spotted her at a nightclub with a young and ambitious lieutenant, a member of the elite presidential guard. I ended the relationship.

Some of my classmates had well-paying jobs in business, the government, or the military. A few of them later became important personalities in Haitian and international communities, such as William Regala, one of a small group of military leaders who ruled the country in the late 1980s; the Reverend Doctor Soliny Vedrine, a graduate of the Dallas Theological Seminary who is now an influential religious and community leader in Boston; and Bonivert Claude, an inveterate competitor who…perhaps a story will provide the best illustration of his character.

Once when we were taking a verbal exam in commercial law, the professor asked me to explain "the effects of export subsidies on world trade." My family did coffee exporting. I had a personal interest in that subject. In addition to reading Professor Gilbert Celestin's notes, I had gone to the library to research it. I took copious notes. I felt comfortable with the subject.

However, for some unknown reason, I said to the professor, "Can I use my notes?

"Go ahead! Go ahead," he replied in a sardonic tone, indicating that, with or without notes, he would get me. He was the big professor with the doctorate from France.

Without being intimidated by his demeanor, I opened my notebook and gave him a dazzling presentation. He stopped me a few times to ask a question or to clarify a point.

When I was finished, he said, "Wow! Gourdet, where are you from?"

"From L'Asile," I replied.

And in local language he said, "But when you go to L'Asile, the people tremble." Then he gave me ninety-five out of a hundred.

That's when the trouble began.

Bonivert Claude had taken his oral exam a few minutes before me, and he had gotten *only* ninety out of a hundred. He was furious. He told the professor that if he had used his notes, he would have gotten a hundred out of a hundred.

In his sardonic way, Dr. Celestin told him, "Go ahead. Go ahead and use your notes."

Another student convinced Bonivert to keep his ninety out of a hundred. As usual, Bonivert Claude graduated as head of the class. Later, he became governor of Haiti's Central Bank and a presidential candidate. I was dealing with a more competitive environment.

A Visit from the Emperor of Ethiopia

One memorable event that took place around that time was the visit to Haiti of His Imperial Majesty Haile Selassie I, emperor of Ethiopia, during his tour of the Caribbean. The tour included Trinidad and Tobago, Haiti, and Jamaica, where he met with the Rastafarian community. In Haiti, I was one of the thousands of people who lined the streets of Port-au-Prince on April 24, 1966, to honor this important visitor. He is said to be a direct descendant of King Solomon and the Queen of Sheba. Since I was raised in the Judeo-Christian faiths, it was important for me to see this man from Africa who came from the same blood lineage as Christ.

CHAPTER 27

It's Good to Listen to Your Wife...Sometimes

Behind every successful man there is a great woman.

AUTHOR UNKNOWN

WHILE ATTENDING MY FIRST YEAR of law school, I became friendly with the son of a widowed neighbor. He was attending secondary school, and his classmate was the young Jean-Claude Duvalier, also known as Baby Doc Duvalier, son of the president and "heir" to the presidency. Along the way, the two of them became friends, and when Jean-Claude Duvalier succeeded his father as president, he requested the presence of his friend by his side.

I visited him a few years after that, on a trip from New York to Haiti. As a gift, I brought him a copy of a book that was published in English by his grandfather Stephen Alexis, who besides being a career diplomat was also a novelist. The book was called *The Black Liberator: The Life of Toussaint Louverture.* I had gone to Macmillan's offices in Manhattan, and they had directed me to an old book dealer, where I bought it. The family didn't have a copy of that book. He was very pleased to receive it.

By that time, he was the assistant to the president, enjoying the president's full confidence. He told me how happy he was to see me, and he added, "Why don't you stay with us in Haiti? You will never have to worry about money. The president is very generous."

It was a tempting offer. Life in New York was hard; I was working two jobs and going to school. I thanked him and told him I would let him know of my decision.

I went home and told my wife about the offer. Her answer was, "I don't want you to see them anymore."

And I never did.

The lure of easy money did not appeal to my wife, and I shared her concern that ultimately there is a price to pay for everything. At some point, the regime collapsed. The president, my friend, and their entourage had to leave the country and go into exile.

The moral of the story is that it's good to listen to your wife…sometimes. No, most of the time!

CHAPTER 28

The Evening Star

Sometimes, remembering hurts too much.

Jess Rothenburg

My relationship with the president's assistant and his mother didn't fade away without a certain benefit for me before I left the country. One day at their house, I was introduced to an interesting young student in social sciences. She was a friend of the family. She worked part time as a radio announcer. She invited me to a beach party she was organizing.

I went to the party, and while we were swimming in the warm blue sea under the heat of the Caribbean sun, I approached her and told her that I was in love with her. Without waiting for her to say anything, I kissed her on the lips. She got angry. I felt apologetic and told her I was sorry. She surprised me with a rationale that left me both perplexed and happy.

She said, "I don't want you to think there is something between you and me just because you kissed me. I have to give you back your kiss."

Then she kissed me with a passion that left me floating on cloud nine. She would become my official girlfriend until I left Haiti.

A Case of Rape

One day while we were together smooching, all of a sudden, her expression changed. She took an air of seriousness as she said, "I have something to tell you."

"What?" I asked, perplexed.

Her eyes displayed concern and melancholy. "You are the first person I ever loved," she said, an air of sincerity in her tone.

"Thank you," I said. "I love you, too."

I thought the conversation was over, but she continued. "That's not all."

"What is it?" I asked, now becoming more puzzled.

Then, in a dramatic way and with tears in her eyes, she explained to me that her mother had placed her in the care of her uncle, her mother's brother, and that the uncle had raped her when she was only thirteen years old. Shocked, I asked her what had happened next. She said that she had told her mother, but she couldn't report him to the authorities because her uncle was a very influential person.

We became even closer after that conversation. Then I left Haiti. Her mother had knitted a beautiful purple sweater for me. I put it in the laundry machine to wash it, and when it came out, it had shrunk to the size of a doll's dress.

Similarly, our relationship faded a short time after I arrived in the United States. My letters to her went unanswered. I thought she had forgotten me. But it turned out that the landlady of my little apartment was a young divorcée who had a crush on me. She intercepted my girlfriend's letters. In any case, I had realized that it would be impossible to provide my girlfriend with the lifestyle she was accustomed to. I was trying to find my way in New York; it would be too hard for both of us. Most likely, our union wouldn't have endured the rigors of life in New York. I had seen it happen to some of my friends. Many marriages were broken once they arrived here in the United States. Some of my friends returned to Haiti after the first year of their experiment in the hard crucible that was 1960s America for a black middle-class Haitian. And just like the sweater her mother had knitted for me, our relationship withered, and she became a memory.

Memories of Haiti

While we were together, we had wonderful moments. We wrote each other beautiful love letters. We went to movies and concerts. During carnival we would wear the colors of our favorite band. Sometimes we went dancing at nightclubs to the music of the new generation.

It was a time of growth in Haitian music, characterized by its richness and originality. Due to its historical evolution, influenced by African traditional music and European and Spanish cultures, Haitian music was very special. *Rara* bands played music with tambours and bamboo shoots. Then there were bands that played music similar to that of other Latin American countries, such as Cuba and Puerto Rico, for the benefit of private parties and for the tourists who visited Haiti in the late forties and throughout the fifties. The musicians were mostly adults. Only a handful made a living out of this profession. It brought so little money.

In the sixties, with the advent of young musicians on the international music scene—such as the Beatles in England and Charles Aznavour, Johnny Hallyday, and others in France—young Haitians became interested in new styles of music. They formed their own bands, such as Shleuleu, Les Ambassadeurs, and Les Fantasistes. I wasn't immune to this new wave that was sweeping over our lives. A couple of friends of mine came to me and asked me to be the impresario of a new band they were forming. They named the band Creole Stars. I didn't play any instrument, but I had managerial skills, and I quickly agreed.

I helped them get organized. I made sure they rehearsed their songs, both original and popular. And finally they were accepted to perform at Rex Theatre, the main attraction in the capital. I went to Radio Haiti, which at that time was the most popular radio station, to request a commercial spot for the Rex Theatre's concert. I gave a flyer to Jean Dominique, the owner of the station. When the ad came out on the radio, the name of the band was changed to the Creole Stars of Petionville. This little addition gave an aura of respectability to the band. Petionville was the city of the elites. It was good for publicity. The concert was well attended and very successful. They did a doo-wop that brought the attendees to hysteria. However, the band didn't last. One by one, the members left the country to find new lives in Canada and the United States.

A sad postscript to this story was that Jean Dominique, who was an important figure in Haitian life, was later exiled, and then after his return to the country, he was assassinated in Haiti for political reasons. As for my former girlfriend, she got married and then divorced. She continued to be friendly with members of my family. She even helped my younger brother Gustave in his schooling. One day, someone told me that she had died. I wrote the following poem in her memory; it is taken from my book *Let It Be Easy.*

The Evening Star

She was the prettiest
And also the brightest.
She could write poetry;
She understood people.
She was a passionate and compassionate lady
Who devoted her life to improving the lot
Of her nation's less fortunate children.
She was destined to do good for humanity.
She was a TV personality on her way to stardom.
One day she disappeared and never came back.
The killer breast cancer hit her, so they say.
The angels came down to carry her into heaven.
Sometimes I think of her, but as you can see,
In the dark of the night, a star looks brighter.
As I lift up my eyes toward the constellations,
I realized that she was there as an evening star.

CHAPTER 29

Coming to America

Two roads diverged in a wood, and I—

ROBERT FROST

AFTER GRADUATING FROM LAW SCHOOL, I took the oath to join the bar association. I borrowed a toga from a lawyer friend of mine to wear for the ceremony. I wasn't ready to buy my own toga.

In his address to us, the president of the bar, an old man who walked with a cane, told us in no uncertain terms, "We have nothing to offer you here; if you find offers from the exterior, do not hesitate to accept them."

But I want to live in my country, I argued in my mind.

A friend and former Boy Scout master named George Craan recommended that I join one of the more prestigious law firms in the country.

When I went for the interview, the firm's senior partner told me, "I am sorry to say that no cases are being litigated in this country anymore. Judicial decisions are rendered solely by the political machine. It would be misleading to offer you a seat here. There is nothing to be done. However, if you have a case, and you want us to help you prepare it, we'll be glad to do so." I went home somewhat disappointed.

While having dinner in the capital at a fancy restaurant called Le Round Point, I noticed the senator of my district. He was in the company of a gorgeous woman from one of the elite families. I went to salute them, and the senator told me that he was happy to learn that I was now a lawyer; he could use my services in his district. He had a job for me.

I went home and told my father about that encounter. He became tense and said, "No way."

It was time for me to appropriate the wisdom of the white-haired authority figure, the president of the bar association, but how?

There were a couple of options. A friend of mine had obtained a contract to work as a teacher in Canada; he said he could help me get the same. A cousin of mine had a contract to work in Zaire, Africa; he gave me an application to fill out for a similar position. I didn't want to go to either place. If I were to leave the country, it would be to go to America. I had studied English. I had read the novel *Moby-Dick*, by Herman Melville, in its entirety, and most of all, I was familiar with Robert Frost's poetry.

"The Road Not Taken," "A Minor Bird," and "Stopping by Woods on a Snowy Evening" were favorites of mine. Besides, I had a couple of friends and a cousin in the United States. That's where I wanted to be.

I told my father about my idea, and he was all for it. But how would I make it happen?

The solution came more easily than I expected. I shared my dilemma with a friend named Marc Vital-Herne, who later became a physician. He was from a prominent family. His father was the pastor of a big church in the capital.

He said, "Why don't you go to the United States as a student? That's what I am doing."

"How do I go about it?"

He gave me the name of a school in, of all places, New York City. I wasn't sure what I would be studying. It didn't matter; it was only a means to an end. I wrote a letter to the school, and a couple of weeks later, I received an application from the Mandel School for Medical Assistants. I filled out the application and returned it with the required fee. They sent me a letter of acceptance that I could present to the US consulate to get a student visa.

I went to the US consulate with my father. He wanted me to leave the country more than I had realized. He had his reasons, but I wouldn't know of them until decades later (see Chapter 25, "Dealing with Politicians"). The consul asked him how he was going to support me in the United States. He showed the consul his bankbook, which had about $5,000.

The consul told him that it wasn't sufficient. As he put it, "The money could be lost in one night at the casino."

My father was taken aback. He had never set foot in a casino his whole life. He told the consul that he had a business and that he owned his house and other properties.

The consul then said, "Bring the titles to these properties."

Now, it's not the habit of any Haitian to let his son or any other unauthorized person see the titles to his properties. These documents can be used to sell the property without the knowledge of the lawful owner. Still, my father had confidence in me. He gave me a shoebox containing the titles of his properties with the admonition, "Anything happens to these papers, you will be responsible for the care of my other children."

I assured him that the papers would be returned to him in the same condition as I had received them. He was satisfied.

Some People Come into Your Life for a Reason

I arrived at the consul's office and placed the unopened box on his desk. He was busy finishing some other matters. Then someone knocked at the door, and the consul said, "Come in! It's open."

The door opened slightly, and this gentleman looked at me and said, "Hi, Gourdet. What are you doing here?"

"I am going to your country," I replied.

The consul looked at both of us and said, "You two know each other?"

"Oh yeah. Gourdet goes to the institute," said the gentleman, still standing at the door entrance.

He was the same gentleman I had met a few years earlier at a reception given by my aunt's diplomat friend. I subsequently met him at the Haitian American Institute, and we exchanged an occasional hello.

The consul didn't ask me any questions. He just signed and sealed my student visa, shook my hand, and said, "Good luck in the United States, Mr. Gourdet."

The gentleman at the door was gone.

Indeed, some people come into your life for a reason! I felt so grateful.

A Gift of One US Dollar and a Message

Immediately after I obtained my visa, my father surprised me by giving me $1,000 in cash. It was money to use for my traveling expenses and to pay for my tuition in the United States. Additionally, he gave me his collection of old US coins and US silver certificates. That was more than I needed.

A friend of mine had obtained a contract with another country, and he didn't have the money for his travel expenses. I loaned him $200, which he later repaid fully. After paying for my passport, airline ticket, and miscellaneous expenses, I was left with over $300 in my pocket. My aunt also gave me some money. She was confident that I would be able to create a better life for myself. She tried to hide a tear, but it was a tear of joy, not of sadness. "How much better is it to weep at joy than to joy at weeping!" wrote Shakespeare.

Mrs. Larius was a woman in my hometown who was a friend of the family. When I went to say good-bye to her, she surprised me with an unexpected gift. It was one US dollar. I appreciated the gift, but I will never forget what she said as she gave me the dollar bill.

She said, "I was saving this US dollar for you. They say there's a lot of money in New York, but I can assure you, you have to work hard to get it. I wish you well."

I said thank you to her, and for a while, I kept this dollar bill in my wallet as my lucky dollar. As I would soon discover, the streets of New York were not paved with gold. However, if you work hard and invest smartly, you can make it in the Big Apple. I did.

With my mother Eumane Gourdet Edouard, 1983

My aunt and adoptive mother
Constance Gourdet Dubos

My stepmother Gloria Dubos Lapaix

My father Lecet Lapaix

Jesse Gourdet, age twenty two

Law School graduating class, 1967
(I am on the front row, fifth from the left)

Chicago, October 1970

East 94th Street, Brooklyn, NY 1970

As a Realtor
Queens, NY, 1977

As a Chemist
NYC Office of Chief Medical Examiner, 1974

Our religious wedding ceremony
Wednesday, September 29, 1971

Our first house, 1976
Birthday celebration, 1987

My family, 1984

With my wife Yanick, 2002

My son Gregory and his mother on TOP CHEF Celebrity cruise, November 2015

Our daughter Jessica and her husband Arthur Murray with their children Morgan and Emery August 17, 2014

Working on the SMAC (Sequential Multiple Analysis Computerized),
a revolutionary chemistry analyzer.
Coney Island Hospital, Brooklyn, NY 1986

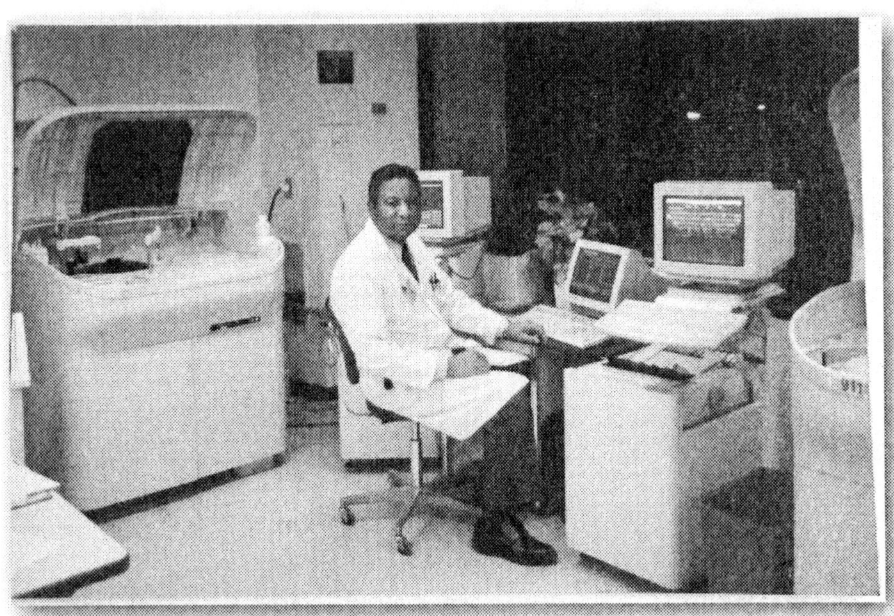

In the chemistry laboratory at the Hospital for Joint Diseases,
New York City, NY, 1995

With friends Iris and Eric White
London, 1986

Dancing with a young woman
Tallinn, Estonia, 2002

Floating on the Dead Sea in Israel, 2008

Having fun in Barcelona, Spain, 2005

Part Three
A Bite of the Big Apple

CHAPTER 30

1968: My First Year in America

Nineteen sixty-eight was one of the most tumultuous and heartbreaking years in American history.

BILL CLINTON

IN HIS BOOK *MY LIFE*, former US president Bill Clinton wrote, "Nineteen sixty-eight was one of the most tumultuous and heartbreaking years in American history."

That was the year I landed at JFK International Airport in New York City—on the evening of Friday, February 16. It didn't take me long to validate Clinton's statement. When I arrived, the city was a heated cauldron whose bubbles of discontent and turmoil were bursting all over the country. Indeed, 1968 was a sad year for America.

A former classmate, Antonio Germain, picked me up at the airport. He and his wife were living in a small apartment on the Upper West Side of Manhattan. I slept overnight on their sofa.

The next day my cousin, Ketty Lherisson, who had been living in New York for many years, came to pick me up in his beautiful car, a 1964 Chrysler Plymouth Belvedere. He gave me a tour of Manhattan. First it was Columbia University, where there was student unrest. Then we drove down Fifth Avenue, and he pointed at the Metropolitan Museum of Art and along the way, he showed me other places of interest, such as Central

Park. I was amazed by the tall buildings and the incredibly beautiful stores on Fifth Avenue.

Around Fiftieth Street, he told me, “Here is Saint Patrick’s Cathedral and Rockefeller Center. You should come back to visit one day.”

On Thirty-Fourth Street, he showed me the Empire State Building, which I knew about and had always wanted to see. Then, as he took FDR Drive on the East Side to cross the Brooklyn Bridge, the Statute of Liberty was right there in front of me. I was baffled by the magnitude of the things I saw on that day. The buildings, the streets, the bridges—everything was so huge.

Since my cousin was separated from his wife, he rented a room for both of us on Parkside Avenue in Brooklyn. He would continue to be my guide in New York City during the months to come.

One day we were talking about the sit-in at Columbia University, which was in the news. My cousin told me about the SDS, the Students for a Democratic Society, which was led by a student named Mark Rudd.

I said to him, “If the sit-in were in Haiti, all these students would have been either in jail or killed by the government.”

He replied, “This is a great country; you wouldn’t believe how great it is. People can say whatever they want.”

I remembered times in Haiti when it had been illegal for three people to gather on the street for a conversation. And I started to develop an appreciation for the First Amendment of the US Constitution, which guarantees the freedom of speech and assembly in this country. However, the events I witnessed over the course of that year would shake the very foundation of the country and change the course of history.

Not long after I arrived in New York, on April 4, I was driving with my cousin when we saw violence erupting on Fulton Street in Brooklyn. People were looting and vandalizing stores. I then learned that the great civil rights leader Dr. Martin Luther King Jr. had been assassinated in Memphis, Tennessee. I used to watch Dr. King on TV, and I was inspired by his speeches. I was so distraught to learn about his death that I wrote a poem in his honor. Here it is, reproduced from my book *Let It Be Easy.*

A Bird's Song

In Memory of MLK

I hear a bird singing.
It's a cry from the heart
That unites all the birds
From mountains to valley.

I hear a bird singing.
It's a song of freedom
That sweeps all over
This great land of ours.

I hear a bird singing.
But on a balcony
In Memphis, Tennessee,
A bullet stops the song.

I hear a bird singing.
The bird is dead
But the song lives on
For other birds to sing.

And if that wasn't enough, two months after Dr. King's assassination, on June 5, I got an early morning phone call from a friend of mine. He told me, "Turn on the TV. Senator Robert Kennedy was shot in Los Angeles, California."

That triggered more unrest and violence. I liked Senator Kennedy. He was sympathetic to the plight of poor people. He had been instrumental in the revitalization of some Brooklyn areas plagued with poverty and crime. Most of all, he was against the war in Vietnam. Many young people were against the war, and confrontations with police in Chicago disrupted the 1968 Democratic National Convention.

Finding My Way

While these tragic events were unraveling, I started to find my way in a world that seemed so strange to me. The great country my cousin had bragged about didn't seem so great to me after all. Yes, there were tall buildings, great museums, impressive bridges, but how did they help me? At this point, I had to take care of more pressing personal matters.

My first goal was to find a job. I had to pay for my tuition, rent, food, and transportation. My cousin took me to a social security office, and I got my social security number. My classes were in the evening. I had plenty of time to work.

I went to an employment office on Fourteenth Street in Manhattan. The employment agent asked me which train I took. I thought she said "plane." I couldn't understand what she was asking me. Finally I told the agent, "Please, write the question for me."

She did, and I said, "Oh, 'train.' I take the IRT number four."

The agent was baffled by the fact that I could read English very well and not speak it fluently. Usually it's the other way around. She sent me to a factory that made clothing. On the second day, they gave me a hand truck full of boxes to deliver to another building. I thought that was beneath my status. I told them I didn't know how to push a hand truck on the street. In the afternoon, the boss called me to his office and told me they had more people than they needed. He gave me my payment for the two days.

I went back to the agency, and they sent me to another place. The job was at night, midnight to 8:00 a.m. My classes were in Manhattan and ended at 10:00 p.m. I figured I had plenty of time to get to the place in Brooklyn. But I didn't take into consideration the chance that I might get lost in the subway. I took the wrong train at the exchange. Now, if you're lost on the New York City subway, you're out of luck because there is nobody to help you. People either don't know or don't want to talk to strangers, especially if you speak with a heavy foreign accent. The subway signs, indicating uptown or downtown trains, had no significance for someone who had just arrived in this country. Finally, just a little before midnight, after a few mishaps, I made it to the place.

It was a plastic factory. They made items such as electrical-outlet covers and large plastic glasses. Today, whenever I go to a restaurant that serves water or soda in these plastic glasses, I say to myself, "Somewhere in the world, probably in China, someone is going through the same thing I went through years ago." They remind me of my nights at the plastic factory.

It was the end of February. The outside air was freezing. Inside, I was working in front of a scorching-hot oven, and the items that came out burned my hands. Still, I worked there for a couple of weeks; the pay was slightly more than what I had been getting at the previous job. On the second Friday morning, I got home around nine. I was so exhausted, I went straight to bed. I didn't wake up until the following Saturday morning. I got scared after sleeping for about twenty hours straight. I didn't return to the job. I decided to go back to the agency for another job.

It was with some trepidation that I walked down Fourteenth Street on my way to the employment agency. What were they going to say?

Suddenly, a man stopped me and asked, "Do you want to work?"

"Yes," I replied.

He sent me to another clothing factory in Manhattan. I liked that place. There was a beautiful young Puerto Rican girl working there. Sometimes I had to fold bedsheets with her. Each of us would hold one end of the sheet to fold it, and at the end we would come hand to hand and face to face. We started to enjoy this little game. Before long we developed a little relationship. That didn't escape the vigilant eyes of her father, who was an assistant supervisor at the place. He got me fired to protect his daughter's innocence.

By then I realized that there were many jobs in the city; all I had to do was find the one that best suited me. I learned how to check the newspaper for jobs; most of them were in factories. I applied for office-assistant jobs, but I was always turned down. I couldn't figure out why, until one day a woman told me that I was overqualified for the job. I had failed to realize that I shouldn't boast about my higher education. The employers were concerned that I would soon find a better job and leave. They wanted someone they could depend on. Besides, they didn't want any troublemakers with higher education. From then on, I gave only the educational information necessary for the job for which I was applying.

"If You're Too Big to Do a Small Man's Job, Then You're Not Big Enough to Do a Big Man's Job."

My next job was in a men's clothing factory. Since my father was a master tailor, I figured I could do better there, even though he had never taught me anything about tailoring. He had a different vision of what I should become. Anyway, I went to work for them, and to my exasperation, they, too, asked me to carry boxes to the post office on a hand truck. Not wanting to push a hand truck on the streets of New York, I told the owner I didn't know where the post office was.

He replied, "I'll send my son with you." That wasn't too bad.

The reason that I didn't want to carry things outside was to avoid encountering anybody from my country who knew me. I felt ashamed that people might see me doing a menial job. And that was exactly what was going to happen. I was pushing the hand truck loaded with boxes on Twenty-Third Street in Manhattan when I heard my name being called. "Master Gourdet!"

I looked around; it was one of my former students. His name was Richard. He was only a couple of years younger than I was. He came from one of the elite families in Haiti that were forced to leave the country for political reasons. He was loading boxes into a truck. I felt so embarrassed, both for him and for me. We talked for a moment.

Then he asked me, "Where are you staying?"

"In Brooklyn," I replied.

"Write down this address," he said. "It's a West Indian club. Meet me there this Saturday after nine at night."

Sure enough, at 9:00 p.m. sharp on Saturday, I met Richard at the address on Avenue G in Brooklyn. There were no signs outside this club. The basement of a two-family house had been converted into a party hall.

Richard introduced me to a beautiful Trinidadian girl named Marge. She became my girlfriend, and every Saturday I would go to the club until Marge insisted that I talk to her parents. I wasn't ready for a commitment.

My encounter with Richard taught me two lessons.

First, if you're afraid to fail, you may never know the reward of success. I didn't want to be seen pushing hand trucks on the streets of New York, and yet, it turned out that by doing it, I met my former student, who introduced me to the appreciation of New York's fine delicacies in the shape of a beautiful Trinidadian girl.

Second, because of him, I also learned that every job carries dignity with it. It didn't take me long to confirm this fact. One day, I took the elevator with the head of a big enterprise. As we came off the elevator, there was a chewing-gum wrapper on the floor. He bent down to pick it up, and he dropped it in the nearest wastebasket.

As I was standing there looking at him in disbelief, he said, "If you're too big to do a small man's job, then you're not big enough to do a big man's job."

It was yet another lesson in humility. I swallowed my pride and decided that this time the lesson was going to stick.

I had other lessons to learn, and one of them had to do with family relationships.

How to Straighten Out a Husband

After I broke up with Marge, my cousin introduced me to an American girl. She was all over me. It was as if I were some kind of novelty toy for her. She told me that she liked my French accent, and she proudly introduced me to her friends. One Saturday evening, on my way to see her, I stopped at a friend's house. He was married, living with his wife and young son. I told him that I was on my way to see my American girlfriend.

He said, "Wow! You have an American girlfriend. Can I come with you to meet her?"

I said, "Of course you can come. She has an older sister." That got him even more interested.

He told his wife he would be right back and then left with me. When we got to my girlfriend's house, we found out that she and her sister were going to a friend's birthday party in the Bronx. They asked us to join them. I said yes because I wanted to be with my girlfriend. But my friend said he would also go with us.

I pulled him aside and asked him, "Are you going to call your wife and let her know?"

He replied, "No, that's not necessary."

Now, from Brooklyn to the Bronx is a long train ride. We got there around ten at night. It was a great party with food, drinks, and dancing. My friend was having a ball.

Finally, around two, I told him, "I think you should call your wife."

He replied, "She is sleeping now. Why disturb her?"

I felt a little guilty, and I asked the owner for authorization to make a phone call. She told me to go right ahead. I dialed the number again and again, and every time, the phone was busy. Finally, by three in the morning, we decided to leave. It was another hour and a half before we reached Brooklyn from the Bronx. When we got to the station, there was a train about to leave. We hurried to take it, but unfortunately, it was an uptown train instead of a downtown train. We lost over half an hour.

When we finally arrived in Brooklyn, it was past five in the morning. We accompanied the two ladies to their house. Then I went to my apartment and my friend to his.

When he arrived home, his house was filled with all the family members and friends that the wife had called over the course of the night to let them know that her husband had disappeared. When asked where he had been, my friend replied that he had been at a party with me. His wife smacked him on the face, right in front of all the people. From then on, he learned how to behave. As for me, I avoided his wife for a long time. I didn't want to get whacked. Years later, husband and wife are happily living together and are still my good friends.

From Congress of Racial Equality to the *New York Times*

My evening classes were progressing nicely. Having graduated from university, where I had grown used to hard studying, I found that the courses were quite easy for me. I was learning medical technology, an area of great expansion in the late sixties and seventies. Many jobs were opening up. Without realizing it, I had entered the field of medicine.

After I had been in school for six months, a friend of mine who was a nurse got me accepted as a trainee at the Brooklyn Cumberland Hospital, where she worked. I didn't get paid, but I needed the hospital's training in order to take the New York City examination. I went to the hospital during the day and to school in the evening. I tried to work the midnight shift for a while, but it took a toll on me. I decided to canvass the newspaper's advertising sections for part-time jobs during the week and on weekends.

I found a job as a telemarketing fundraiser for an organization called CORE, Congress of Racial Equality. They had an office in the Wall Street area, where a bunch of us would make phone calls to business executives, asking them for contributions to the CORE organization in order to promote black businesses. If they were not forthcoming, we would use scripts that practically threatened them with riots, and that usually got their attention. The leader of that organization was a civil rights activist named Roy Innis. He later became a mayoral candidate for New York City.

After I had honed my skills as a telemarketer with CORE, I went to work for the *New York Times*. We were given a list of names and phone numbers to call, asking people to subscribe to the newspaper. A favorite pitch was "It's such a delight to enjoy your morning coffee with the *New York Times* in your hand." During our short orientation, someone asked a question about the *Daily News*.

The supervisor immediately said, "That trash? Don't mention it."

I thought there was a little war being waged between the *Daily News* and the *New York Times*. And then the supervisor went on to give us a little speech about a great leader, Mr. Arthur Sulzberger. He insisted the *New York Times* was the only respectable newspaper worth reading. I became a

New York Times reader myself. Up until then, I had been reading the *New York Post*, which I started to read as soon as I came to this country, and sometimes the *Daily News*. I had enjoyed the articles of two columnists: Art Buchwald, who was hilarious, and William F. Buckley Jr., whose conservative views gave me things to think about. But I became intrigued by the fact that the two of them didn't like each other. And that had aroused my interest.

After my stint at the *New York Times*, I continued with the habit of reading it, especially on Sundays. The paper was so large and so voluminous; the hardest thing was to learn how to fold it in half lengthwise, then in quarters, and then in eighths while reading the articles, especially on the subway, which was always full of people. It was an art that bestowed an air of respectability on the person who mastered it. To quote the *New York Times*, "It's the hallmark of a true New Yorker." Today many young people read the news on their smartphone, whose screen size is minuscule when compared to the broadsheet *New York Times*.

By year's end, I had worked in eleven different places, an average of one per month. Most of them were factory jobs that you wouldn't find in New York City today. Whenever I was tired, humiliated, and in despair, I remembered why I came to this country, and I also remembered the words of the lady from my hometown: "They say there's a lot of money in New York, but I can assure you, you have to work hard to get it."

That gave me the inner strength to muster the courage to move forward with the hope of creating a respectable future for me and my family. The year went by pretty fast, and I graduated from the school for medical assistants in January of 1969.

CHAPTER 31

New York City Office of Chief Medical Examiner (OCME)

I believe luck is preparation meeting opportunity.

Oprah Winfrey

After I completed my courses, I continued my training in medical technology at the hospital. Then I passed the written examination given by the New York City Department of Health. They gave me a letter indicating that I had passed the exam. And most important, they gave me a list of over fifty hospitals in New York City throughout the five boroughs of Manhattan, Brooklyn, Queens, the Bronx, and Staten Island. I told myself that out of all of these hospitals, one of them had a job for me, and I was going to get it, even if I had to visit all of them. Little did I know that a job was waiting for me on my second stop.

The Shaping of a Mentor

As I came out of the New York City Department of Health's building on Twenty-Seventh Street and First Avenue in Manhattan, I checked the list of hospitals they had given me. First Avenue itself had many hospitals. There were Beth Israel, the VA, Bellevue, New York University Medical Center, and Memorial Sloan Kettering. Additionally, there were other hospitals in the nearby vicinities on the East Side of Manhattan: Cabrini, Special Surgery, Mount Sinai, Metropolitan, New York Presbyterian, and the Rockefeller Institute—the list goes on.

I started with Bellevue Hospital, which was right across the street from the Department of Health. At Bellevue's personnel department, a young lady told me that they didn't have any open positions, but that I should try NYU, a couple of blocks north on First Avenue.

I walked up First Avenue, and at the corner of Thirtieth and First, I noticed a building with the sign "Institute of Forensic Medicine, New York University. Office of Chief Medical Examiner, New York City." I thought it was NYU Medical Center. I went there, and I met a receptionist. I gave her my letter from the Department of Health and told her that I was looking for a laboratory position.

She looked at the paper and said, "Mr. Gordett—did I pronounce your name right?—please sit down for a moment. The administrator will be with you shortly."

In the left corner of the lobby, sitting at a big desk, a man in a dark suit was dictating a letter to his secretary. When he was finished, he rubbed his hands together in a sign of satisfaction. The receptionist still had my letter.

She gave it to the man behind the desk and introduced me to him. "Mr. Gordett—did I pronounce your name right?—this is the administrator, Mr. Kupperman. You can talk to him." And then she left.

Mr. Kupperman extended a hand and said, "I am Harry Kupperman, the administrator. How can I help you?"

I told him I was looking for a job in the laboratory. He looked at the letter, which had the heading of the New York City Department of Health, and told me, "Take the elevator to the third floor and ask for Dr. Umberger, the laboratory director. He might be able to help you."

As I got on the elevator, I tried to remember the name Umberger. It sounded a little hard at first, but then I remembered the name Sulzberger from the *New York Times*. I put the two names together, Sulzberger/Umberger. I had it. I got off the elevator on the third floor, and to keep things simple, I didn't ask for Dr. Umberger; I asked for the laboratory director.

The lady I was speaking with responded, "Dr. Umberger is not in his office. You should try the fourth floor."

I took the elevator again, and as I was getting off on the fourth floor, a tall man with gray hair, a white shirt, and a bow tie, and over it all, a white lab coat soiled with chemical spots, was waiting by the elevator. I told him I was looking for the laboratory director.

He said, "Come down to my office." I figured he must be Dr. Umberger, the laboratory director.

I entered the elevator again, and he pressed the button for the third floor. We went to his office, and he offered me a seat as he sat behind his desk. I knew he was indeed Dr. Umberger, the director, because a cast bronze nameplate on his desk read, "Dr. Charles J. Umberger, PhD, Toxicology Laboratory Director."

Slowly, he pulled a big cigar from a cigar box on his desk and lit it. Then, looking straight at me, he said, "What can I do for you?"

I repeated the same routine by introducing myself and showing him my letter from the New York City Department of Health, which by now was transformed into a letter of introduction.

He looked at the letter and asked me, "Where are you from?"

"Haiti," I told him.

"It's tough down there, isn't it?" And without waiting for my answer, he said, "Tell me about you."

This was the first time someone had addressed me in these terms: "Tell me about you." I found it very interesting, and later on, after I had become a manager, I would use the same phrase to open a job interview. I would say to my interviewee, "Tell me about you." A simple invitation to open a conversation, but it's amazing to see how some young people are taken aback, not knowing where to start.

I told Dr. Umberger that I had graduated from the Medical Assistants School here in Manhattan. I also told him that I had studied law at university in Haiti and that I had moved here for a better life.

He then asked me, "Have you taken any chemistry courses?"

I said, "Yes, I had two years of chemistry."

Then he asked, "What did you learn in those classes?"

I answered him. "One year covered inorganic chemistry, and the second year covered organic chemistry."

Then he asked me, "What did you learn in both classes?" I remember telling him about the periodic table of the elements and about some metals. I also mentioned to him that we called our chemistry teacher Professor Kekulé, after we learned from him that a German scientist by the name of Frederick Kekulé had discovered the benzene ring in a daydream. He kind of smiled when I said that.

Then I added, "I can get a letter from my school in Haiti to certify that I took these courses."

He said, "Yes, do that. Ask for the letter."

Dr. Umberger took a puff on his cigar. As he was slowly expelling the smoke, I remembered my grandfather Dor smoking his pipe and telling me, "You're a big man now."

Dr. Umberger leaned back in his seat to a more comfortable position, and then he looked at me and said, "Come to work tomorrow at nine in the morning."

I couldn't believe it. I had been ready to check fifty hospitals. On the second one, I had found a job.

As it turned out, I had also acquired my first mentor in the United States, Dr. Charles J. Umberger. Indeed, some people come into our lives for a reason or a season.

Wrong Address

I thought I was working for New York University Medical Center. Unbeknownst to me, I had landed at a place that wasn't a hospital at all; it was the New York City Office of Chief Medical Examiner, otherwise known as the city morgue. The Institute of Forensic Medicine had an affiliation with NYU Medical Center. I was happy to have a good job. I was working for the City of New York, with all the benefits attached to that position, including paid sick days and vacations.

When I reached home, I wrote to my former school requesting a letter certifying that I had taken chemistry for two years. I was kind of doubtful the school would reply. But they surprised me. About three months later, I received the letter. It was a well-executed document that originated from my secondary school and was certified by the Department of Education and the Office of Foreign Affairs. It was signed by Roger Larose, Director; Alexandre C. Antoine, Assistant Director for Secondary Education; Emmanuel Saget, General Secretary for National Education and the Director of Legal Affairs, Office of the Secretary of State for Foreign Affairs. It also had the official seals of each one of these offices. It was the most official document I had ever seen coming out of the Haitian bureaucracy. I was very pleased.

I brought it to Dr. Umberger, who asked his secretary to put a copy in my file and to give me back the original. He had good reason to ask for such a document, as will be seen later.

A Change of First Name from Gesner to Jesse

The day after my interview with Dr. Umberger, I reported to work before 9:00 a.m. He referred me to his secretary, a tall, beautiful young German lady named Carol. She went with me through the formalities associated with new employment: job application, fingerprints, picture, and so on.

After completing these tasks, she took me to see Dr. Lorenzo Galante, the laboratory assistant director. Dr. Galante was an affable man, about five feet seven inches, maybe in his forties. He spoke with an Italian accent. He asked me my name, and I told him it was Gesner Gourdet, but he couldn't say it. It sounded too difficult for him.

I told him, "You can call me Jess."

Then he said, "Jesse. That's easy."

I said, "Yes." And I became Jesse.

Then he asked me, "Are you sure you can handle this job?"

I said, "Why not?"

He then called one of his assistants and said something to him in Italian. Larry opened a walk-in refrigerator, came back with a labeled container, and opened it for me to see. Inside I found half of someone's brain, a large piece of liver, one kidney, a small bottle of urine, a full tube of blood, and another bottle containing something I didn't recognize. I inquired about it. Dr. Galante told me it was gastric content—that is, whatever the dead person had ingested before dying. Everything was neatly labeled. They both looked at me with inquisitive eyes, watching for my reaction.

I said, "I can handle it."

I had never seen a human brain prior to that day, except once when I had witnessed a little girl being hit by a truck and her brain had been scattered all over the street. But I needed a job, and this one would do.

Dr. Galante took me to his office, where he explained the nature of the job to me and the medico-legal implications of the work done by the forensic laboratory. Science and technology were used for the investigation and determination of the causes of death. I actually became enthused about working in legal medicine, which they called forensic medicine. They also were involved in research. They were developing newer techniques to establish causes of death, which is why they were affiliated with New York University School of Medicine.

My first year in New York ended, and so did the extreme hardship I had experienced. With my new job came my new name, something closer to my mother's favorite name—Jess. I could start thinking about a new direction for my life.

CHAPTER 32

How to Find Your Ideal Mate

Act as if it were impossible to fail.

Dorothea Brande

Now that I had a real job, things began to get easier. It was time to move to a more mature phase of my life. It was time to think of an ideal mate. One of my classmates at the school for medical assistants was a young girl from my country. She was extremely beautiful, tall and slim, with nice features. We became friends. We would go to a show, take a walk in the park, and sometimes see a movie. One of them was a war movie—*Where Eagles Dare,* with Richard Burton and Clint Eastwood. I enjoyed it, but I could tell she didn't like it very much. She just leaned on me, not paying too much attention.

A Night on the Town and Not a Token to Go to Brooklyn

Once, the famous French singer Charles Aznavour performed in New York at Carnegie Hall. My friend and I were great fans of Aznavour. We knew most of his songs by heart. It was a wonderful opportunity to see him perform live for the first time. I got tickets for both of us, and after the show, I took her to dinner. It was a very pleasant night out. Afterward, I accompanied her on the train to her apartment in upper Manhattan. Then I went back to the subway station to take the train to Brooklyn. I realized I had used my last token, and I also didn't have any money left. I had used my last few dollars as tips in the restaurant. I had just started my job at the medical examiner's office, and it would take six weeks to get my first paycheck. I had spent my last dime on this girl. First I panicked, and then I remember laughing at myself. Here I was, after a night on the town with the most beautiful girl and not a token to go back to Brooklyn.

I stood at the turnstile searching my wallet and my pockets. I even looked on the ground to see if someone had lost a token. I remembered that the streets of New York are not paved with gold. They're not paved with tokens either, although that would have been useful indeed. All I saw was a policeman standing by the token booth, looking at me suspiciously, even though I had my nice suit on. I went straight to him and told him what had happened. He asked me for my identification. I showed him my ID card from the medical examiner, which bore the insignia of the City of New York. He smiled and told me I could go without paying. As he turned around to open the gate for me, I jumped over the turnstile and took the next train to Brooklyn, free of charge.

I didn't tell my date about this incident because I was starting to have this grand vision about her, and I didn't want to embarrass myself in front of her. Anyway, soon afterward, a common friend told me to lower my expectations because she was engaged to a medical student out of the country. I stopped seeing her. Then I decided to look for another girlfriend—or better yet, a life partner.

Taking Control of My Destiny

Was it Woody Allen who said, "If you want to make God laugh, tell him about your plans"?

He forgot to mention that "God helps those who help themselves."

Around the time I found myself in Manhattan without a token, I took a one-day course on setting goals at the Roosevelt Hotel. I wanted to learn as much as possible about how to take care of myself. They called that self-help. I became immersed in the field, which was new to me. I read every book I could find on the subject, including *Wake Up and Live,* by Dorothea Brande; *The Magic of Believing,* by Claude M. Bristol; *The Secret of the Ages,* by Robert Collier; *Think and Grow Rich,* by Napoleon Hill; *It Works,* by RHJ; *Psycho-Cybernetics,* by Maxwell Maltz; *The Greatest Salesman in the World,* by Og Mandino; *The Power of Your Subconscious Mind,* by Dr. Joseph Murphy; *The Power of Positive Thinking,* by Norman Vincent Peale; and *The Magic of Thinking Big,* by David J. Schwartz.

Four of them—*Wake Up and Live, Think and Grow Rich, The Magic of Believing,* and *It Works*—had a profound impact on me.

In *Wake Up and Live,* Dorothea Brande stated that people have a will to fail that is just as powerful as the will to succeed. She revealed a simple success formula, which is to "act as if it were impossible to fail." In other words, "Fake it till you make it."

In *Think and Grow Rich,* Napoleon Hill told how, at the request of Andrew Carnegie, he interviewed hundreds of distinguished people in order to distill their wisdom and their formula for success.

In *The Magic of Believing,* Claude Bristol explained how belief makes things happen, and he gave a series of techniques to help along the way.

The fourth book, *It Works,* was only twenty-five pages, but it encapsulated the basic idea of the other three books by exhorting you to write down what you want in detail and in order of importance, with the idea that "if you know what you want, you can have it."

People are so busy making a living that they have no time to think about what they really want. Every year, hundreds of self-help books are published. I have read my share of them. They all boil down to knowing what you want, see it in your mind, preparing yourself for its achievement, and taking a first step toward your goal.

Before William Henley wrote in 1888, "I am the master of my fate. I am the captain of my soul," Archimedes, the famous Greek inventor and mathematician from circa 200 BC, stated, "You as a man can take control of your own destiny." More recently, Andrew Carnegie added, "The man who acquires the ability to take full possession of his own mind may take possession of anything else to which he is justly entitled."

I thought I was entitled to a good wife, and one of the exercises in that seminar I attended at the Roosevelt Hotel focused on how to find your ideal mate.

We were given half an hour to think about our ideal mates and put our thoughts down on paper. Besides physical characteristics and attractiveness, it involved jotting down other attributes such as ethnicity, religious beliefs, education, financial status, moral values, general interests, and compatibility.

With these new resources in my tool kit, I embarked on an expedition to find my soul mate, and it didn't take long for her to manifest.

CHAPTER 33

A Perfect Match

When you find your perfect other self, you will know it in an instant.

KAHLIL GIBRAN

AFTER READING THE PREVIOUS CHAPTER, you might say that I made finding a life partner too complicated. You might wonder, where was the charm? Let me say that while I was having dinner with a lovely couple in their eighties, the wife described to me the exact same procedure she had used to attract her husband years earlier. You should have seen the way her eyes lit up when she said, "I wrote down that I wanted a tall and handsome man who will love me forever."

It worked for her, and it worked for me also. I have been married for over forty years—yes, to the same woman.

LOVE AT FIRST SIGHT

On Saturday, March 27, 1971, I attended a friend's wedding. During the presentation of the bridal party at the reception, my eyes fell on one of the bridesmaids. She was about five feet ten inches tall, with a radiant face and graceful body. She was perhaps in her early twenties. I was instantly lovestruck. It was love at first sight. Deep in my heart, at that very moment, I felt that the universe had custom-tailored this girl especially for me.

I turned to my friend and told him, "You see that girl over there?" I pointed my finger at the girl. "I am going to marry her."

My friend thought I was infatuated, and to get me down out of the clouds, he said, "How do you know she doesn't have a boyfriend?"

Confidently I answered, "She's going to be my wife."

As soon as the presentation of the newlyweds ended, I went to the lovely bridesmaid and introduced myself with these words: "Hi, my name is Gesner. I'd like to be your friend."

"But I don't know you," she immediately said.

"You'll get to know me. We have a lot in common," I replied.

"Like what?" she asked.

"I can name three similarities," I said. "Number one, we're both from Haiti. Number two, we're both young. Number three, we have a beautiful future ahead of us."

She was listening very attentively, and then she said, "That's true."

I smiled because I was happy that she was in agreement with me on something. That was a good start. Then I continued. "What's your name?"

"Yanick," she said.

"Can I call you Yane?"

"That's fine," she said. It turned out that's what her family called her.

Then, moving right along, I continued to build my relationship with Yane. Like Pharrell Williams, I told myself, "Jesse, you've got all night to get lucky."

I wasn't going to let anyone approach her, and no one did. We were too busy establishing the foundation for our beautiful future together. At the end of the wedding reception, she allowed me to drop her off at her aunt's apartment, where she was staying. I promised to call her. As I drove home, I was so excited about my discovery that I started to sing. It was a popular song of that time called "Venus." They say that music is the language of the heart. My heart was happy, and the song was most appropriate. It summarized my feelings at that moment.

She's got it.
Yeah, baby, she's got it.

Well, I'm your Venus.
I'm your fire
At your desire.

There Is a Purpose to Everything

It suddenly dawned on me that I was head over heels in love with someone I knew nothing about, but I was confident that I was going to win Yane's heart. After two weeks of silence, I called her and asked if I could visit her. The answer was an immediate yes. It turned out that she had been hoping to hear from me sooner. I had promised to call her, and I did not.

When I arrived at her house, she instantly won me over with her short pants, which revealed a pair of long legs suitable for exhibition at the Met. I asked her if I could take her to a movie. She said yes, and we went to see *On a Clear Day You Can See Forever*, starring Barbra Streisand and Yves Montand. It was playing in a theater on Flatbush Avenue in Brooklyn. I remember buying popcorn and offering her some, but she said no. (A sign of class?)

I wound up eating it all by myself. However, she was willing to share with me something more appetizing and more precious than popcorn: a first kiss. After that we became inseparable. Since she was living within walking distance of my house, I would see her every single day, except for occasional travels.

I wrote little poems and essays for her or about us.

I told her:

When I met you, I thought I found Haiti in you. You are its sun that brightened my days, its splendor that threw me into rapture, and its rivers that ran through the mountains. Haiti's natural glamour emanates from you. The candor that characterizes its people animates your heart. For me, you are everything that I loved and left in Haiti: my village, my parents, my first friends, and my past.

O girl who saw the day on the land that gave me birth, you bring back to mind the memorable joys of my childhood. Here in this

> *country, on the road to the future, the last snows have melted. Winter is gone. The trees have become aware of their nudity and are hurrying to put on their green costumes. Slowly, nature is coming back to life. Timidly, but surely, spring is moving forward, and with it, the need to see you, to be with you, to admire you, and to love you, grows stronger in my heart every single day. You have cleared my heart so that you can occupy it all by yourself; you have purified my soul so that you can penetrate my essence. Be the one that will enchant me forever. And when the seasons have run their course and spring comes back again and again, may it find us like today, united in the same communion, working for a common future, sharing common joys and pains, until the final conquest of whatever happiness is possible in this life.*

We knew each other for only a short time, but it was a perfect match. The intensity of our love transformed into a fire that consumed both of us. I had never experienced such love before and never have since. It didn't matter to me that she didn't have a profession or even a job. She was going to school and had a little part-time job that couldn't even pay for her tuition. Her aunt was helping her out. Unlike some of the girls I had dated, who were either American-born citizens or permanent residents in this country with well-paying positions, she was just like me, on a student visa that would expire at some point, and then we would be asked to voluntarily leave the country or be deported. That's exactly what happened to me. But if you trust in the universe's order, you'll discover that there is a purpose to everything.

CHAPTER 34

How An Immigration Judge Became My Ally

There is a chord in every heart that has a sigh in it if touched aright.

Ouida

Soon after I started to work for the city, it was discovered that I was in the country on an expired student visa. My boss, Dr. Umberger, by now my mentor, had taken it upon himself to file the necessary papers with the US Department of Labor to get me a permanent visa while I continued to work. My application was being processed at the US consulate in Haiti, but I was uncertain how long it would take to have the change of status.

Somehow, I decided to go to Montreal, Canada, to visit some friends. Someone told me that I needed a permit to do so and that I should go to the US Immigration and Naturalization Service in Manhattan to obtain such a permit.

Big mistake!

I went to the INS, and they almost arrested me. I was told that I had overstayed my visa in this country and that I should either leave the country immediately or be deported. I explained that I was working for the City of New York. They answered that I was an illegal alien and told me I had to report to immigration court. Instead of a visa to go to Canada, I went home with a court appointment for deportation to Haiti.

I immediately went to see an immigration lawyer, who gave me a detailed picture of doom and gloom while at the same time asking me for $2,000 to keep me in this country for another six months. I told him I would get back to him. I then decided to go to the immigration court by myself, without representation.

What made me so cocky was the fact that I had studied law, and I thought I could defend myself. Another big mistake! Even the best trial lawyers are advised not to represent themselves in a court of law. But I didn't learn that in law school. The other reason was obvious; I wasn't going to spend my meager savings on legal fees.

On the appointed day, I showed up at the immigration court by myself. A security guard ushered me to a large courtroom and left me in the creepy room by myself. Then the prosecutor and the judge entered the room. It was just the three of us in the room—the judge, the prosecutor, and me. After a preliminary introduction, the judge explained to me why I was there and that I had a right to counsel. I told him that I would defend myself. The prosecutor was reviewing some papers, and the judge made a sign to him.

He then got up, and in a malicious manner, he asked me loudly, "How many people have you killed?"

I looked around the courtroom to see if he was addressing someone else. No, the question was addressed to me. I instantly doubted the wisdom of coming to the court without a lawyer to represent me.

I answered, "I never killed anybody."

The next question: "Are you or have you ever been a member of the Communist Party?"

I hurried to answer. "No." But in the back of my mind, I was doubtful. In secondary school, communist literature had occasionally popped up. At the university, I had come across *The Communist Manifesto*, by Karl Marx and Friedrich Engels. It contained the ideology that influenced both Lenin and Mao to establish communism in their respective countries.

I hadn't read it, but I had seen it. Did this knowledge make me a communist? The answer would be yes in the Haiti of Papa Doc, where even owning a dictionary meant danger because it had the word "communist" in it. I was in America, not in Haiti. But it didn't seem to make a difference in this court.

I decided I had to do something to protect myself; otherwise, I was going to be deported. As the prosecutor was readying himself to fire the next question, I looked at the judge as if to ask him to rescue me from this lunatic who wanted to bury me alive.

That's when I noticed the judge's nameplate. It read, "Judge Francis J. Lyons."

An idea came to me. I raised my hand. The judge noticed it and said, "Mr. Gourdet, you want to say something?"

"Yes, Your Honor," I answered.

"You can talk," he said.

The prosecutor was looking at me. I could tell he wasn't happy to see me interrupt his line of savage questioning.

I asked the judge, "Your Honor, do you know Dr. Michael Lyons? He is a professor at Rutgers University in New Jersey, and he also works as a pathologist at the New York City Office of the Chief Medical Examiners, where I also work."

The judge appeared a little bit surprised at my question and seemed to ponder for a short instant. Then, in an almost inaudible voice, he said, "No, I don't know him."

And as the impatient prosecutor was burning to resume his callous grilling, the judge said, "Mr. Gourdet, you said you have applied for permanent visa status."

I answered, "Yes, Your Honor."

Then he asked, "How long is it going to take you to get it?"

I replied, "I don't know, Your Honor, but I have received a letter from the US consulate in Haiti indicating that my application is being processed."

The judge didn't say anything, but with a wave of the hand, he invited the prosecutor to approach the bench. They talked quietly for a few minutes, while I was nervously awaiting the next assault from the hard-nosed prosecutor. But after a while, I saw him going head down to his seat and back to his papers, writing without looking at me.

As I was trying to make sense of this new development, the judge said, "Mr. Gourdet, I am going to give you an order of voluntary departure without expense to the government on or before October fifteenth, 1971. If by then you don't have your permanent status, let this court know. An extension may be granted."

I then realized that, as the English novelist Ouida puts it, "There is a chord in every heart that has a sigh in it if touched aright." I had touched that chord in the heart of Judge Lyons. Christmas had come in the middle of June with a nicely wrapped present. I could legally stay in the country for at least another four months.

"Thank you, Your Honor," I exclaimed.

As I thanked Judge Francis Lyons, I couldn't help thinking of Dr. Michael Lyons, a man who hardly knew me but whose name had come to my rescue in time of adversity.

Indeed, some people come into your life for a reason.

True Joy, Mazel Tov!

The month of June ended; July came and went. August was advancing, and with the passing of the days, I was getting very nervous. Then, toward the end of August, I received a package from the US consulate informing me that my application for permanent residency had been granted and that I should travel to Haiti to get it. I immediately placed a phone call to the US consulate in Haiti. Luckily for me, the receptionist connected me directly with the consul. I thanked him for the letter indicating that my request had been approved, and I told him that I was getting married. I asked him if it would be possible for them to give my wife permanent residency at the same time.

He answered, "Yes, sure, come with your wife. I'll send you a letter for her."

I thanked him and hung up the phone. Somewhere out there, someone was watching over me.

It had been less than five months since I first met Yane, and I knew that eventually I would marry her, but we had not talked about such plans.

I went to her house that same evening and proposed to her. I did it without high formalities. I didn't even kneel in front of her and ask, "Will you marry me?" I didn't even have a ring. There was no time for that. I just asked her if she wanted to be my wife. She answered in the affirmative.

Then she asked me, "When do we get married?"

I said, "Now."

That threw her completely off balance.

"What do you mean 'now'?" she asked.

I then told her about Judge Lyons at the INS and the conversation I had had with the consul in Haiti, who promised to give her a visa if she went to Haiti with me as my wife.

She was happy that she would be able to go back home and see her family. Neither she nor I said anything to her aunt Keke.

At that time, it was necessary to take a sexually transmitted disease test before getting a marriage license in New York City. I told Yane we would go for the test the next day after work. She agreed. When I went to pick her up the next day, she met her aunt, who was coming out of work.

The aunt asked her, "Where are you going?"

"I am going to get married," she shouted at the aunt as she left in a hurry.

When we came back, Aunt Keke was in bed, a wet compress on her forehead. She had an elevated body temperature and a splitting headache. We then told her the whole story about our upcoming trip to Haiti to obtain permanent US visas for both of us. I ended the conversation with a quote from Voltaire in *Candide*: "All is for the best in the best of all possible worlds."

Upon hearing these words, she instantly recovered and said, "You two must be famished. Let me prepare a meal for you, and then I will call my sister, Yane's mother, to tell her this important news."

In less than an hour, Yane and I were sitting at the table, enjoying a nice dish of poulet en sauce over white rice with sweet peas. Mm-mmm, good.

The following day I took Yane to the Diamond District on West Forty-Seventh Street in Manhattan to get her an engagement ring. When we got there, she told the jeweler, a jovial Jewish man named Sam, that she wanted the tiniest diamond possible. He showed us a few rings, and Yane picked a small gold ring with a tiny diamond. Sam showed us the inscription written on the inner side of the ring: *TRU JOY.* I asked him what had happened to the E in "true." He said it was better that way. The cost of the ring was fifty dollars.

Yane tried it, and it fit perfectly. She said, "I'll take it."

I asked her, "Are you sure you don't want a more expensive ring?"

She replied, "That's all I want."

We bought the little ring. Sam wished us "Mazel tov" (good luck), and we left very happy.

When Yane showed the ring to my friends and told them the price, one of them told her, "Your boyfriend is too cheap. A girl like you deserves a more expensive ring."

I had already opened a joint savings account with her at the Dime Savings Bank, with the promise that one day it would have $100,000 in it. She knew how much money I had. She was already frugally controlling the purse.

A Blessing by the Pope

My coworker Steve Goldner was going to a scientific meeting in Rome, and since his grandpa was an influential business leader who had met Pope Paul VI, the first pope to visit the State of Israel, he secured an appointment with the pope for his grandson Steve. The New York Archdiocese arranged it.

I took advantage of this opportunity and asked Steve to have the pope bless my wife's little engagement ring. Steve took the ring with him to Rome, and when he came back, he assured me that he had met with the pope in a small group setting at a private ceremony and that the pope had blessed my wife's ring along with other articles from the faithful. After over forty years, she still wears the same little ring with the inscription TRU JOY, even though she now has more expensive ones. I recently heard that

Pope Paul VI was beatified in 2014 and is on his way to sainthood. My wife's little ring will have an even greater spiritual value since a saint will have blessed it.

On Friday, August 27, 1971, five months to the day of the date that I met her, we went to City Hall in Manhattan and got officially married. Along with us were Mercedes Bogat and Jacques Deshommes, our witnesses. On our way home, we got soaking wet from a heavy rain. Someone said it was good luck.

Our wedding reception was scheduled for the next day, which was Saturday.

We went to her house, her aunt's apartment, and I stayed with her until nine at night when I told her I was leaving.

She asked me, "Are you going by yourself?"

I didn't quite understand what she meant until she said, "We are married."

Thank God for smart women! It never occurred to me that I now had a wife, and she belonged in my bed. She took some sexy lingerie that she had secretly purchased for the occasion. She was going to show me a little more than those gorgeous legs I had admired on my first visit to her house. And we've been together ever since.

A Visit to My Hometown

We went to Haiti, where our families made arrangements for a religious wedding ceremony and a big reception. On the lovely tropical afternoon of Wednesday, September 29, 1971, we made our vows for the second time. Bishop Louis Kébreau officiated at the wedding ceremony. It was in front of a couple hundred family members and friends. Yane's younger sister, Mona, had selected for the bridal party some of the most beautiful young girls in Haiti. Looking at them during the reception, I asked myself which one of them was going to find her ideal mate at such a propitious moment.

Since Yane was a former Girl Scout leader, her troop attended the wedding in full uniform and gala lineup. For the honeymoon, we spent a couple of days in a country hotel in the mountains near Petionville. Then I took her to my hometown to see my place of birth. She fell in love with it as she had with me. Yane was a city girl, and I was a country boy. I wanted to make sure she understood where I came from. As the saying goes, "You can't know where you're going until you know where you've been."

At the US consulate, everything went smoothly. We both got our permanent residency visas. As the consul shook my hand to say good-bye, he asked me a question that left me both puzzled and grateful. He said, "Do you know a judge by the name of Francis Lyons?"

Surprised, I said, "Yes, that's my immigration judge. Is there a problem?"

"No, no problem," he said with a smile. And I left.

Judge Lyons, the immigration judge with the power to deport me from the country, turned out to be my greatest ally in obtaining my permanent visa. For that, I was so grateful. Some people come into your life for a reason.

My wife and I flew back to New York. At the airport, her mother cried. It would be a while before she would see her daughter again, but she was happy that her little girl was now a young woman and about to start a family of her own.

My two-week vacation was over, and it was time to go back to work and learn how to be a forensic toxicologist.

CHAPTER 35

On Becoming a Forensic Toxicologist

Challenge is a dragon with a gift in its mouth.
Tame the dragon and the gift is yours.

NOELA EVANS

I WENT BACK TO WORK at the Office of the Chief Medical Examiner (OCME). My new assignment was to rearrange dozens of chemicals that filled many closets. There were enough dangerous substances to kill a whole population, and many of the chemicals were carcinogenic. The concept of MSDS (Material Safety Data Sheets) had not yet been invented, and no one had heard of OSHA (the Occupational Safety and Health Administration). It wasn't unusual for the New York City Fire Department to be called to schools for fires or explosions caused by the handling and storage of dangerous chemicals.

Most of the chemicals I had to reorganize were dangerous substances such as acids, bases, and organic solvents, chemicals used in the preparation of reagents for toxicological testing. They all needed special handling; some had to be placed in special cabinets, and others had to be refrigerated or even frozen. Others could be kept at room temperature. A chemist named Tony worked with me on this project. It gave me an opportunity to learn about the properties of these chemicals, and it also taught me how to keep an inventory, which was an essential part of laboratory management. Later,

I would study and take a test with the New York City Fire Department to become a chemical safety officer for my place of employment.

When I completed this assignment, Dr. Galante complimented me on work well done and gave me a new assignment. I would work in the clerical aspect of the laboratory, managing biological samples. That included receiving, documenting, numbering, registering, storing, retrieving, and distributing the samples collected during autopsy. I worked with another technician named Larry. Our work was done under the watchful eyes of a chemist supervisor. The chain of custody had to be kept perfectly because many of these cases wound up in legal trials, and Dr. Umberger had to answer in court, not only to the integrity of the samples and accuracy of the tests results but also to the good management of his toxicology laboratory.

Slowly, I learned the techniques used in the preparation of specimens for chemical analysis, such as homogenization, distillation, extraction, and purification. I also learned the difference between acidic and basic compounds; about volatile substances, such as alcohol, cyanide, and chloral hydrate; and about dangerous metals, such as mercury, lead, and arsenic. I learned about water-soluble and organic-solvent-soluble compounds, and I also learned about prescription drugs like barbiturates, which were causing accidental poisonings and fatalities. Most importantly, I learned about human dignity in the handling of the biological samples. Many of the deceased were distinguished personalities, and some were deeply religious and well-respected individuals who died while they were not being attended by a physician or whose deaths had occurred in unusual or suspicious circumstances.

The Price of Drug Addiction

During my time at the New York City Office of the Chief Medical Examiner, heroin addicts were dying regularly, sometimes many at a time, especially when the doses were pure and not cut with an adulterant such as quinine. This was a humbling experience for me. Some of these people had everything. They spoke good English; they had a name; some were young and beautiful, famous and rich; a few of them were worth millions of dollars, and they were all addicted to drugs. Here they were, on their backs on a table at the OCME. A piece of their brain or liver was in my hand to help determine what had killed them, prompting the question—why did they have to die so young? I left the answer to that question in the hands of the master of the universe. My heart was broken; empathy could not describe my feelings.

Unable to control heroin addiction, the authorities introduced methadone to help these people cope in a controlled manner with their craving for narcotics. Unfortunately, some people died of methadone overdoses as well.

Then there was a wave of cocaine addiction. Once I was called to the autopsy room along with my supervisor to pick up autopsy specimens. In addition to the usual biological samples sent to the lab for toxicology analysis, we were given a large jar containing a bunch of little balls made of condoms filled with cocaine. They had come from the large intestine of a man who had died on a plane traveling from South America to New York. The body was brought to the OCME. Some of these balls had busted, and a high dose of cocaine had penetrated his bloodstream, killing him. I remember writing a little epitaph for this poor guy:

Amigo Mío

He kissed his girlfriend good-bye
Under the South American blue sky,
Heading for New York as told,
Hoping for a pot of gold.

Coke got into his bloodstream.
He felt like in a bad dream.
He kicked the bucket on the plane
With his belly full of cocaine.

Did You See Me on TV?

Actual toxicology analyses were done by experienced chemists and physicists, some with master's and PhD degrees. Dr. Galante and Dr. Umberger reviewed their work. They had at their disposal an array of techniques for the isolation, identification, and confirmation of the substance of interest.

Analysis for carbon monoxide involved a technique that used large amounts of mercury, which was a dangerous substance; however, later a new analyzer was developed that eliminated the use of mercury. Many accidental deaths occurred due to carbon-monoxide poisoning, not only because of fire but also for other reasons. Here are a couple of real-life examples.

One winter, a young couple wanted to be together. They enclosed themselves in their detached garage with the car running for heat. They died without feeling a thing, due to carbon-monoxide inhalation. Similarly, an old couple parked their car in their indoor garage, inadvertently leaving the car running, and went to sleep. Two days later they were found dead. Now this gets a little bit complicated because of inheritance policies. Who died first? That's a question for the medical examiner to determine, but it's also an issue that will create a nice little fight for family members on both sides and a field day for estate attorneys.

Occasionally, there were cases of particular interest to the media. Once, Gabe Pressman of NBC News came into the lab with his cameraman and reported on us in action. I was doing the distillation of somebody's brain to extract alcohol and other volatile substances. On these occasions, Dr. Umberger would put on his dirty lab coat and be directly involved in all stages of the procedural analysis. He wanted to know every detail. As I observed him, I started to develop an investigative eye myself, which would take me to the next important stage in my life. But before I get to that, let me relate how I learned about baseball.

CHAPTER 36

A Passion for Baseball

You can observe a lot by just watching.

Yogi Berra

One of the chemists I worked with was a man named Mr. Shanker. He was already in his sixties. His lab coat was always dirtier than Dr. Umberger's. He constantly wiped his hands, soiled with chemicals, on his laboratory coat. He taught me how to test for volatile substances. At that time, the tests involved chemical reactions in test tubes. He was a very serious man. He seldom laughed. One day, I saw Mr. Shanker dancing the hora in the lab while singing "Hava Nagila." He was all energized. Never had I seen him in such good humor. Something good must have happened.

I asked him, "Why are you so happy, Mr. Shanker?"

"The Mets, my son. The Mets are champions. They won the World Series, beating the Baltimore Orioles."

He grabbed my hands and got me into a few dancing steps while turning in a circle. It was a dance of happiness that I would later witness at Jewish weddings or bar mitzvahs.

He had never called me "son" before. He was really thrilled, and he wasn't the only one. On my way home that evening, I saw people embracing each other on the streets and in the train. New York City was consumed with a passion only baseball could create. It was contagious. The game of my childhood was soccer, but I soon became consumed with this love affair with baseball. I became a Mets fan, and I went to some games at Shea Stadium in Queens. Later, I would also catch an occasional Yankees game in the Bronx.

Mr. Shanker's euphoria didn't last long. Soon after that, the top boss, the legendary Dr. Milton Helpern, caught him signing out at ten minutes to four.

Dr. Helpern must have been in a bad mood that day. He asked Mr. Shanker, "What's your scheduled work time?"

Mr. Shanker replied, "Eight a.m. to four p.m."

Dr. Helpern called the administrator, who was right there, and told him, "Deduct twenty minutes from his paycheck."

Mr. Shanker objected. "It's ten minutes to four. Why twenty minutes?"

Dr. Helpern replied, "In order for you to be here at ten minutes to four, you had to leave your station at least another ten minutes early, to give you time to take off your lab coat, wash your hands, and take the elevator."

Mr. Shanker was so distraught he didn't come back to work. He retired on the spot.

Not long after that incident, the administrator saw me signing in at 8:10 a.m., when my shift started at 8:00 a.m. He didn't say anything to me, but he sent a note to Dr. Umberger advising him to deduct ten minutes from my salary for the lateness.

Dr. Umberger replied, "Mr. Gourdet came in on time. I stopped him in front of the building to talk to him about his assignment for the day; that's why he signed in ten minutes late. Officially, he was on time."

The reality was that a subway delay had caused my lateness. But Dr. Umberger used this opportunity to even a score with Dr. Helpern for interfering in the management of his laboratory since Mr. Shanker had worked directly under Umberger. On the other hand, Dr. Helpern wanted to show Dr. Umberger that he, Dr. Helpern, was the big boss and that he made the rules.

It was a case of office politics, an ego clash between two big bosses. As for me, I was relieved that the dignity of Mr. Shanker had been restored. He was a dedicated worker who had shared his passion for baseball with me.

CHAPTER 37

How I Met a Famous Scientist

In the field of observation, chance favors the prepared mind.

Louis Pasteur

While processing autopsy specimens, I noticed that many blood samples were white instead of the usual red color. In school, I was told that condition was called lipemia, but why were there so many? Since I had access to the final analysis files, I checked them and found out that more than 50 percent of these lipemic samples were also positive for morphine, a by-product of heroin. I went to Dr. Umberger and asked him about it.

Without answering me, he picked up the phone and talked to someone. Then he told me, "Go see Dr. Weiner on the fifth floor. He is waiting for you."

Dr. Alexander S. Weiner, head of the forensic-serology department, was one of the most famous men in blood typing. He and Dr. Karl Landsteiner had discovered the blood Rh factor, a major discovery in blood transfusion that saves people's lives every single day. Dr. Karl Landsteiner had discovered the blood ABO system, for which he was awarded the Nobel Prize in Physiology and Medicine.

I went to see Dr. Weiner in his office. He was very kind. I introduced myself and told him what I had observed. I showed him a sample I had brought with me.

He became informal and started to chat with me, asking me a series of personal questions unrelated to the subject at hand: "Where are you from? Do you have a family? How is it in Haiti? How long have you been working at the Medical Examiner's Office? How do you like New York City?"

I was starting to ask myself if he was ever going to answer the question that had brought me to his office, when the tone of his voice became more subdued.

Looking at me, he said, "It's good to be observant and to pay attention; you never know what you may discover. The change in the color of the serum that you observed is due to a fatty diet. Most drug addicts eat junk; they don't eat properly."

"Thank you, Dr. Weiner," I said.

And then he added, "If you notice anything unusual, let me know. My door is open."

I got up, and as I was leaving, he picked up the phone, and I heard him say to Dr. Umberger, "Keep an eye on this young man."

Cheers!

There was a supervisor named John. Dr. Umberger called him to his office and told him to work with me on anything of interest to me. John worked closely with a young PhD graduate from Columbia University named Dr. Hoffman and another chemist named Steve, the one who had met with Pope Paul VI. They had one thing in common. Every Friday evening on their way home, they would stop for a beer at an Irish bar on Second Avenue called Limericks. That Friday evening, I was invited to have a beer with them. Again, I became a member of an elite group.

There was one problem: I didn't know what to order at a bar. I wasn't a beer drinker. I had only been to a bar once, at the place in Haiti where Margarita worked, and I hadn't gone there for a drink. Steve asked the bartender, "What's on tap?"

The bartender answered something that I didn't understand.

Steve said, "Fine," and we were served large chilled mugs full of frothy beer.

John raised his glass followed by the others, and, looking at me, he proposed the familiar Irish toast:

May the road rise to meet you.
May the wind be always at your back.
May the sun shine warm upon your face.
And rains fall soft upon your fields.
And until we meet again,
May God hold you in the hollow of His hand!

A Test for Marijuana

At that time there was no test for marijuana or THC (tetrahydro-cannabinoid) in biological specimens. The three members of my team were deep into research to come up with such a test. Dr. Hoffman would comb the New York University Medical Center's library for the latest articles on that subject. (There was no web surfing at that time.) They got me involved in the analysis of urine samples. Later, when scientific papers were published, I was happy to see my name as coauthor. It was an honor to be part of something that was greater than me, a team that wanted to make an impact on the field of toxicology. We worked very hard to develop a test, using a freeze-dry technique, but one company named Syva beat us to the punch by coming up with a new technique called EMIT (enzyme multiplied immunoassay technique). It allowed for the screening of THC and other drugs using antibodies. It became very popular and is still in use.

My interest in science was developing, but I lacked the formal basic science education to match it. It was time to go back to school.

CHAPTER 38

Life on Campus

Adaptability is defined as the ability to perceive when a new kind of behavior is called for—and to respond appropriately.

Richard Wedemeyer and Ronald W. Jue, Ph.D., *The Inner Edge*

While all these things were happening, one day Dr. Umberger called me to his office and informed me that administration had told him that I couldn't continue to work in my job title because it required twenty-four credits in chemistry. The letter from my school in Haiti didn't indicate how many credit hours I had, so it was practically worthless. Dr. Umberger suggested that I register for chemistry classes at New York University, his alma mater. In the meantime, he managed to keep me on the job.

He went to City Hall and requested the creation of a new title for the OCME that didn't have the twenty-four-chemistry-credits requirement but did have a comparable salary to what I was making. The wheels of bureaucracy turn very slowly. The process would take another three years to complete. A new title, senior toxicology technician, was created. By that time, I had more chemistry and other science course credits than were necessary; however, life would take me along a different path.

But first I followed Dr. Umberger's advice and registered at New York University for two chemistry classes (a total of eight credits) in the summer. For the fall term, I registered for another chemistry class that was being taught by an NYU professor who also taught chemistry on TV. He was an interesting professor. He told us that during the summer, he went to countries in Europe and Latin America, advising them on how to preserve the monuments that were being corroded by sea air. He said he discovered the formula for Rolaids antacid and sold it to a company in New Jersey. They had paid him a pittance while they made millions.

Besides regular science students, the class had some aspiring nurses and a lawyer who worked for a chemical company. On the first day of class, the teacher told us, "You can ask me questions about anything; if I don't know the answer, I'll fake it."

Everybody smiled. Nervous students could relax.

I raised my hand. He asked me to speak.

"How come you can light a match by striking it on a one-hundred-dollar bill?" I asked.

He looked at me somewhat curiously, and calmly he said, "I've never seen a one-hundred-dollar bill. Have you?"

This time, instead of smiling, the class cracked up laughing.

But I had the last laugh. I got an A in his course.

Rules Are Meant to Be Broken

During the spring semester, I took another chemistry course at NYU. It was with Professor Gettler. I was familiar with the name because there was a large portrait of a Dr. Alexander Gettler at the OCME. I asked him about it, and he told me that was his father; he had been chief medical examiner.

On the first day of class, Professor Gettler laid down the ground rules: "No student is admitted to my class ten minutes after starting time." He made sure to lock the door once the ten minutes had elapsed.

One day, there was a major snowstorm. Most of the class was on time, but Professor Gettler wasn't there. Ten minutes after the class was supposed to start, one student closed and locked the door. Professor Gettler showed up a good twenty minutes later, with his hair up in the air, wet like a cat out of the shower. He tried to open the door, but he couldn't because the door was locked. He made signs through the small rectangular glass window of the door. Nobody paid attention. He knocked at the door really hard, and someone opened it. He apologized for being late. He explained that he was coming from Westchester, and traffic was terrible because of the storm.

We sympathized, but we didn't forgive. From that day on, the ten-minute rule disappeared, and the door was left unlocked.

One student wrote a note on a piece of paper and passed it to me. The note said, "Rules are meant to be broken."

Smart by Association

As I was completing that fourth chemistry course at NYU, Dr. Hoffman informed me that Saint John's University in Jamaica, Queens, was starting a graduate program in toxicology. He suggested that I apply. I did, and I was accepted. I needed two more organic-chemistry courses as prerequisites. I registered for them at Saint John's during that summer.

I arrived in class early, and the room was almost empty. I took a seat somewhere in the middle of the room. Along came another student, and of all places, she decided to sit right by me. I made believe I hadn't seen her, but I had already observed her. She was a beautiful young lady with blond hair and a nice shape. She looked a little older than most of the students, who were in their late teens or early twenties.

She introduced herself to me. "My name is Joan. What's yours?"

"Jesse."

"Nice to meet you, Jesse."

After the first session, as we were on our way to the bookstore to buy our textbooks, she asked me an innocent question that left me puzzled. "Jesse, can I borrow a dollar from you? I am short one dollar to buy my book. I'll give it back to you tomorrow."

I am a little slow in the assimilation of high concepts of human behavior, but I didn't need to be a genius to realize that this gorgeous girl wanted to befriend me. I gave her a dollar bill, and the next day she sat right by me again so that she could repay the loan. We became friends. I told her that I was married; she told me she had a boyfriend in medical school. She had graduated from college with a degree in math, but now she wanted to be a pharmacologist. That's why she had wound up in the organic-chemistry class. She was in a situation somewhat similar to mine.

She became the biggest help to me. We studied together and took breaks together. When the teacher noticed that I had such a smart and beautiful girl as my class partner, he automatically assumed by association that I was just as smart as she was, and he gave me a very good grade.

My relationship with Joan didn't go unnoticed by some of the students. One day, she and I went to lunch with two white students who were going together. The boyfriend asked me, "Jesse, how does it feel to have such a pretty white girl by your side all the time?"

Before I figured out what to say, Joan answered for me, telling the student, "Jesse feels the same way you feel to have your girlfriend by your side all the time."

I couldn't have come up with a better answer. As our class schedules changed, we lost contact with each other, and we never saw each other again. Some people come into your life for a season.

By then, I had already been at the Office of the Chief Medical Examiner for more than four years. I was familiar with all the techniques being taught in my classes, and I did very well in the toxicology courses. In the meantime, Dr. Umberger found ways to keep the city bureaucrats off my back; he said someone had buried my file under a desk, where it was forgotten.

Dr. Umberger was my first mentor and my greatest benefactor. My interaction with him didn't stop at the OCME.

CHAPTER 39

Memories of Dr. Charles J. Umberger

Some people enter our lives and forge such an impression on our heart and soul, it lasts forever.

Author unknown

Dr. Umberger loved country living. He had a large farm with two dozen horses in upstate New York. That's where he preferred to spend his weekends. I spent many weekends on the farm with him before I got married. His two well-behaved young daughters would come to spend an occasional weekend with him, and they enjoyed helping their father in the collection of hay and other farm activities. I enjoyed my stay there because it gave me an opportunity to ride horses and be away from the city.

I remember one time when I was riding a horse and the one ahead of me was going really fast. My horse didn't want to be left behind. All of a sudden, it took off at a super speed, and for a few minutes, I experienced this euphoric sensation of being transported in the air, as if time had stopped. As the horse slowed down, I came back to reality. I never had such an enjoyable experience until years later, when I took a ride with a friend of mine who had just bought a new Porsche. I asked him to show me what the car could do. He took off on one of the country roads on Long Island, and for about a couple of miles, I was breathless, as though I was on the Cyclone at Coney Island in Brooklyn.

I told Dr. Umberger that my father was an avid horse rider but that the horses in Haiti were not as big and beautiful as his horses. He told me he would give me one of his horses to send to my father. I checked on pricing for the horse's transportation from New York to Florida by land and from Florida to Haiti by sea. It was more than I could afford. I had to decline the offer, but I appreciated the gesture.

He would have a vegetable garden during the spring, where he planted corn, tomatoes, eggplant, peppers, cabbage, and other summer vegetables. Since his birthday was during the summer, we would then have a huge party for him at his ranch, attended by most of the lab workers and their families. Each family would bring a dish. I remember one year my wife brought a dish of macaroni au gratin. It was so good, years later people were still talking about it. My wife is a great cook, and to this day her food is still the best.

Sometimes when I went to the farm, I would take books with me to read. One of them was *The Godfather*, by Mario Puzo. The book was so exciting I read it in one weekend. That was before the movie came out. It wasn't too difficult for me to picture some of the mob scenes described in the book. I had once witnessed the shooting, in broad daylight, of a small-time bookmaker in the East New York section of Brooklyn, where I lived for a while. When the movie came out, I was one of the thousands who packed the theaters.

Dr. Umberger retired before I left the OCME. We wanted to have a nice and memorable retirement party for him. We invited all of his friends and acquaintances. Many of them were the lawyers and judges he had come across during his career. Earlier, the office had thrown a big party for Dr. Milton Helpern, the iconic chief medical examiner. It was at the Waldorf Astoria, where for the first time I had seen chandeliers that were bigger than anything I could ever have imagined. But we ruled out the Waldorf for Dr. Umberger's party; it was too fashionable. We wanted a chic, more down-to-earth place where people could relax and have a good time. We chose the Tavern on the Green restaurant in Central Park. The food was excellent, and the park atmosphere was more in line with Dr. Umberger's style.

As a member of the organizing committee, I was responsible for the music. I contracted a famous Haitian band, composed of black musicians experienced in the entertainment of American tourists in luxury hotels in Haiti. They happened to be on tour in New York at that time. We got a call from Tavern on the Green informing us that they couldn't play. They told us it had to do with some union issue. But we figured there was more than that. We told Dr. Umberger about the situation. He made one phone call, and all the problems vanished. The band provided music for the party, and it turned out to be a great success. All the guests enjoyed themselves.

Dr. Umberger wasn't going to tolerate any prejudice.

After I got married, while I was going to school at NYU, I decided to move from Brooklyn to Manhattan to be nearer my workplace and school. An employee of the lab was vacating her apartment on Second Avenue. I applied for the apartment, and I was told I could have it. But when I met the building management in person, they saw my face, and all of a sudden the apartment became unavailable. Here again, Dr. Umberger picked up the phone, and as if by magic, the apartment became mine again. But my wife and I didn't want to live in a place where we were not welcome, and we didn't take it.

Dr. Umberger passed away only a few short years after he retired. By that time I had already left the OCME. I went to the funeral and met a brother of his, who told me he was an engineer and was living in West Virginia. I told him about my relationship with Dr. Umberger, the man who opened the way for me to succeed in New York. His memories will stay with me forever. Indeed, some people come into your life for a reason and a season.

Part Four
How to Succeed in New York

CHAPTER 40

A Childhood Dream Fulfilled

It's not where you start—it's where you finish that counts.

Zig Ziglar, *Over the Top*

In 1975, New York City came to the verge of bankruptcy. It was a total financial disaster. The federal government didn't want to provide any assistance. The October 30 front page of the *Daily News*, which alluded to President Gerald Ford's stated intention to veto any bailout for New York City, made nationwide news. The headline read, "Ford to City: Drop Dead."

It is believed that President Ford did not utter those two words and that the media came up with the catchy headline. But for President Ford, the damage was done. He lost the next election to Jimmy Carter. Ultimately New York City was rescued with a big federal loan.

The slashing of city agencies' staffs was inevitable. The OCME lost many workers. I lost my job during that time, and my life was redirected toward another path. The crisis opened up new opportunities for me.

Learning to Roll with the Punches

When word got out that I was out of a job, people came to the rescue. A friend and former classmate, Dr. Joseph Balkon, was supervisor of the toxicology laboratory at Long Island Jewish Medical Center; he offered me a technologist position there, and I took it.

While I worked there, another friend of mine, Eleones Anglade, called me and told me, "Real estate is the place to be. Many houses are being sold. There is much money to be made."

It was a time of exodus to the suburbs. Many affluent white people were fleeing the city and Queens to move to the quiet villages of Long Island. It didn't matter if they had to commute three hours a day. New houses, large shopping malls like Green Acres, Roosevelt Field, Fortunoff, movie theaters, and expensive restaurants were being erected for their enjoyment. That gave black people, especially West Indians, an opportunity to buy nice single- or two-family residences on large piece of property in certain neighborhoods of Queens, like Laurelton, Cambria Heights, Springfield Gardens, Hollis, and Queens Village.

My friend introduced me to real-estate sales, and it became my second field of employment during all my active working years. I would work my regular hospital job during the day, and in the evening and on weekends, I would do real-estate sales.

At that time I was living in a recently built little community in Brooklyn, about ten minutes from JFK Airport. The landlady, who was single, had set a condition for the apartment rental: "No children in my house."

I thought it was a hard thing to say to a young couple, and I vowed that nobody was going to tell me something like that a second time. And when our son, Greg, was born in July of that year, my wife and I decided that it was time to buy our house.

A house in our neighborhood in Brooklyn caught our attention, and I considered buying it. I told my friend Dr. Balkon at Long Island Jewish Hospital about it, and he said to me, "Jesse, why would you want to buy a house in Brooklyn?"

He was a Long Island man, living in the quiet town of Huntington, the same town where Walt Whitman was born. I took his advice and decided to raise the bar. We bought a house in a nice residential section of Queens.

It was a four-bedroom, finished-basement house with two and half baths and a large backyard on a sixty-by-one-hundred-foot lot.

My wife was saving most of our income. She knew how to do that. In our account at the Dime Savings Bank, the dimes had turned into dollars, the dollars into hundreds, and the hundreds into thousands of dollars. For the six years I worked at the OCME, I ate at the Bellevue Hospital's cafeteria, which was subsidized by the city. I had three meals a day Monday through Friday. The meal tickets were twenty cents for breakfast, thirty cents for lunch, and forty cents for dinner; for that you got a balanced meal with dessert and drinks. No way to beat that in New York City. My wife was working full time and attending college in the evening. On weekends, she would make a nice meal. Occasionally we would go to a Chinese restaurant or a pizza place for dinner.

The price of the house was $40,000. It had a mortgage of $15,000 at a low interest rate of 4 percent. We took over the mortgage, thus avoiding employment verification and the credit check. The sellers gave us a $5,000 second mortgage for five years. We came up with the other $20,000.

Controlling the purse, my wife had saved $15,000. We borrowed $3,000 from my cousin Ketty and $2,000 from her sister Micheline. On the morning of the closing, I realized that I was still short on closing fees. I stopped at the First National City Bank and borrowed $1,000 in cash from my bank credit card.

Our lawyer, Raphael Rhodes, found ways to get money from the sellers. It was revealed at the closing that the detached garage did not have a certificate of occupancy. He threatened to kill the deal if the sellers didn't make adequate compensation. They had already bought their one-way tickets to the Sunshine State of Florida; they complied with whatever was required of them to consummate the sale. After all expenses were paid, I returned home with $800. I used that money to redo the landscape of the house's front yard. I called a nursery, and they did a magnificent job. Instead of a dull front yard with dying grass and an old pine tree that had seen better days, I wound up with a display of green shrubs and colorful flowers that transformed the front yard into an oasis of colors for the admiration of visitors and passersby.

By the way, at the height of the real-estate market in 2006, that same house was listed for over $400,000—a nice tenfold increase in thirty years. By that time, I had already sold it at a hefty profit, and I didn't regret anything. We had many years of enjoyment in that house. Family members stayed with us until they got a foothold in this country. Others came for a vacation and had a nice place to stay. Every year we would have backyard parties attended by family and friends. We installed a large aboveground pool, and the kids enjoyed swimming in it. As it was my first house, I was emotionally attached to it, and so were my children. My daughter was born while we lived there, and my son had a place in New York he could call home. Most of all, it was the realization of a childhood dream, to have my own beautiful house with electricity, indoor plumbing, and an indoor kitchen.

When my wife and I visited the Western Wall in Jerusalem, I noticed some young Orthodox Jews at a booth with a picture of Rabbi Menachem Mendel Schneerson. I walked over to them and told them that I was from Queens, New York, and that the rebbe (master) was buried in my neighborhood. One of them was from Canada but had lived in New York; he asked me a few questions about Queens. "Do you know Francis Lewis Boulevard?"

Of course, I knew the street; I'd lived on 131st Avenue, a few blocks away from Francis Lewis Boulevard, for many years. The cemetery is located at the corner of 121st Avenue and Francis Lewis Boulevard.

Here, taken from my book *Let It Be Easy,* is a little poem evoking the four seasons in that house.

Good-Bye

Good-bye sweet home.
I never thought I would leave you so soon,
And in my heart the feelings start to grow.
May the passing of the seasons teach me to let go.

I will remember your beauty in spring hours:
The multiple colors of your splendid flowers,
The friendly creatures that your environment nurtures
In the garden and pond by some miracle of nature.

Summer will bring back the sweet memories
Of moments shared with friends under cherry trees,
The sight and sound of children playing with water,
A bird walking on the lawn in clement weather.

Raking leaves in the fall was a family ritual,
Working together while singing a spiritual,
And the wind blowing leaves in my face
As it cleared the land's surface.

Winter under your roof was most enjoyable;
Leaving footprints in the snow is not always bearable.
I wish I could write your name on the walls of Time.
Your memory is engraved in my heart like a shrine.

CHAPTER 41

How I Acquired a New Mentor

Prosperity in life is derived more from who you know, not what you know.

JACK CANFIELD, MARK VICTOR HANSEN, LES HEWITT: *THE POWER OF FOCUS*

SOMETIME AFTER OUR SON, GREG, was born, his grandma, my wife's mother, took him with her to Haiti. He would return during the summer so that we could celebrate his birthday. That gave my wife the opportunity to continue with schooling while working full time. She eventually got her master's degree in microbiology and public health at Wagner College and later became a supervisor at Montefiore Hospital, followed by head of the microbiology department and AOD (administrator on duty) at Brookdale Hospital.

I was contemplating resuming law. My application to the Brooklyn Law School was being processed, and at the urging of my friend Paul Jourdan, I even took a course on how to take the bar exam. However, I didn't follow through with that plan. Instead, I went to school again for a master's degree in administration.

My position at Long Island Jewish was a temporary one. I was replacing someone on maternity leave. When the time came for me to leave, my friend Dr. Balkon managed to pull some strings and kept me there for a full year. In the meantime, he recommended me for a toxicologist position with the New York State Police in Albany, the state's capital, where he had friends.

I did the interview with the captain of the police department, and he was very courteous. He showed me their collection of guns that went back many years. He asked me if I liked hunting, a sport I could enjoy there during the season. Then he referred me to an investigator who was assigned to do a background check on me. I went to see the investigator in his office at the World Trade Center in New York City. That was before terrorists brought down the twin towers in 2001. The investigator asked me to tell him every place I had lived and everything I had done since birth. Soon afterward, I got a call from my father in Haiti. Somewhat alarmed, he wanted to know what kind of trouble I had gotten myself into. Someone from the US embassy in Haiti had visited him, asking all kinds of questions about me. I assured my dad that I was doing just fine, and that put him at peace.

After a couple of months, I was called back to Albany for another interview. The captain told me that the job was mine, but due to budget constraints, my contract would be for only two years. I went back home, thought about it, and decided to decline the position. I went full time in real estate, and I did fine. Two years later, I got a phone call from a friend of mine; his name was Fritz Jean-Baptiste.

He asked me, "Jesse, why did you leave the medical field?"

I told him I was doing well. Indeed, I was making a good living. The only drawback was that I was working seven days a week, especially on weekends, when most people look for real estate.

He said, "Real estate is a roller coaster; you should have a plan B." And then he added, "Working in the medical field will always assure you a job. It is open twenty-four hours a day. There is a great need for licensed clinical laboratory technologists; I can ask the director of the laboratory where I work to accept you in their training program."

Up until then I had worked in toxicology, where tests were done for two purposes: to determine the cause of death and to determine drug abuse. Working at a hospital's clinical laboratory was a completely different matter. Tests were done for the purpose of determining the diagnosis and prognosis of sick patients and for preventive medicine. It was a good opportunity.

I told Fritz, "Make the appointment for me."

When I showed up at Coney Island Hospital, I was met by a beautiful young technician. She inquired about my visit and asked me where I was from. I told her I was Haitian.

She said, "You're the first Haitian I really like."

I had just met her.

And then she took me to Mr. Albert Hanok, the laboratory director, and told him point blank, "You should hire him." (Another angel?)

I sat down with Mr. Hanok and his second in command, Dr. George Abraham. They looked at my credentials and asked me a few questions. Then they glanced at each other in an acquiescing way without uttering a word, but by their eyes, I could tell it was an acceptance.

Mr. Hanok then said, "You're admitted to the clinical chemistry training program. It's starting on Monday."

When I went there on Monday, I was surprised that there were only two of us trainees in chemistry. The other trainee was a college student on internship. There were other trainees, but they were assigned to other sections of the laboratory department, such as microbiology, hematology, and the blood bank.

Training consisted of both practical work and didactic classes. We were assigned to work one on one for about a month with a technologist who would teach us the techniques of his line of work. At the end of training, we would receive a grade. Then we would go to another technologist, and so on until we'd rotated through all the sections. Additionally, supervisors and heads of different sections were teaching courses.

On the first week of training, I attended a statistics course given by Dr. Abraham. He gave us homework assignments on the subjects covered: graphical representations of data, standard deviations, means, confidence intervals, and such. I went home, and not only did I do the assignment well, but I also typed it and placed it in a folder, with his name nicely typed in bold letters on the cover page. I presented it to him the next morning even though it wasn't due until the next class. He couldn't believe that a student could be so diligent and professional. He showed the paper to Mr. Hanok, who wrote on it, "Congratulations, job well done."

What Dr. Abraham didn't know was that I had already taken statistics courses on the graduate level. Still, from then on, he adopted me as his protégé, and he became my mentor and friend. He would open many doors for me, both professionally and in the community.

One year later, after I completed the training, Mr. Hanok wrote a letter to the New York Department of Health on my behalf, and I got my license as a clinical laboratory technologist. There was one position open in the laboratory, and it was mine. I was assigned to work with yet another elite team, this one in charge of instrumentation and purchasing. The other trainee got a position with a diagnostics company.

I had gone backward to start all over again, only this time, I was on a step that would take me to a higher level. But it came with a price.

CHAPTER 42

"All Truths Are Good, but Not All Truths Are Good to Say"

Let no one take your goodness away from you.

Author unknown

It was the late seventies; automation was transforming the clinical laboratory field. That's when the concept of chemistry test profiles was developed. Results of laboratory tests that used to take hours, sometimes days, were reaching doctors in minutes, thus saving many lives. New computerized laboratory analyzers were being manufactured by companies such as Technicon, Beckman, Coulter, DuPont, Abbott, Kodak, and others. This offered opportunities for technologists to spend a week or two in other states around the country to learn these new technologies. Since my team, which consisted of supervisor John Saviano, Iris White, and me, was in charge of instrumentation, I got to go away on training for every new laboratory analyzer that was being purchased by the hospital. Over the years, besides New York and New Jersey, I visited cities in states such as California, Florida, Illinois, Texas, Indiana, Kansas, and others.

At that time we were treated like VIPs. The hospital wanted us to succeed, and the analyzer's vendor depended on us to be their representatives in the workplace, a win-win situation. We stayed at the best hotels and had carte blanche to eat at the best restaurants in the city where training took place.

One Chicken for Twelve People

On two such occasions, I came across individuals who, in their innocuous ways, made me feel that I was navigating territories where I did not belong.

In the first instance, I was having dinner at a five-star restaurant with some colleagues; I placed an order for the double lobster tails. The waiter tied my bib around my neck; I looked really stylish. Through the course of the meal, I noticed a well-dressed gentleman at another table looking at me. He also had his bib tied around his neck.

At some point, he got up and came to my table and said, "Hi there," and then he told me, "I am very impressed; you're having the same dish I am having."

Then he gave me his card and told me, "If there is anything I can do for you, do not hesitate to contact me."

He was the sales manager for some big corporation. Was he trying to be nice and helpful, or was it a curiosity for him to see a black person with a bib around his neck, enjoying lobster tails at a fancy restaurant?

Whatever it was, he made me feel self-conscious, and my lobster didn't taste so good afterward. As Dr. Wayne Dyer wrote in his book, *The Power of Intention: Learning to Co-create Your World Your Way,* "A sense of belonging is one of the highest attributes on Abraham Maslow's pyramid of self-actualization…Respect yourself and your divinity by knowing that everyone belongs." And Dr. Dyer added, "This should never come into question." But I would be tested a second time.

The second instance was more direct and humiliating, to say the least. I was at another expensive restaurant with a friend of mine who had also traveled for this training. On my plate was a medium-rare thirty-two-ounce steak. I was enjoying my juicy steak with baby carrots and asparagus. Sitting at the table near me was a couple having dinner.

The man struck up a conversation with me. "That's a nice steak you have there!"

I said, "Yeah."

"Where are you from?"

"New York."

Then he said, "You were not born in New York, were you?"

"No."

"Where are you from?"

"Haiti," I answered.

"Oh, Haiti, I have been there. You must feel very privileged to eat such a big steak because in Haiti, it's one chicken for twelve people."

My partner was fuming; he was about to deliver a punch to this SOB. I stepped on his foot under the table. The guy continued to rub it in, and at some point he said that he worked as a mercenary in Haiti, trying unsuccessfully to overthrow the government.

I listened to him politely, although I didn't think he deserved my attention. Then his wife asked us what brought us into town. I told her that our company had just bought a state-of-the-art medical analyzer worth a quarter of a million dollars; we were here to be trained so that we could teach other people how to use it.

She said, "Where did you go to school? Our son would like to do something like that."

I told her, "You should send your son to MIT, the Massachusetts Institute of Technology."

She said, "Thank you."

Neither my friend nor I had graduated from MIT. We attended colleges in New York. But MIT was the university where the groundwork for the revolutionary technology of this new analyzer had been developed. I felt I could restore my dignity with a display of superior knowledge. "No one can make you feel inferior without your consent," wrote Eleanor Roosevelt.

Later, I read a book called *How to Win Friends and Influence People*, by Dale Carnegie; it totally changed my relationship with all kinds of people. I became immune to prejudices. When people try to hurt me, and some have, I just feel empathy for them, and I send them a thought of love. Many people have commented on my calm demeanor and the feeling of peace that I project. Does that make me a guru?

To quote the Buddha, "The man who foolishly does me wrong, I will return to him the protection of my most ungrudging love; and the more evil come from him, the more good shall go from me."

Still, I couldn't escape the reality. The man at this restaurant was telling the truth. He brought me back to my early childhood in Anse-à-Veau, where indeed one skinny chicken was sliced into as many pieces as there were people in the house. One person would get the feet, another one the head, and so on.

Still, as my former boss would have put it, "All truths are good, but not all truths are good to say."

As luck would have it, the next person I met gave me the tool that empowered me to reach my dreams and aspirations.

CHAPTER 43

A Five-Year Plan

Nothing can bring you peace but yourself.

Ralph Waldo Emerson, *Self-Reliance*

The director of the pathology department at Coney Island Hospital retired, and a new medical director came in. He was a firm believer in human potential.

Soon after he took the position, he invited each employee to sit down with him to discuss plans for the future. When I met with him, he asked me, "Where do you see yourself professionally in the next five years?"

I had never thought of my future in those terms, but I knew I wanted to advance. So I told him, "I want to be in charge of a laboratory."

I kind of felt afraid after I said that. I thought I had made a mistake by telling my boss about such an ambitious goal. But he seemed appreciative.

He asked me, "What are you doing now to prepare yourself for that position?"

I told him, "I don't know yet, but I'll think of something."

He shook his head as if to indicate that something was missing. Then the conversation turned to trivial issues, and I left his office.

As I came out, I spoke to another tech, named Oscar, who had met with him just before me. Oscar asked me, "What did he ask you?"

And without waiting for me to answer his question, he went on a tirade. "This guy is really a nutcase. Do you know, he asked me what I wanted to be five years from now? How would I know? I can't even tell if I am going to make it until tomorrow."

I listened to Oscar, and I didn't say anything. He was my friend, and he had taught me a lot about computers. In fact, a few days before this meeting, I had been passing by Junior's restaurant in Brooklyn; I got him a nice strawberry cheesecake to share with his wife. He had confessed to me that his wife had had sex with another man in their house while he was there; that left him devastated. I thought that sharing something as good as a Junior's cheesecake with his wife would restore their union. Unfortunately, he died a few short years later of liver disease, at a young age. He was driven to drugs and alcohol.

On my part, I took the five-year-plan idea planted by the medical director very seriously, and so did he. To my happy surprise, he decided to put me a step closer to my goal. He gave me a promotion at the first opportunity that arose. Then he asked me to give lectures, which everyone attended.

One day, I was addressing another tech in the lab, and I said loudly, "Nobody is indispensable; anybody can be replaced."

He just happened to be passing by, and he heard me say that. He looked at me and said, "I am the director; I am indispensable."

Less than one month later, he was gone. He took a better position in the city. Some people come into your life for a season.

The five-year plan he taught me became a model for me to follow in all aspects of my life, and I found it very useful in reaching my goals. (I've got to talk to Woody Allen.)

CHAPTER 44

It's Who You Know

We make a living by what we get, but we make a life by what we give.

Winston Churchill

Sometime after I had my one-on-one meeting with the medical director, my mentor, Dr. Abraham, informed me about a master's degree program in health-services administration that was being offered by the New School for Social Research in Manhattan. He recommended that I apply for it.

"This will give you a foothold in management," he added.

It was a three-year evening program of fifty-two graduate credits. My union (local 1199) was paying for it; I had nothing to lose, but everything to gain. I enrolled in the program.

After I had taken about thirty credits and received mostly A's, the school invited me to participate in research they were conducting for the Manhattan-borough president and other organizations in the city. One of them had to do with the reinstallation of the carousel in Prospect Park. It had been out of order for some time. Our research team later recommended going for it. Another project was to come up with the best cafeteria benefits for employees.

The school gave me a letter for my place of employment, requesting that they grant me two weeks of paid time off to devote exclusively to the special projects. The letter also indicated that I was on the dean's list and that courses taken during that term would be free of charge. I gave the letter to my boss, Mr. Hanok, who took it to administration, and the request was rejected. Not to be deterred, I took a two-week vacation and worked on the projects.

I was part of a small group of students dedicated to these projects. First we found out that in New York City there was a large group of single mothers whose biggest concern was day care for their children. We set out to visit any institutions that provided such benefits for their employees. My partners and I visited Chase Bank, the Lady Garment Workers Union, and a couple of other places. When I found out that International Paper had a day-care center for their employees' children, I was anxious to interview one of their vice presidents. I tried to reach out to them on numerous occasions, but I just couldn't get through due to constant travel and meetings. I remember one day getting off the phone very distraught, having once again failed to secure an appointment.

My friend and coworker Iris White saw me with a long face, and she asked me, "What's the matter, Jesse?"

I told her, "I've been trying to reach a VP at International Paper for one week now, and they keep giving me the runaround."

"Did you say International Paper?" she asked.

"Yes," I replied.

"My husband knows some of the top people there," she added. My friend made one phone call, and I had my appointment the next day.

We recommended setting up a day-care center for the children of employees. Luck would have it that one day I was watching the evening news on television when they showed the graduation from day care of a group of adorable little children. It was exactly what my team had recommended. I was so happy.

Labor Day Weekend in London

Later my colleague Iris and her husband, Eric White, went to live in London for business. They invited me and another coworker to visit them over the Labor Day weekend. When we got to Newark Airport, my friend realized that he had taken his old expired passport instead of the renewed one. As he started to freak out, we heard a voice over the airline's PA system indicating that they had overbooked and whoever hadn't checked in yet would receive a free round-trip ticket for next-day travel to London. We quickly got a refund for our original tickets and spent an enjoyable weekend in London.

We visited some major historical sites, including Trafalgar Square, Buckingham Palace, and Westminster Abbey. We went shopping at Harrods. We saw the play *Starlight Express*, which was hugely successful in Europe but didn't do as well on Broadway. We had dinner at a couple of famous restaurants. All of this was courtesy of our friends Iris and Rick.

Talk about who you know!

CHAPTER 45

Write It Down: The Power of a Clear Vision

When you want something, all the universe conspires in helping you to achieve it.

PAULO COELHO, *THE ALCHEMIST*

AFTER I OBTAINED MY MASTER'S degree in health-services administration, my written goal was to have a supervisory position in the city. I had missed working in Manhattan. Life was more exciting there, with more restaurants, more entertainment, and more social life. I decided that the ideal position for me was laboratory supervisor at New York University Medical Center. I called NYU's human resources department to inquire about such a position. It was my lucky day.

"Yes, there is an opening for laboratory supervisor; you can apply for it," I was told.

They set up an appointment for me with the director of the laboratory. I met the director in his office for about half an hour. I already knew of him. He was the well-respected publisher of a newsletter I was familiar with. After a few minutes, the interview became less formal and more conversational. He asked me some pertinent questions about my background and my ability to handle the work. I asked him a couple of questions about the structure of the organization.

At the end, he told me, "Someone will contact you."

I waited for a couple of weeks; I didn't hear from anyone. After a month, I called human resources, and I was told the position was no longer vacant. I checked with a friend who worked in the lab at NYU. He told me they had promoted someone from within. So much for my written goal, I thought.

Another few months passed, and I got a call from a former colleague. She told me she was moving to Irving, Texas, and invited me to apply for her supervisory position at the Hospital for Joint Diseases in Manhattan.

As I reached this crossroad in my journey, I turned to Dr. Abraham, my boss and mentor at Coney Island Hospital, for advice on how best to proceed.

He told me, "You should go for it."

"What about salary?" I asked him.

He took his Texas Instruments calculator and came up with a number that was 25 percent greater than what I was making. I was scared.

I went to the interview well prepared. When I arrived there, I was surprised to find the NYU lab director, the same one who had interviewed me, in the room with the head of the department at the Hospital for Joint Diseases. He was a renowned pathologist somewhat new to the city. He introduced the NYU lab director to me as a consultant. Then he told me that he would let the lab director interview me first, and afterward, he would have a few questions for me.

The NYU lab director looked at me with a smile and said, "I have already interviewed Jesse."

Totally dumbfounded, the pathologist looked at him and said, "When? Where?"

His answer was, "I interviewed Jesse for a laboratory-supervisor position at NYU. He is qualified."

The pathologist then came back to earth and asked me some technical and logistic questions that he had prepared earlier. I saw him referring to his notes. At the end he said to me, "Should there be an emergency in the middle of the night, would you be able to provide coverage for the laboratory?"

I told him that I was proficient in both the technical and managerial aspects of the laboratory and that I lived only half an hour away. He seemed content with my answer.

Then, the talk turned to money. He asked me how much I wanted to be paid. With much trepidation in my heart, I told him the figure Dr. Abraham had given me.

He expressed surprise and said, "But that's way more than what the previous supervisor was making."

Boldly, I answered, "You are not hiring the previous supervisor; you are hiring me."

His head tilted slightly to the right. I took it to mean that he understood. But that didn't solve the problem. He then asked me, "Is this salary very important to you?"

My answer was simple. "It's expensive to work in the city. You have to dress properly and pay for transportation and lunch. If I cannot get a decent salary, I'll stay in Brooklyn, where I work now. I like it there."

I thought I resonated with him. As I said above, he was a newcomer to the city. He must have considered the same issues.

Then, turning toward me, he said, "Please wait in the lab. We'll call you in about fifteen minutes." Then both of them left the office, and I saw them taking the elevator.

After about half an hour, they came back, and the pathologist called me into his office. "We got you what you wanted, but it is short five hundred dollars."

"That's fine. I'll take it," I said calmly, hiding my excitement.

When I told Dr. Abraham about the salary, he said, "Damn it, we should have asked for more."

After twelve years, I bade farewell to Coney Island Hospital with a big party. I was now a New York City man with a job title to match. This time I promised myself that I wasn't going to eat the thirty-cent lunch at Bellevue Hospital. I had earned the right to experiment with the many fine restaurants of the city.

Still, it didn't end there.

In *The Alchemist*, the Brazilian writer Paulo Coelho wrote, "When you want something, all the universe conspires in helping you to achieve it." I was going to experience this truth in the most personal way.

Two weeks after I started to work in the city, my friend Sara Mook, who was the laboratory manager at Bellevue Hospital, invited me for lunch. While savoring roasted duck at a nice Chinese restaurant, she told me, "There is a vacant weekend supervisory position at Bellevue. It's an NYU position. If you know of someone who would be interested, let me know."

I told her, "I will," and I forgot all about it.

A few days later, she called me and said, "Jesse, I was talking to you about the NYU supervisor position."

It didn't occur to me that the universe was still working on my request to have a laboratory-supervisor position at New York University Medical Center. I did not plan on having a second job. Still, I went to NYU and filled out the application. My goal to work for New York University Medical Center in a supervisory position was fulfilled without me lifting a little finger. The City of New York had an arrangement with NYU Medical Center to provide medical, technical, and managerial resources at Bellevue Hospital. My position came out of that affiliation.

Still, I failed to realize that I had also achieved another goal. One day I met the former medical director of Coney Island Hospital at a conference, and he asked me, "How are you doing, Jesse?"

Only then did I realize that I had accomplished my five-year plan as per the conversation I'd had with him four years earlier.

"Where do you see yourself professionally in the next five years?" he had asked me.

"I want to be in charge of a laboratory," I had answered.

In my lectures to young people entering the workplace, I usually relate that story to demonstrate that if you know what you want and prepare yourself for its achievement, chances are that it will come to pass. Many of the things I have accomplished in life, such as writing a book, buying ideal houses, earning a specific amount of money a year, and meeting a distant relative with a connection to my French ancestors, resulted from written goals. There are those who think that this is all hogwash, but talk to successful people like Suze Orman or Jack Canfield, and they will agree with me regarding the power of a clear and written vision. I emphasize *written* because a goal not written is like a seed without soil.

As for me, my goal to work in a supervisory position in Manhattan was realized, and I had a field day in New York City.

CHAPTER 46

I Love New York

It's up to you, New York, New York.

FRANK SINATRA

FOR THE READER WHO IS not familiar with New York, let me start by saying that New York City is made of five boroughs: Manhattan, the Bronx, Brooklyn, Staten Island, and Queens. Manhattan is often referred to as New York City because it is the main borough, with the center of government, and also because it was called New York City when it was the only borough, long before consolidation with the other four boroughs to make a bigger city. Manhattan is also called New York, same name as the state. For post-office purposes, letters are addressed not to Manhattan, NY, but to New York, NY. And, of course, Manhattan is also called the Big Apple. The names Manhattan, New York City, or the city are interchangeable, depending upon the context.

Besides its position as the center of world business, three things are noticeable in New York City (I mean Manhattan specifically). First, there is always new construction going on. Second, people are always in a hurry, going somewhere. Third, New Yorkers love to partake in cultural and recreational activities and restaurants. There is so much to see in New York City. Just walking in Central Park is an enjoyable experience.

There were always new plays that we had to see. Radio City Music Hall had something for the kids. A season ticket for the opera at Lincoln Center was fashionable. Madison Square Garden always had a sporting or musical event that couldn't be missed. The many museums constantly offered new exhibitions.

I remember once reading an article in the *New York Times* about the Metropolitan Museum of Art's acquisition of a Renaissance painting for which they paid over $45 million. Like many New Yorkers, I was anxious to see what the Met had acquired for such a hefty sum. I decided to go and see the painting with my wife. At the information desk, someone directed us to the location of the painting within the museum. It was a *Madonna and Child* by Italian master Duccio di Buoninsegna. When I got there, I was disappointed by the dimensions of the painting; it was about the size of a sheet of paper. On top of that, the frame had burn marks at the bottom.

As I was complaining, my wife said, "It's so beautiful."

I shut my mouth, and from then on I learned not to question the value of art.

It was philosopher Henry David Thoreau who said, "The question is not what you look at, but what you see."

And comedian Flip Wilson would add, "What you see is what you get!"

A Multiethnic Mosaic

In New York City, one gets to mingle with people from all ethnic and religious backgrounds. The city is paved with a multiethnic mosaic. This diversity is also reflected in the workplace. I have worked with people from all the continents of the world, and I got to be exposed to many other cultures besides those of the Americas, the Caribbean, and Europe. As such, I was afforded the opportunity to experience different customs firsthand by attending a wedding, a bar mitzvah, a night of dancing at an ethnic club, or sometimes just an invitation to dinner at someone's house. I made new friends, and I went from restaurant to restaurant. I've tasted all kinds of ethnic cuisine, from the many Asian restaurants to expensive steakhouses. A Sunday-morning Chinese dim sum in Chinatown was always delightful. I learned how to use chopsticks and to appreciate sushi with a glass of sake. I also learned the different wines that go with a twelve-course French meal, and I've put a charge on my American Express gold card that made me cry while they were laughing.

Some of my closest friends are those whom I have met at work. In 2008, my wife and I went to Israel with Henry Huber, who was born there, and his wife, Fayna, whom I worked with. This gave me the opportunity to witness firsthand the horror of the Israeli and Palestinian conflict. We had dinner at his cousin's house and visited the resting place of his family members who were killed in the suicide attack of March 27, 2002, at the Park Hotel in Natanya, during a Passover seder. His cousin lost her husband, her twenty-year-old daughter, and her daughter's fiancé in that attack. Needless to say, I was heartbroken.

As I reflect on these experiences, I have come to realize that we are so fortunate to live in America. As human beings, we share many characteristics in common. One of these is the desire to pursue happiness, an inalienable right for humankind that is embedded in the US Constitution but that is hardly noted in many parts of the world. Here in America today, people can pursue their dreams and develop their God-given talents. More and more, opportunity is based on merit, not on pedigree. That's why people come to America. It doesn't matter whether we are from Australia, China, Egypt, India, Iran, Israel, Korea, Mexico, Nigeria, Pakistan, Philippines, Russia, Syria, Thailand, Tibet, Ukraine, Vietnam, Zimbabwe, or someplace else. We are here for the same reason: the pursuit of a better life.

In his book *Over the Top,* motivational speaker Zig Ziglar wrote, "If you don't like who you are and where you are, don't worry about it because you're not stuck either with who you are or where you are. You can grow. You can change. You can be more than you are" (Ziglar 1997, 59). Human beings have been migrating ever since our ancestors left Africa, and I predict that migration will continue until we conquer space. We cannot change the place where we were born, but we can change the place where we live. It's a small world; we just have to learn to live together. New York is the best example of such a utopia where people from everywhere live together regardless of ethnic or religious backgrounds.

In my travels, I've heard people say, "New York is not a good place to visit."

I'd always tell them that New York has both good and bad, but once you discover the good side, you will say, "I love New York."

CHAPTER 47

A Commitment to Excellence

It is not enough to do your best;
you must know what to do, and then do your best.

W. Edwards Deming

At the Hospital for Joint Diseases in New York City, one of the best hospitals in the United States, I learned the art of perfection and a commitment to excellence. The hospital specialized in orthopedic surgery and other disciplines. Besides the general public, famous athletes, musical divas, religious leaders, and all kinds of celebrities go there for their medical care.

At the hospital I became a member of the CQI team (Continuous Quality Improvement). It was made up of heads of departments such as anesthesiology, nursing, nutrition, radiology, information technology and others.

The doctor who chaired the meetings summarized our task in these terms: "We have to strive for perfection. The patient must be provided with an all-around super experience in every area."

Then he added, "The surgery can be successful, the bed comfortable, the nurses wonderful, but if the meatloaf that goes with the mashed potatoes is cold, that will spoil the whole hospital experience."

To improve our skills, we attended lectures by outside consultants, experts in management who taught us the principles and methods devised by W. Edwards Deming and Joseph Duran. I got the message, and I took notes. I became proficient with TQM (Total Quality Management) and the Six Sigma. These are concepts designed to continuously improve products and services for customer satisfaction.

I set out to run my department striving for excellence. I learned to look at processes before blaming people. Every aspect of the lab operation was measured, and the charts were posted for everyone to see our progress. When it became apparent that my main chemistry analyzer wasn't efficient enough, I asked for state-of-the-art instrumentation technology. The administration didn't understand why I needed new analyzers. I enlisted the support of the head of the anesthesiology department. I got what I wanted.

Later, the CEO of the hospital found out that I was on the executive board of the American Association of Clinical Chemistry (AACC), a professional organization, along with a friend of his, the world-renowned Dr. Arthur Karmen, professor of pathology at Albert Einstein College of Medicine of Yeshiva University. He signed all my requisitions without asking a thousand questions.

Like all institutions, the hospital had periodic inspections from both federal and local agencies. Once, we had a surprise inspection from the Joint Commission on Accreditation of Healthcare Organizations (JCAHO), which is now called the Joint Commission (TJC). At some point in the process, the inspector said, "It's amazing; everything is so wonderful."

The lab administrator, always vigilant, didn't want to let such an opportunity go by without benefiting from it. She asked the inspector, "Would you tell that to top administration?"

The inspector replied, "Yes, I will." And she kept her word. In her summation, she told top management that the lab was doing a wonderful job.

My staff was committed to excellence, and they reminded me when I failed to live up to my own high standard. One time my VP asked me to jot down some notes for her on my department's budget. I started to prepare the notes, and one of my technologists, Monica Yuen, told me, "Don't listen to your VP and give her just some notes. Prepare a formal departmental budget for her. You never know where little pieces of paper may end up."

I took her advice and prepared a comprehensive budget along with a two-page narrative, explaining my vision and my goals for the lab. It was as if my colleague had been prophetic. During that week, I was invited to a budget meeting, and the CEO asked me to read my budget narrative. He was pleased with it. This little incident reminded me of my French class assignment of long ago, when I'd had trouble reading my excellent paper on seventeenth-century classic writers. By now, I was comfortable with public speaking.

Sometime during the summer months, we would get students from Stuyvesant High School, one of the top public high schools in the country. I was amazed to see how they always strove for speed and perfection. Members of my staff, Gisele Joseph, Marylou Whitley, and Ruby Cooper, would make sure to keep them busy with interesting assignments. They were part of a breed that subscribed to *a commitment to excellence.*

CHAPTER 48

Love and Appreciate What You Have, for It Will Soon Be Gone

Be thankful for what you have; you'll end up having more. If you concentrate on what you don't have, you will never, ever have enough.

Oprah Winfrey

One day I got a visit from Dr. Malcolm Hyman, the former head of the pathology department at Coney Island Hospital. He had already retired. As my former boss, he knew me well and had even sent me a beautiful letter of congratulations after I had taken the position of laboratory supervisor at the Hospital for Joint Diseases. As he lived in the area, I was now working in his residential neighborhood.

Upon greeting him, I noticed that he did not exhibit his usual cheerfulness. He had a concerned look on his face. I told him how pleased I was to see him and inquired about the nature of his visit. He told me that his wife was a patient in the hospital; he had come to the lab to pay me a visit.

During the time his wife was in the hospital, he stopped by every day, and with the approval of his wife and his wife's doctor, I showed him the results of his wife's lab tests. Then his wife was transferred to NYU Medical Center. I didn't hear from him for many months.

Then one day I got a letter from him. He informed me that his wife had passed away, and he wanted to thank me for my support and the good care she had received at the hospital. He offered to have lunch with me someday. Then he closed the letter with these words: "Love and appreciate what you have, for it will soon be gone."

I am known to collect nuggets of wisdom upon which I build the foundations of my character. This one was the most significant piece of advice I had received in a long time. I wrote it on a piece of paper and stuck it in my wallet. It would become my new mantra.

It didn't take me long to verify the validity of this advice in a tangible way. Unbeknownst to all, the Hospital for Joint Diseases was secretly working on a merger with New York University Medical Center. When I found out, I went to my boss and told him that should a merger happen, my position would be eliminated. He assured me that I would be working there for many years to come.

Then one day the administrator was off, and I was asked to attend a meeting at NYU, representing the Hospital for Joint Diseases. I sat quietly at the meeting. The merger was being discussed, and when I looked at the proposed table of organization, I noticed that it didn't include my position. Routine lab work would be sent to NYU; only a stat laboratory would be kept at Joint Diseases. I didn't say anything; I just knew that I had to make my move before it was too late. I was a member and a past president of the New York section of the American Association for Clinical Chemistry (AACC). Many people in the field knew me; I sent word out that I was looking for a new position. Soon after that, I got three job offers. One of them was an evening-laboratory-supervisor position with the Brookdale University Hospital and Medical Center.

CHAPTER 49

Dialing God

You will call upon Me and go and pray to Me, and I will listen to you.

JEREMIAH 29:12

I WAS ALREADY FAMILIAR WITH Brookdale University and Medical Center. That's where both my kids were born. I worked there part time in the early 1980s. And on a couple of occasions over the years, they had invited me to join the department of laboratories, a position that I had turned down. My wife was working there as the microbiology section manager, and I didn't want to bump into her every minute. It wouldn't have been healthy for our relationship. This time, things were different. I needed a job, and the position was in the evening. We would have no interaction at the workplace.

When I went to Brookdale for the interview, I met briefly with Dr. Herbert Elliott and Dr. George Pringle, respectively the chair and director of the department. I had met them earlier at a conference, and both told me that the position was mine if I wanted it. Dr. Elliott asked me to go and see the director of human resources. He was a tall man with gray sideburns. He wanted to talk to me about salary. Here again, I went through the same game being played by management regarding my starting salary. He offered me the same salary the previous supervisor had been making. I used the same technique I had used at Joint Diseases with a little twist, and it worked out.

I told the human resources director, "You're hiring me, not the person before me. I know how to save money for my department."

Saving money! That got his attention.

"How would you do that?" he asked.

Confidently, I talked to him about economy of scales, sections consolidation, improved technology, control of overtime, and a host of other techniques I was familiar with. Luckily, in addition to my higher degree in administration, I had recently completed a one-year weekend certificate program in laboratory management at Hartford University in Connecticut. The courses covered tools like the ones I mentioned. They were theoretical models learned in school, and although I had used some of them in my previous work, I didn't know whether they were applicable in this environment. I threw them at him, and he bought the concept. I could see it on his face. He excused himself to go to the phone in a different room.

After a few minutes, he came back and told me, "You'll get the salary you requested. However, you cannot get overtime."

That was irrelevant because my position was in management, and managers don't get paid overtime, except maybe bonuses. Still, there was a point to it. I put this incident together with the one at the Hospital for Joint Diseases, where they had shorted me $500 of my asking salary, and I saw a pattern. When it comes to negotiation, neither party wants to come out empty-handed. Each one wants at least a win-win situation, a concept I learned from management expert Stephen R. Covey in his book *The Seven Habits of Highly Effective People.* It reminded me of the incident I mentioned earlier, when a girl I had kissed during "negotiation" got angry and kissed me back so that we could be even—a real win-win situation.

The Blizzard of 1996

On my first day of work, January 8, 1996, New York City was hit by a major blizzard. The city was buried under two feet of snow. A friend of mine, James Limage, had a four-wheel-drive SUV. He came to pick me up and drove me to work, stating, "No excuses for missing work on your first day."

My shift started at 4:00 p.m. I arrived at Brookdale at two. I met the chairman of the department, Dr. Herbert Elliott. Jokingly, but as a way of expressing my commitment, I clicked my heels and gave him the military salute as I yelled, "Captain Gourdet, reporting for duty!"

He looked at me with a smile and shook my hand with amazement, as if wondering what kind of crazy guy he had hired. Since I was coming from Queens, sixteen miles away, he hadn't expected to see me. From that day on, he held me in high regard.

I got involved with staff coverage for the night and with the assignment of hospital beds for me and for staff members who couldn't go home. History repeats itself. It was the second time this kind of thing had happened to me. Eighteen years earlier, on February 6, 1978, on my first day as an employee at Coney Island Hospital, I had had to sleep over because of the blizzard of '78, a major snowstorm that paralyzed New York City and much of the northern Unites States, including New Jersey, Connecticut, Rhode Island, and Massachusetts.

Anyway, the next day after I started at Brookdale, the receptionist transferred a phone call to me. It was from the wife of one of my technicians. She was inquiring about her husband. She hadn't heard from him since the day before. She wanted to know if he was at work. I was so embarrassed. I was on my second day of work, and I didn't know who the employee was. It turned out he had spent the night on the Long Island Rail Road. The train was going nowhere; the tracks were covered with snow. After that incident, I made it a point to learn the names of the staff right away.

Kidney Stones

When I started at Brookdale, a few employees remembered me from my time there years before. During the physical exam at that time in 1980, it had been revealed that I had kidney stones. Tests showed a trace of blood in my urine, and an IVP (intravenous pyelogram) had confirmed the presence of a kidney stone.

Then I started having excruciating pain, to the point that I didn't know who I was. The doctor told me the stone was trapped in my ureter, and it was too big to pass. I needed surgery. Lithotripsy was just coming out, and my doctor wasn't trained in that procedure.

On the day of the surgery, I was in the waiting room on a stretcher feeling very cold. I looked around. On my left was a little old lady, all white hair, very emaciated, and she looked really peaceful. On my right, there was an agitated old man who kept on saying, "I don't want to die. I don't want to die."

I got scared, and I said to myself, *Is this the way I am going to go?*

Then a doctor I knew walked in and saw me. He asked, "What are you doing here, Jesse?"

"Kidney-stone surgery," I answered.

He put his hand over mine in a compassionate manner and jokingly said, "What you really need is a plumber." I relaxed and smiled.

My surgeon told me he was going to do a little incision and take the stone out. When I came out of surgery, he had cut half of my waist to remove the little stone, the size of a sweet pea. To cheer me up, my friends placed a big stone by my bedside and teased me by saying, "Here is your baby. It was delivered by C-section." Every woman I have spoken with has assured me that a kidney stone is more painful than delivering a baby.

Another incident at the hospital had a palliative effect on me. I was sharing the room with another kidney-stone patient. He didn't like the food being served to patients, and every evening he would sneak down to the hospital's cafeteria to buy real food. Before he took the elevator back, he would call me, and I would check the hallway to make sure it was safe for him to come up without being caught by the nurses.

He told me the story of something sad that had happened to him. Ironically, instead of eliciting sadness, the story made me laugh to the point that my wound started to hurt.

He said, "I passed three kidney stones at home. I gave one to my doctor; he lost it. I gave him the second one; he said this time the laboratory lost it. Since the doctor wanted me to spend a few days in the hospital for observation, I brought the third stone with me. I put it, wrapped in a paper napkin, on the night table. The nurse thought that it was a soiled napkin and threw it away." Poor guy!

My wound healed, and since then, I have never had any problem with kidney stones. Today, kidney-stone surgery is done in an outpatient setting, and you don't need a month to recuperate.

Later, I wrote the following poem about my experience in the waiting room. People have found it inspiring. It even got an Editor's Choice Award from the International Library of Poetry. I gave the poem to a young woman who was undergoing surgery; it gave her the strength to go through the ordeal. It is reproduced here from my book, *Let It Be Easy.*

Dialing God

I was dreading the outcome
I felt afraid of what's to come.
My heart was pounding,
My body was shaking.
What's going to happen?
Was it the end?
My mind was set on doom and gloom.
Am I heading straight to the tomb?
I closed my eyes and made a call
To God who is always there for us all.
I felt a hand touching my hand.
"Let it be" was the command.
Then I heard a voice singing this song
That has the power to make us strong:
"We shall overcome!"
"We shall overcome!"
A sense of peace overtook me.
"Just let it be. God is with me."
Whatever the outcome, it's fine.
"Thy will be done, not mine."

That experience gave me a sense of priorities. I wrote a list of the important things I wanted to accomplish in my life, one of which was to visit Europe. Soon after that, in 1981, I took my wife on a tour of Europe. In Paris, we visited the Louvre, where I saw Leonardo da Vinci's *Mona Lisa*, a painting that is said to hold many hidden mysteries. Then we visited the Château de Versailles, built by King Louis XIV. We were amazed by its splendor and its magnificent gardens. After Paris, we took trains to Rome, Florence, and Venice. We enjoyed the trip so much that we would return to these cities over the years.

During my second round at Brookdale, my time was pretty much routine, with no catastrophes and no major excitement, only some lingering financial constraints. A new laboratory was completed the year I started. The lab was physically spacious and designed with an open-space concept that allowed for multiple configurations. The instrumentation was state of the art, and my staff was up to date with the latest in laboratory technology. The years went by very fast.

Occasionally, the hospital would provide care to firefighters with burns over their bodies and carbon-monoxide intoxication. Mayor Rudolph Giuliani would stop by, to be by their sides and to make sure they got the best care. I always have a special thought for these heroes who put their lives in great danger to save other people's lives. They called them New York's bravest; I think they deserve the appellation.

In December 2010, I retired from Brookdale Hospital. They had a big party for me, attended by my daughter and her husband and other friends and former coworkers who came to say farewell.

CHAPTER 50

Real-Estate Years

Only when the tide goes out do you discover who's been swimming naked.

Warren Buffett

In 1975, while I was working at the Long Island Jewish Medical Center as a toxicology laboratory technologist, a friend of mine called me and told me about opportunities in real-estate sales in Queens. All I needed was a license and to register with the Department of State. New York had two levels of licensing: licensed real-estate salesperson and licensed real-estate broker. A salesperson must work under a broker, who holds the salesperson's license. A broker can be responsible for his or her own license.

I obtained the salesperson license and started to work in real estate part time, on evenings and weekends. Soon afterward, I was doing it full time. When I found out that New York University's Division of Business and Management had a one-year certificate program in real estate, being an eternal student, I applied for it. Later, I took and passed the broker's license exam. I made sure it never expired by meeting all of the state's requirements, including mandatory continuing education. In short, I kept my license even when I wasn't active in the business. Real estate goes up and down, and I used it as a vehicle to supplement my income. I was in it if it was hot and going up; I was out of it when it cooled off.

Former clients remembered me and recommended me even at those times when I was not active in the business. It was such a situation in 2002 when I went on an errand in my neighborhood of Little Neck, Queens. As I passed a Century 21 real-estate office, I suddenly had the urge to enter that office. It just so happened that a few days earlier, two people had called me to ask if I could help them find a house. I went into the office and asked to speak to the manager. A sales agent asked me what it was in reference to.

I told her, “I am a licensed real-estate broker, but I am not active in the business. Two friends of mine are looking to buy a house. Would someone in the office be willing to work with them? I don’t expect a referral fee.”

She replied, “Our company is looking for brokers. Why don’t you meet with the recruitment manager? She is at the central office; here is her name and address.”

I drove to Greenvale, Long Island, and I met with Heather Moskovic, Larry Braden, and Emmet Laffey. Before I realized what I was doing, I had enlisted as an agent with Century 21 Laffey, one the top real-estate agencies in Long Island and Queens. They had about fourteen offices, but they decided to keep me at the headquarters in Greenvale.

My first sale came shortly thereafter. I was asked to go and meet a young man from out of state who wanted to sell his grandma’s house. One of the Laffey brothers, Mark, told me, “Do not leave the house without securing the listing.”

I knew I had to do my best. There were other brokers after the listing. Additionally, the next-door neighbor had made an offer to the seller for a private sale.

I wore my well-pressed suit with the Realtor’s pin on my jacket lapel. My shoes were shining clean. The owner was a young man in his early thirties. He gave me a tour of the house. It was a large house and probably the nicest in the upscale neighborhood.

I made a professional presentation to him. I indicated my qualifications as a Realtor and my affiliations with Century 21, the Long Island Board of Realtors, and the Multiple Listing Service (MLS). I also presented the seller with a professionally done market analysis of his property. The color display of graphs and charts indicating recent sales for comparable houses in the neighborhood seemed to impress him. Together, we came up with a listing price. Then I explained to him my marketing strategy. It included prominent display on the Internet and advertising in the weekend edition of the newspapers, including the *New York Times*. By the time I left, I had a signed listing agreement in my briefcase along with my 6 percent broker's commission agreement. The next-door neighbor would have to compete with the greater public.

The following Sunday I had a well-attended open house. I collected six offers. I asked the six competing buyers to provide me with a mortgage commitment and final offer.

Two of the six, including the next-door neighbor, decided to drop out. Of the remaining four, two of them were business owners. They had stellar credit scores in the eight hundreds. However, all four of them qualified for a mortgage. I gave them my office number and told them to fax me the best offer they felt comfortable with by 2:00 p.m. on the Thursday of that week.

On that Thursday, one of them called me and asked, "Jesse, how much do you think I should bid?"

I told him the same thing I told the other ones. "Whatever you feel comfortable with."

He faxed his bid and immediately called me again. He told me, "If my bid is too much over the closest bid, reduce it for me, just so I can win. I'll be nice to you."

Obviously, the guy didn't know me. I don't do monkey business.

By 2:15 p.m., I had the seller on the line, and I reviewed the bids with him, along with the buyers' qualifications, for a smooth deal. All four buyers qualified. The seller could pick any one of them. He chose the one with the highest bid. The gentleman who thought his bid was way over came in third.

After the closing, the owner sent me a beautiful thank-you letter expounding on the professional way in which I had handled the sale of his property. I gave a copy of that letter to the manager for my file. On my first sale, I had earned more money than I had made in six months in my extra weekend job at that time. I left it and concentrated on real estate.

The Poor Old Lady

Another memorable incident in my real-estate career is worth mentioning because it exemplifies a motto by Aesop: "No act of kindness, no matter how small, is ever lost."

I was selling the beautiful English Tudor house of a retired woman. The house was mortgage free but filled to the brim with items collected over the years and remnants of an antiques-store business. In the garage, there were two expensive foreign cars, bought new but hardly driven. By my estimate, she was worth at least a couple million dollars.

One day I stopped by her house to talk to her about an impending open house, and I found her crying. I asked her, "Mrs. Gordon, what's the matter?"

She replied, "It's the end of the month, I have used all my social security money to pay my bills, and I have no money for food."

I asked her, "Why don't you sell some of the items you have in your house to cover your food expenses?"

"I am not selling anything in my house. I am moving with all of it."

Realizing that I wasn't going to change her mind, I told her that I'd be back in a few minutes. I went to the nearest West Indian restaurant and bought her a nice plate of food. She was very happy.

When I got home, I told the story to my wife, and every weekend she would bring food for Mrs. Gordon until the house was sold, and she moved to another state. (You guessed it—with all her stuff.) She needed two huge trailers to carry her possessions; she never sold even one item.

A few years passed, and I hadn't heard from her. Then one day I got a phone call. It was one of her daughters on the line.

She told me, "My mother passed away, and we're going to have the funeral services in New York so that she can be buried near my father.

Before she died, she asked me to invite you to her funeral services. She thought very highly of you and your wife." It was a great honor for me.

I went to pay my last respects to Mrs. Gordon. As I reflected in front of the open casket, I thought that Ben Franklin would have been proud of her. She personified five of Franklin's thirteen virtues: temperance, industry, frugality, resolution, and humility. She believed that a penny saved is a penny earned. She had the kind of mentality that puts your face on the one-hundred-dollar bill.

I will always remember Mrs. Gordon. It is an amazing grace to have the blessing of a dying person.

Too Much of a Good Thing Can Be Wonderful

It was Mae West who said, "Too much of a good thing can be wonderful." The Century 21 Laffey brand was very popular in Queens and Nassau counties. They had an aggressive marketing strategy and handled the sale of some of the most exclusive residences in Long Island, giving the sales agents access to expensive houses. From 2002 until 2007, the real-estate market did nothing but move up. Money came in easily. I took cruises with stops in European and Baltic cities.

In Saint Petersburg, the beautiful city founded by Peter the Great, I visited the Hermitage Museum. I was struck with awe at the sight of the original painting, *The Return of the Prodigal Son,* by the Dutch master Rembrandt. This painting has always stirred great emotion in me because of its beauty and its message of love, repentance, and mercy. As human beings, we are prone to express our lowest basic instincts, but if we repent and return to our father in heaven, we are sure to be received with open arms of love and forgiveness.

In Copenhagen, Denmark, the melancholic beauty of *The Little Mermaid* touched my heart: "Every man's life is a fairy tale written by God's fingers" wrote Hans Christian Andersen.

In Barcelona, Spain, I was sitting at an upscale outdoor café, having lunch with my wife, when my cell phone rang. On the other end was a lawyer in New York, informing me that everything was finalized for the closing on a deal I was working on.

I remember telling my wife, "Sometimes, God is really good to us. *Carpe diem*, let's seize the day; it doesn't get any better than this."

In Florence, Italy, I bought gifts for my friends and coworkers. And it went like that until early 2007, when the real-estate market crashed.

What Goes Up Must Come Down

A few months earlier, I remember giving a lecture to a group of businesspeople, and one of them asked me if the real-estate bubble was going to burst. My answer was simple: "What goes up must come down; it's a law of nature."

By the time the real-estate market crashed, I had already secured a high-paying position as a hospital laboratory administrator.

CHAPTER 51

Tales from the Trenches

Personally, I enjoy working about eighteen hours a day.

Thomas A. Edison

While I worked at Brookdale Hospital, sometimes I would go to inspect other laboratories under the auspices of CAP, the College of American Pathologists. This is a professional peer-review program that aims to improve the quality of laboratory services and at the same time to meet requirements for CMS, the Centers for Medicare and Medicaid Services. This gave me the clout to work as a consultant in my field, and occasionally I would be called upon to help both private laboratories and hospital laboratories to prepare for their inspections.

One such organization was the New York Community Hospital in Brooklyn, a member of the New York-Presbyterian Healthcare System. In 2003, my boss at Brookdale asked me if I could go there and help them out. Their administrator had resigned one month prior to a federal inspection. I worked with them, and they did very well on the inspection. They offered me the administrator's position, but I declined. Over the following years, they would call me for consultations, and I would help them.

On April 26, 2007, at about five in the evening, I was sitting in my office at the Brookdale Hospital Medical Center when my phone rang. I picked it up; it was the medical director of New York Community

Hospital's laboratory department. I had known the director for about four years, ever since I had started to work for them as a laboratory consultant.

She asked me, "Would you be able to come to the hospital tomorrow afternoon? I have set up an appointment for you with the CEO at three."

I said, "Yes, I will come."

She didn't tell me what the meeting was in reference to, and I didn't ask her. The next day I went to the meeting. Present were the head of human resources, the senior VP of nursing, the VP for ancillary services, and the lab medical director. The CEO explained to me that the laboratory administrator had just resigned and that they were expecting an unannounced federal inspection any day now. I thought they wanted me to help them out as I had in the past. But it wasn't so. This time they wanted me to stay.

The CEO told me, "We would like you to take over the position of laboratory administrator here at New York Community Hospital. You will work under my direction."

I told him that I didn't mind helping out, but I was happy with my evening position at Brookdale, and I didn't intend to leave it.

He replied, "Brookdale is only fifteen minutes away; you have plenty of time to get there."

Obviously, he didn't mind if I had two jobs. For a moment I got concerned that this would have a negative effect on my health. Then, thinking like a Ferengi, these strange creatures from *Star Trek* who always focus on profit, I decided to take a chance. *Why not?* I thought. I was close to retirement; an extra salary would only sweeten my retirement pot.

Coming back again to a written goal, I wanted to make a certain amount of money. This was an opportunity to achieve my goal. The real-estate market was coming down, but here again the money came to me in a most unexpected way.

It was Jessie Belle Rittenhouse who wrote the following:

For Life is a just employer,
He gives you what you ask,
But once you have set the wages,
Why, you must bear the task.

In plain English, "There ain't no free lunch."

The next Monday I was working as laboratory administrator for the New York Community Hospital during the day while keeping my evening-supervisor position at Brookdale. I continued to work at New York Community Hospital for a few years, even after I had retired from Brookdale.

I directed the lab at New York Community Hospital with the same high standards and commitment to excellence I had learned and applied at the Hospital for Joint Diseases. In both cases, I had a hand in the management and decision making for the laboratory. I passed all the regulatory agencies' inspections and patient surveys with flying colors. My departmental budget was handled efficiently. I developed good relationships with the other departments. All in all, I had a good experience there. It was good for the hospital, good for patient care, and good for me—a win-win-win situation.

When in Rome...

When I took the position at New York Community Hospital, I was invited to classes given by the CEO, a former university professor. He couldn't rid himself of the teaching bug. Classes started at 7:00 a.m.

My Brookdale job ended at midnight, but I didn't want to miss courses given by the supreme boss of the place. So, after only four hours of sleep, I was back in Brooklyn to listen to his Tales from the Trenches. (That was the title of the course.)

Besides departmental mission and vision, classes were devoted to the basic concepts of leadership, and they included sessions like communication, goals for patient care, standards of practice, evaluation of outcomes, performance improvement, open-mindedness and proportionality, inner strength, and unwillingness to yield under pressure. My favorites were titled "The Lay of the Land" and "When in Rome..."

To illustrate his points, the CEO drew examples from ancient and modern history with a strong reliance on political leaders and old movie characters. He wanted to infuse into each one of us a deeper understanding of the principles of leadership. His goal was to empower us so that we could motivate our respective staffs for greater efficiency and effectiveness.

I was so caught up in the moment and enjoying what I was doing so much that it never occurred to me that I was sleeping about four to five hours a night on weekdays. I caught up on sleep over the weekends. Sometimes on my way home at night, I would find myself sleeping while driving on the dangerous Jackie Robinson Parkway, which connects Brooklyn and Queens; however, I was never involved in any accident, although there were plenty on that parkway.

The Homeless Man Who Gave Me Three Dollars

Occasionally, on my way home at midnight, I would stop at a gas station to fill up, despite warnings from those who cared for me that it was too dangerous to do so at that late hour. A few times at the station, a beggar would come to me and ask for money. I always gave him one dollar. He was about thirty years old, somewhat skinny, and he seemed pretty quiet. One time, after I gave him a dollar, he stood near me while I was pumping gas.

In a subdued and respectful manner, I asked him, "You seem to be such a nice young man. Why is it that you don't have a job?"

He confided in me, saying, "I used to be a teacher. I have a master's degree in education. I started taking drugs, and I lost my job. My family doesn't want to have anything to do with me. I became homeless."

His words wrenched my heart. I said to him, "I am sorry," and I meant it.

I left, and I didn't see him for a while. One day, I stopped for gas at another nearby location after midnight. There he was again, asking me for money. Politely, I told him I had only five dollars and that I needed it for gas to go home. He put his hand in his pocket and pulled out some money.

He handed it to me and said, "I only have three dollars; you can have it to buy gas."

I said, "Thank you, brother. That's very nice of you, but I am all right."

I never saw the homeless man again, but his generosity will stay with me forever.

This period in my life when I was working two jobs was very tough for me. I learned to adapt to the many challenges I faced along the way. When the road got rough and the battles were many, I found strength in a poem that I wrote and kept on my desk. Here it is:

Great Spirit

Great Spirit of light and force,
Shed your light upon my heart,
Enlighten me for a great start.

Great Spirit of light and force,
Shield me from distraction,
Lead me into inspired action.

Great Spirit of light and force,
Inspire me to excellence,
Embolden me with confidence.

Great Spirit of light and force,
Cover me under your wings,
Shower me with your blessings.

Great Spirit of light and force,
Grant me your invincible power,
Be with me until the final hour.

There you have it—"Tales from the Trenches."

Part Five
Giving Back

CHAPTER 52

An Attitude of Gratitude

The purpose of life is to discover your gift. The meaning of life is to give your gift away.

David Viscott

As a kid raised in Haiti, I saw firsthand what poverty is, and early in life I made a commitment to improve my life and the lives of those close to me. We were fortunate to live in New York City, where opportunities abound. The road wasn't always smooth; life is full of bumps and bruises, but we developed the stamina to reach the finish line. Ultimately, what we worked for wasn't money but a measure of comfort, safety, and peace.

As any parent knows, raising kids is one of the challenges of life. Sometimes you have to go through an inferno to reach paradise. Both our children attended local Catholic elementary schools and out-of-state prep schools. We felt privileged to be able to provide them with good educations. Greg became a well-known executive chef who competed in television shows such as *Top Chef, Cutthroat Kitchen*, and others. Jessica became a health care coordinator. Looking back, I can see that the most important thing we probably gave them was the love that binds our family. I never cease to love my wife, and our love for the children never wanes. We love them for who they are and not for what they do. In return, they show affection for us as parents, and that brings us a lot of happiness.

We are blessed with two wonderful granddaughters. They are a delight and a lot of joy. Additionally, our godchildren, family members, and friends make life so meaningful for us. As Mahatma Gandhi said, "Where there is love, there is life."

Stewardship

It was Mark Victor Hansen of the *Chicken Soup for the Soul* series who taught me the word "stewardship," which means being the trustee of our wealth with the responsibility of passing it on to the rest of humanity. That's the kind of attitude being exhibited in a big way by luminaries such as Bill and Melinda Gates, Warren Buffett, Oprah Winfrey, and others. That's also the attitude of countless numbers of everyday people who contribute selflessly to the betterment of humanity in their own communities. When disaster strikes in some parts of the world threatening human survival, people of all religious faiths and political persuasions open their hearts and wallets to come to the rescue, revealing the inherent goodness of human nature. Such was the case after the catastrophic earthquake that hit Haiti on January 12, 2010. It was a humbling experience.

Throughout this book, I have indicated how scores of people contributed to whatever success I have achieved. At the end of the day, what really counts is not the amount of money you make or the good life you live, but how you improve the lives of your fellow human beings. This is the philosophy I have lived by.

I am able to connect with all kinds of people, and I can make friends easily. This ability has allowed me to participate in professional and community-service organizations with the goal of passing on what I have received to others in need.

For thirty years, I was actively involved in the New York section of the AACC (the American Association for Clinical Chemistry). As a former Chair and executive board member of the association, we provided continuing education for the members of the New York section and the general public. This allowed us to attend lectures given by the brightest minds in the field of laboratory medicine. They were the pioneers who made significant contributions to the development of accurate methods and technologies for the diagnosis and prevention of diseases. One such scientist was Dr. Arthur Karmen, who developed the first biochemical test for myocardial infarction; another one was Dr. J. Craig Venter, who decoded the human genome in 2000, paving the way for personalized medicine, and the list goes on.

As president of a Lions Club, I helped to provide for children's education. As treasurer of the Rotary Club and member of many other charitable organizations, I participated in the distribution of Thanksgiving food baskets to families in need and the provision of clean drinking water for the people of an impoverished village. Most of the money from the sale of my book *Let It Be Easy* was given to charity, and I intend to do the same with the proceeds from the sale of this book. That will be my "footprints on the sands of time" as Longfellow wrote in his poem "A Psalm of Life":

Lives of great men all remind us
We can make our lives sublime,
And, departing, leave behind us
Footprints on the sands of time;

Footprints, that perhaps another,
Sailing o'er life's solemn main,
A forlorn and shipwrecked brother,
Seeing, shall take heart again.

CHAPTER 53

The Morning After

When you arise in the morning, think of what
a precious privilege it is to be alive,
to breathe, to think, to enjoy, to love.

Marcus Aurelius

As our train's journey neared its end, I woke up, realizing that while I was in a semiconscious state, my whole life had unfolded in front of me. Ultimately, I had fallen asleep. It was early morning; the sun was just coming up on the horizon. I could contemplate its deep yellow and orange colors with the blue sky in the background. We were already crossing through small villages in Georgia, approaching Florida. I couldn't help but think of all the people who came into my life for a reason or for a season and made me who I am. I remained inspired by the lessons I had learned from them.

Still, as my journey went forward and toward God, I had three good reasons to be grateful. One, I almost didn't make it out of my mother's womb. Two, I survived typhoid fever and even saw a glimpse of heaven. Three, I made it past fifty-two years old, the age at which I was predicted to die.

As I sat by the train's window watching the trees disappear and admiring the natural beauty of the landscape, the words of Walt Whitman came back to my mind:

Henceforth I ask not good-fortune, I myself am good-fortune...
Strong and content I travel the open road...
All seems beautiful to me.

My life was filled with divine grace. I am grateful for the love and protection bestowed upon me and for my ability to adapt to challenges.

So much emotion permeated my being on the day I left New York! It was indeed a journey of gratitude. I wiped a tear from the corner of my eye, and I started to sing.

Amazing Grace, how sweet the sound
That saved a wretch like me...

ACKNOWLEDGMENTS

One of the tenets of my core beliefs is that our DNA doesn't determine our destiny; however, it does influence who we are. That's why I want to pay tribute to both my French and African ancestors. I carry their genetic makeup, and for that I am grateful.

The writing of this book involved numerous people who helped to shape my life and make the journey easier. I am indebted to all of them even though I mentioned only a few. Some of you did good deeds for me that I am not even aware of. You know who you are. If you come upon this book, know that whatever you did for me is greatly appreciated.

I want to thank the author of the poem "A reason, a season, or a lifetime" for its inspiration.

A small group of people read the manuscript and provided me with helpful insights. For that, I want to thank my daughter, Jessica Gourdet Murray; my son, Gregory Gourdet; my brother, Gustave Edouard; my friends Max and Denise Kénol, James Rogers, Manassé Décady, Marilyn King-George. I am particularly grateful to Wynne S. Wharff, who was gracious enough to write the book's introduction and who offered valuable advice. Additionally, I'd like to thank my wife, Yanick. Without her support, this book wouldn't have been possible.

I learned so much from my editors. They deserved my special thanks. To the many other people who helped me along the way, I extend my cordial thanks.

REFERENCES

Alexis, Stephen. 1949. *The Black Liberator: The Life of Toussaint Louverture.* Translated by William Stirling. New York: Macmillan Publishers.

Aurelius, Marcus. 2002. *Meditations: A New Translation.* New York: The Modern Library.

Bach, Richard, and Russell Munson. 1970. *Jonathan Livingston Seagull.* New York: The Macmillan Company.

Brande, Dorothea. 1936. *Wake Up and Live.* New York: Tarcher.

Bristol, Claude M. 1969. *The Magic of Believing.* New York: Simon & Schuster.

Byrnes, Rhonda. 2006. *The Secret.* New York: Atria Books.

Camus, Albert. 1942. *L'Étranger.* Paris: Gallimard.

Canfield, Jack, and Mark Victor Hansen. Chicken Soup for the Soul series. Florida: HCI Books.

Carnegie, Dale. 1982. *How to Win Friends and Influence People.* New York: Pocket Books.

Carter, Jimmy. 2001. *An Hour before Daylight: Memories of a Rural Boyhood.* New York: Simon & Schuster.

Clinton, Bill. 2004. *My Life.* New York: Knopf Publishing Group.

Coelho, Paulo. 2007. *The Alchemist.* New York: Harper Collins.

Collier, Robert. 1959. *The Secret of the Ages.* New York: Robert Collier Publications.

Cooper, James Fenimore. 1982. *The Last of the Mohicans.* New York. Bantam Classics.

Covey, Stephen R. 1990. *The Seven Habits of Highly Effective People: Powerful Lessons in Personal Change.* New York: Simon & Schuster.

de Buck, J. M. 1961. *Dieu Parlera ce Soir.* Paris: Desclée de Brouwer.

de Saint-Exupéry, Antoine. 2001. *The Little Prince.* Translated by Richard Howard. San Diego: Harcourt.

Dumas, Alexandre.1846. *Le comte de Monte-Cristo. Paris: L'écho des Feuilletons.*

Dyer, Dr. Wayne W. 2004. *The Power of Intention: Learning to Co-create Your World Your Way.* California: Hay House.

Frost, Robert. 1962. *Selected Poems.* New York: Rinehart Editions.

Gourdet, Jesse. 2010. *Let It Be Easy.* New York: Blue Diamond Press.

Hill, Napoleon. 1963. *Think and Grow Rich.* Minnesota: Fawcett Publications.

Huffington, Arianna, and Françoise Gilot. 1993. *The Gods of Greece.* New York: Atlantic Monthly Books.

Hugo, Victor. 1862. *Les Misérables.* Bruxelles: A. Lacroix, Verboeckhoven & Cie.

Kushner, Harold S. 1983. *When Bad Things Happen to Good People.* New York: Avon Books.

Longfellow, Henry Wadsworth. 1992. *Favorite Poems.* Mineola, NY: Dover Publications.

Maltz, Maxwell. 1960. *Psycho-Cybernetics.* New York: Simon & Schuster.

Mandino, Og. 1968. *The Greatest Salesman in the World.* New York: Bantam.

Manigat, Lesly F. 2001. *Evantail d'Histoire Vivante d'Haiti.* Port-au-Prince, Haiti: Collection du CHUDAC.

Melville, Herman. 1851. *Moby-Dick.* New York: Harper & Brothers.

Métraux, Alfred. 1972. *Voodoo in Haiti.* New York: Schocken Books.

Murphy, Joseph. 1963. *The Power of Your Subconscious Mind.* New York: Tarcher Penguin.

Orman, Suze. 1997. *The 9 Steps to Financial Freedom: Practical & Spiritual Steps so You Can Stop Worrying.* New York: Crown Publishers.

Peale, Norman Vincent. 1952. *The Power of Positive Thinking.* New York: Ballantine Books.

Plato. 1974. *The Republic.* Translated by G. M. A. Grube. Indianapolis, IN: Hackett Publishing.

Puzo, Mario. 1969. *The Godfather.* New York: G. P. Putnam's Sons.

RNJ. *It Works.* 1962. New York: Scrivener.

Schwartz, David J. 1959. *The Magic of Thinking Big.* California: Wilshire Book Company.

Swift, Jonathan. 1986. *Gulliver's Travels.* Mineola, NY: Dover Publications.

The Arabian Nights. 1981. Translated by Sir Richard Burton (1885–1888). Connecticut: The Easton Press.

The Good News Bible: *Today's English Version*. 1993. Edited by the American Bible Society. New York: Harper Collins.

Voltaire. 1947. *Candide.* Translated by John Butt. New York: Penguin Books.

Ziglar, Zig. 1997. *Over the Top: Moving from Survival to Stability, from Stability to Success, from Success to Significance.* Nashville, TN: Thomas Nelson.

ABOUT THE AUTHOR

Jesse Gourdet graduated with a degree in law in Haiti before immigrating to the United States when he was twenty-four. Gourdet spent the next forty-three years in New York City. He worked as a clinical chemist and realtor. He attended New York University and St. John's University. He received a master's degree in health services administration from the New School for Social Research in New York City.

Gourdet is now retired in Florida with his wife, Yanick. He is also the author of *Let It Be Easy*, a collection of inspirational poems and short stories.

You can contact Jesse at: jesse@jessegourdet.com